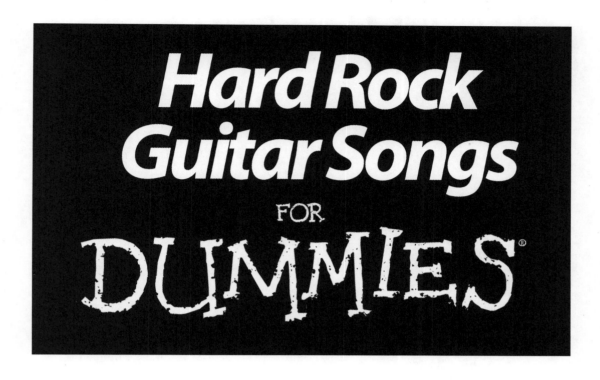

Hard Rock Guitar Songs FOR DUMMIES®

Performance Notes by Greg P. Herriges

ISBN-13: 978-1-4234-2622-6
ISBN-10: 1-4234-2622-3

HAL•LEONARD®
CORPORATION
7777 W. BLUEMOUND RD. P.O. BOX 13819 MILWAUKEE, WI 53213

Visit Hal Leonard Online at
www.halleonard.com

Table of Contents

Introduction

. . . .

*W*elcome, aspiring shredders and screamers, to *Hard Rock Guitar Songs For Dummies!* Everything you need to play some of the greatest and most popular songs in hard rock and heavy metal is here, including note-for-note transcriptions of the tunes (in tab and notation), and performance notes that can help you through the hairier parts — without the need for a music degree to understand the terms.

About This Book

For every song, you get a brief intro with a little background on the artist (in case you're not already a rock trivia god), followed by the essential info you need to learn the song:

✔ A run-down of the parts you need to know, not including those parts that are clones of other sections of the song.

✔ A breakdown of some of the special techniques you need to play the song — the trade secrets you won't see on the sheet music.

✔ When necessary, some info you need to navigate the sheet music (such as pickup measures). Be sure to familiarize yourself with codas, repeats, and other navigational details explained in the Guitar Notation Legend.

You may already know a lot of this stuff, so if you know it, skip it — unless you find the writing especially witty and eloquent (yeah, right). The best strategy is always to go through the song and find all the main chords and their positions (the chord chart at the back will help), then try working in all the licks and tricks.

How to Use This Book

The music in this book is in standard notation and tablature (also known as tab) — which is just a diagram of the guitar strings with numbers that tell you what frets to play. Assuming you know a little something about reading tab or music, a Guitar Notation Legend in the back helps translate all those strange words, alien symbols, and hieroglyphs that are the written language of guitarheads. I also assume you know some things about the guitar itself — like how to hold it, where the neck and frets are, how to tune it, basic chord strumming, and how to look cool while doing it.

There's also a chart of common chords and scale positions in the back. This is handy, because where a line of tab gives you fret numbers, these diagrams show you the visual shape of the chords and scales and which fingers work best for them.

New techniques and concepts are introduced as they appear, and referred back to when necessary. So you can skip around the book and pick out your favorite songs first, without missing out on essential information.

Conventions used in this book

Here are some common rock guitar terms you'll see discussed throughout the book:

- ✔ **Barre** *chords* (chords in which one finger holds down a few strings at once)
- ✔ **Open strings** (strings played in **open position**, without a finger holding them down)
- ✔ **Riffs** (repeating bits of music that are noteworthy enough to mention) and **licks** (common lead guitar tricks)
- ✔ **Strumming** (using a guitar pick to "fling" across the strings, often in a pattern of **downstrokes** — strumming down toward the earth — and **upstrokes** toward the sky)
- ✔ **Power chords** (those chunky two-note chords, labeled with a "5," that make rock what it is)
- ✔ **Pentatonic** (five-note) **scales** (the basis for most of the hot licks and screaming solos you're about to learn)
- ✔ **Other terms** that are explained in the Guitar Notation Legend. In the performance notes, when you see an unfamiliar word in *italics*, that's your cue to flip to the back of the book.

Your other left

No two guitarists are the same, and some of the greatest ones happen to play left-handed — so forgive your author/teacher for sometimes referring to the picking hand as "right" and the fretting hand as "left." Sometimes there's no better way to say it.

Down is up

When I talk about low and high strings, I'm talking pitch-wise, in terms of what you hear, not what you see. Your low E string, for example, is the string on "top," the fattest one with the lowest sound (sometimes tuned down to D or lower). The high E string is the skinny one on the "bottom," and so on. I try to be as clear as possible on whether I'm talking about sound or sight. Speaking of which, the names of the open strings in standard tuning, low to high, are E–A–D–G–B–E.

Icons Used in This Book

In the margins of this book are lots of little icons that will help make your life easier:

Optional parts, like insanely fast solos, that may be too challenging for many guitarists, but are discussed anyway for the learned and/or ambitious "champion" players among you. There's no way to walk you through every lick, but you'll get some tips that might make them less painful. In these discussions I may have to throw lots of strange terms at you, all of which can be found in the Guitar Notation Legend.

Details (such as tunings and special techniques) that you need to know, and will probably need again in the future.

Notes about specific musical concepts that are relevant but confusing to the layperson. Sometimes it's just something that's musically very cool!

Shortcuts and suggested ways to get through some of the hard parts without tangling your fingers.

A reason to stop and review advice that can prevent damage to your fingers, ears, guitar, or ego.

Am I Evil?

Words and Music by Sean Harris and Brian Tatler

Intro
Moderate Rock ♩ = 160

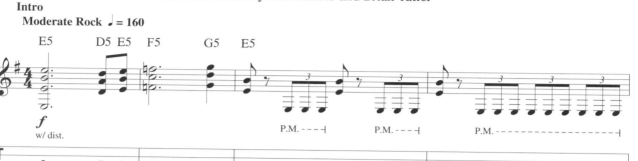

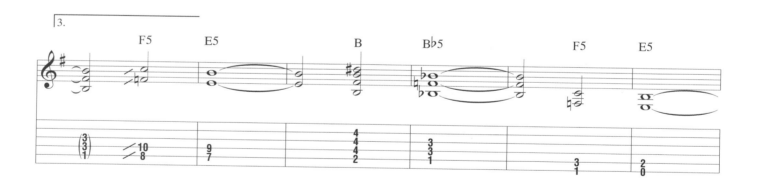

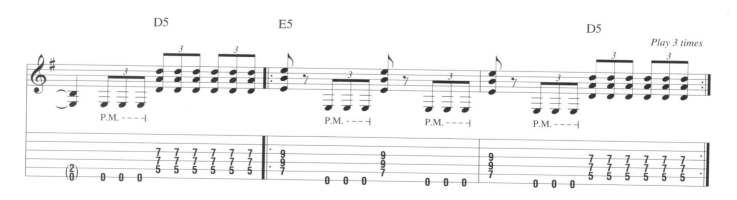

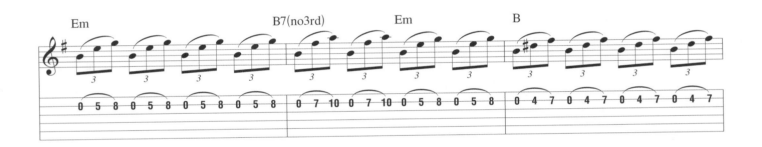

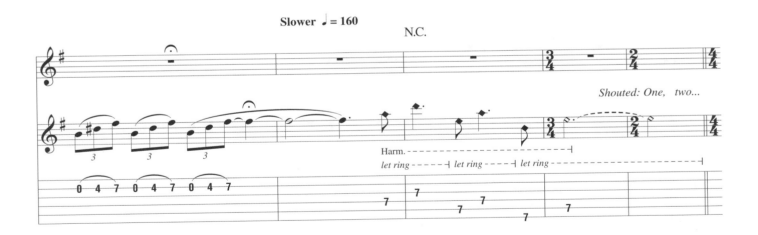

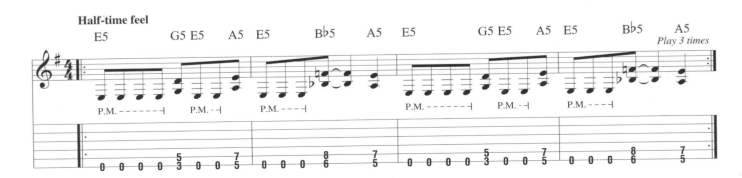

1. My

Verse

moth-er was a witch,
she was burned a - live. ____
2. *See additional lyrics*

End half-time feel

Thank-less lit - tle bitch
for the tears I cried. _____

Take her down now,
don't want to see her face. ____

All

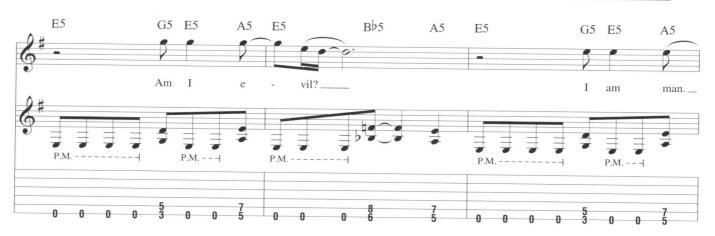

Am I e - vil? _____   I am man._

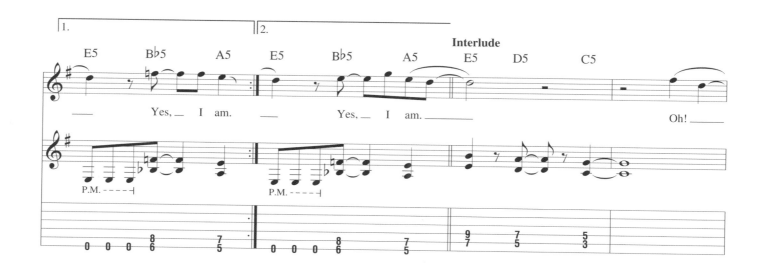

— Yes, _ I am. —   Yes, _ I am. _____   Oh! _____

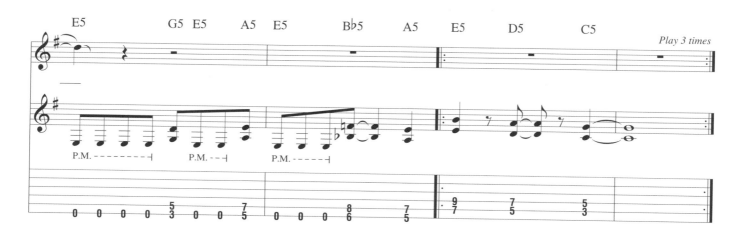

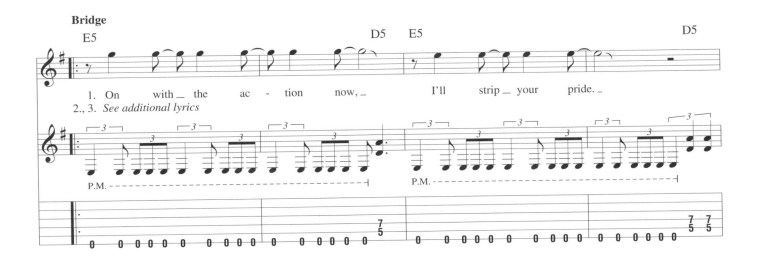

Bridge

1. On with the ac - tion now, I'll strip your pride.
2., 3. *See additional lyrics*

I'll spread your blood a - round, I'll see you writhe.

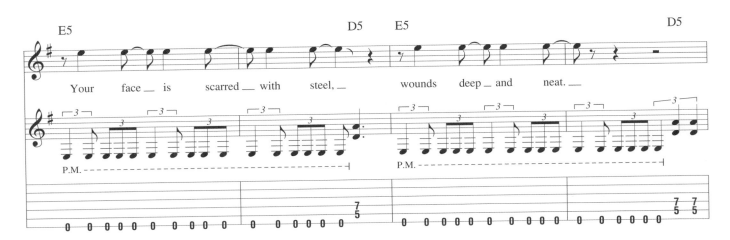

Your face is scarred with steel, wounds deep and neat.

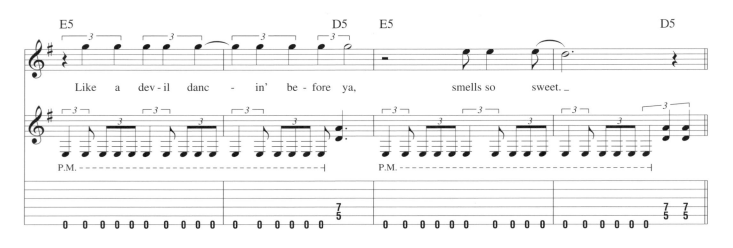

E5 .... D5 E5 .... D5

Like a dev - il danc - in' be - fore ya,   smells so   sweet. __

P.M.

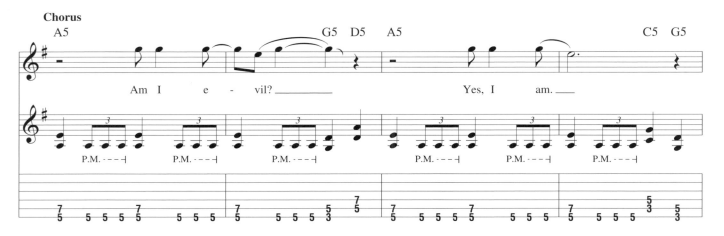

Chorus

A5 .... G5 D5 A5 .... C5 G5

Am I e - vil? _____   Yes, I   am. __

P.M.

3rd time, To Coda

A5 .... G5 D5 A5 .... C5 G5

Am I e - vil? _____   I am man. __

P.M.

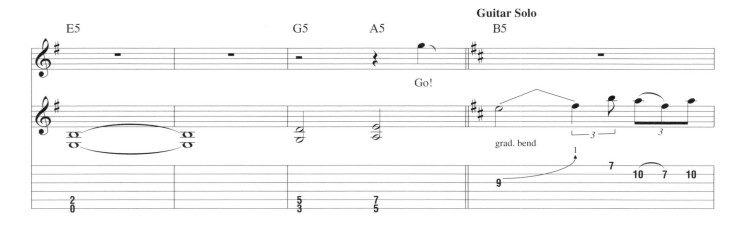

Guitar Solo

E5 .... G5   A5   B5

Go!

grad. bend

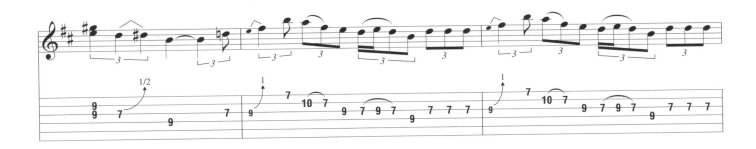

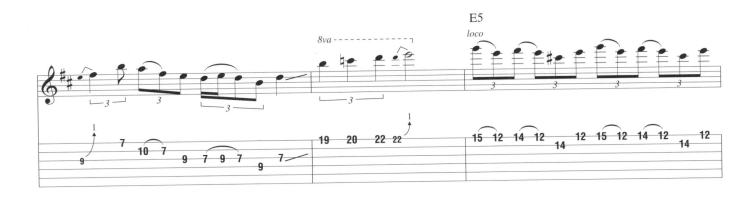

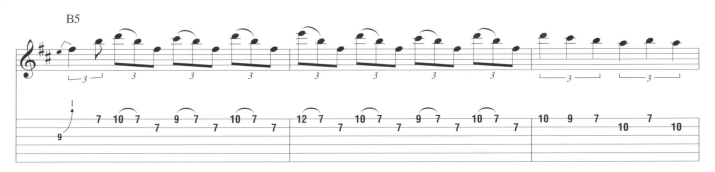

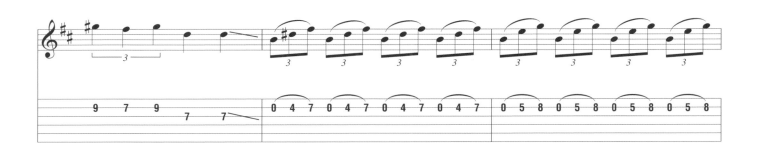

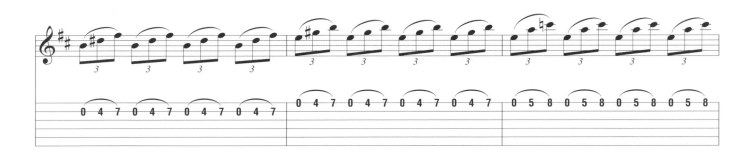

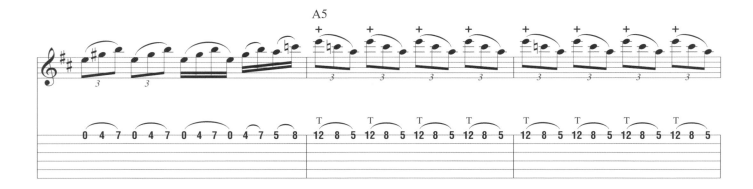

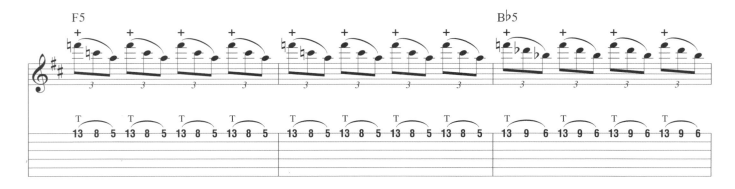

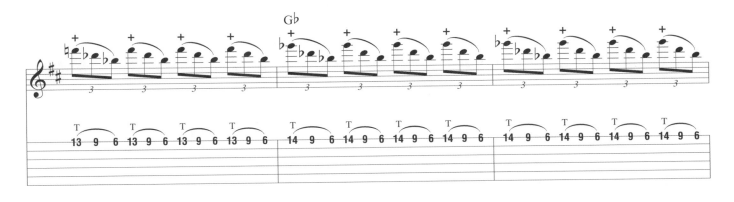

B5

D.S. al Coda

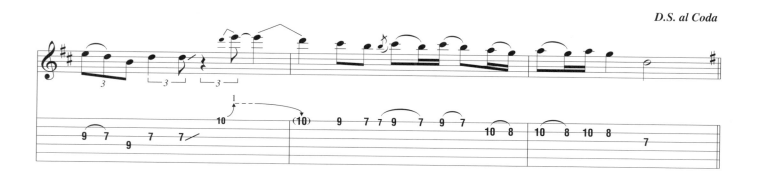

 Coda

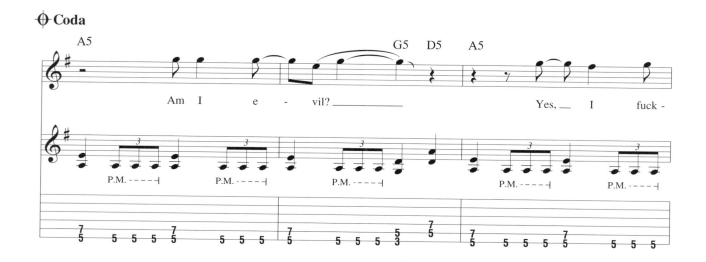

A5

G5 D5 A5

Am I e - vil? _____ Yes, __ I fuck-

C5 G5 A5

G5 D5

ing am. _____ Am I e - vil? _____

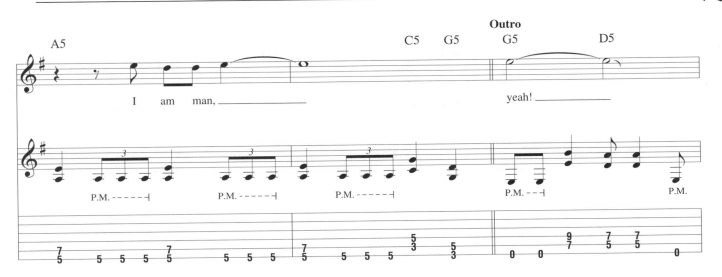

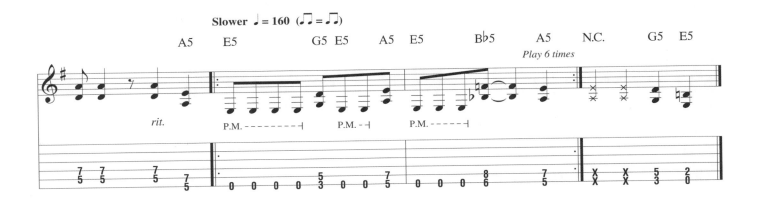

Additional Lyrics

2. As I watched my mother die, I lost my head.
   Revenge now I sought to break with my bread.
   Takin' no chances, you come with me.
   I'll split you to the bone, help set you free.

Bridge 2. I'll make my residence, I'll watch your fire.
   You can come with me, sweet desire.
   My face is long forgotten, my face not my own.
   Sweet and timely whore, take me home.

Bridge 3. My soul is longing for, await my hell,
   Set to avenge my mother, sweeten myself.
   My face is long forgotten, my face not my own.
   Sweet and timely whore, take me home.

Bark at the Moon

Words and Music by Ozzy Osbourne

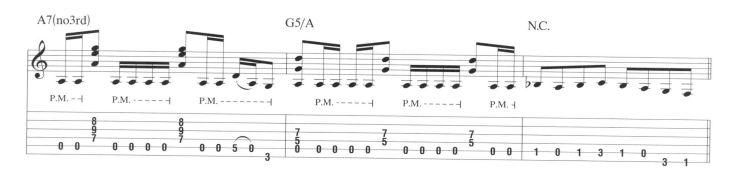

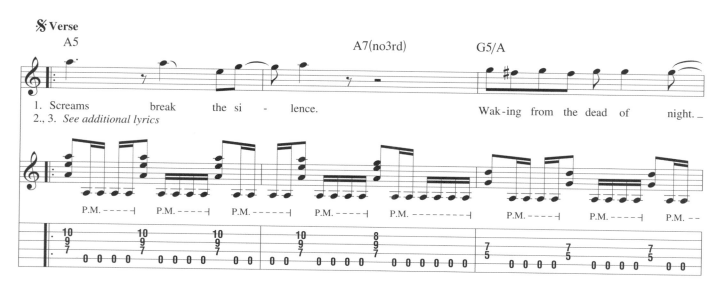

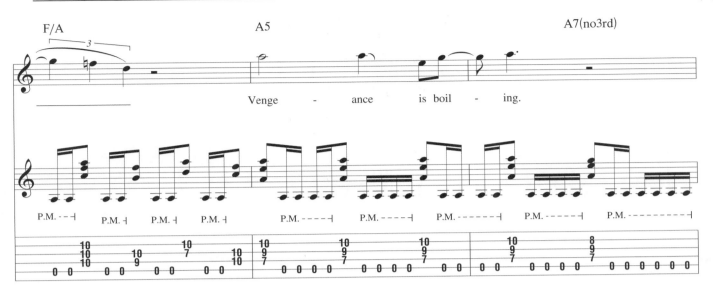

Venge - ance is boil - ing.

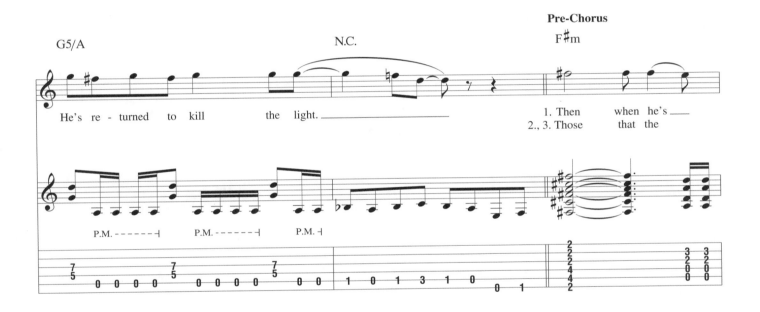

He's re - turned to kill the light.

1. Then when he's
2., 3. Those that the

Pre-Chorus

found who he's look - ing for,
beast is

*Bass plays F#, next 2 meas.

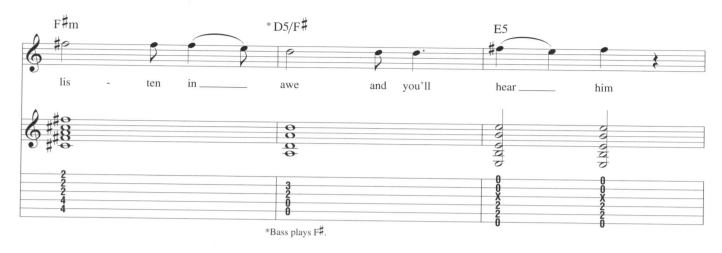

F#m   *D5/F#   E5

lis - ten in _____ awe   and   you'll   hear _____ him

*Bass plays F#.

1.

Interlude

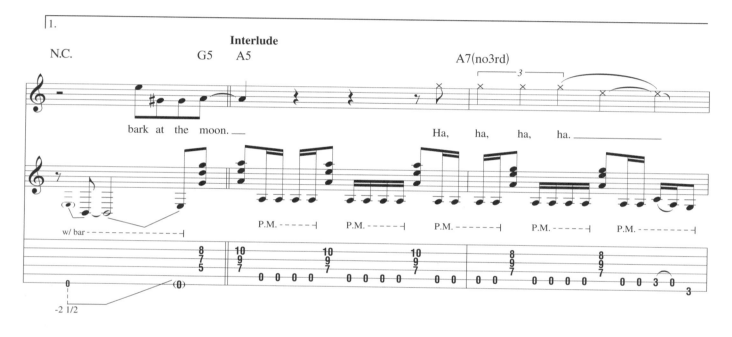

N.C.   G5   A5   A7(no3rd)

bark at the moon. ___   Ha,   ha,   ha,   ha. ___

w/ bar

-2 1/2

P.M. P.M. P.M. P.M. P.M.

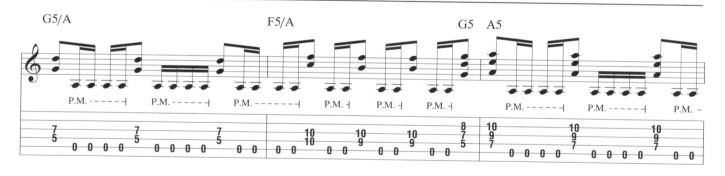

G5/A   F5/A   G5   A5

P.M. P.M. P.M. P.M. P.M. P.M. P.M. P.M. P.M.

A7(no3rd)   G5/A   N.C.

P.M. P.M. P.M. P.M. P.M. P.M.

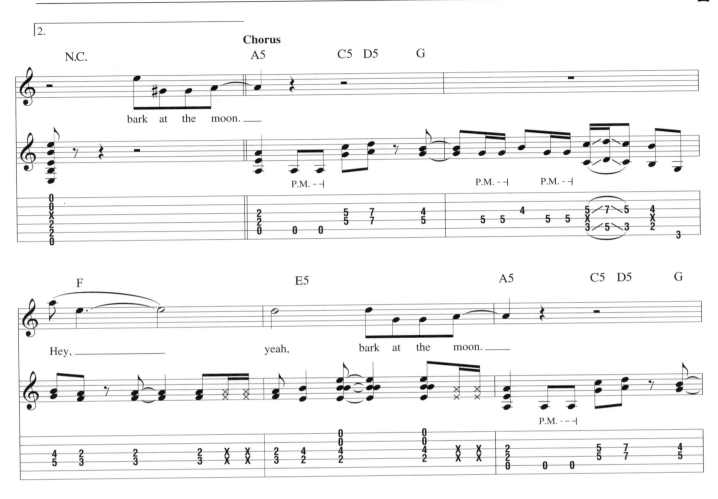

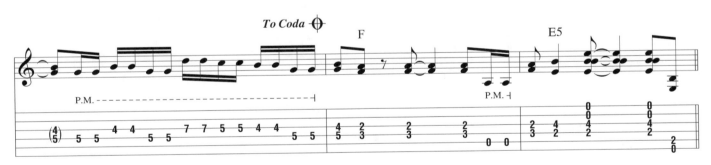

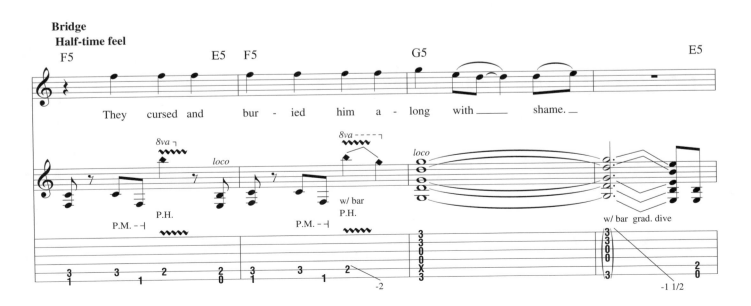

And thought his time-less soul had gone, _____ gone. _____

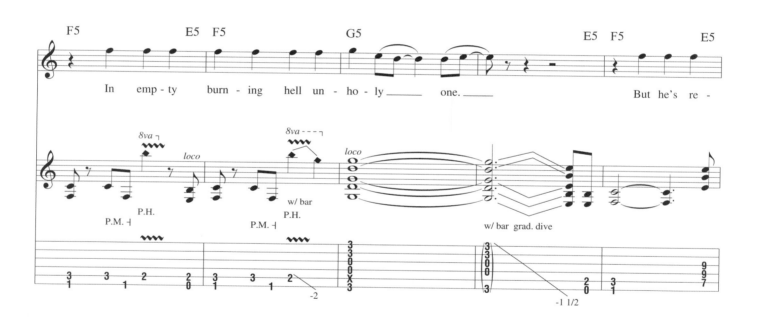

In emp-ty burn-ing hell un-ho-ly _____ one. _____ But he's re-

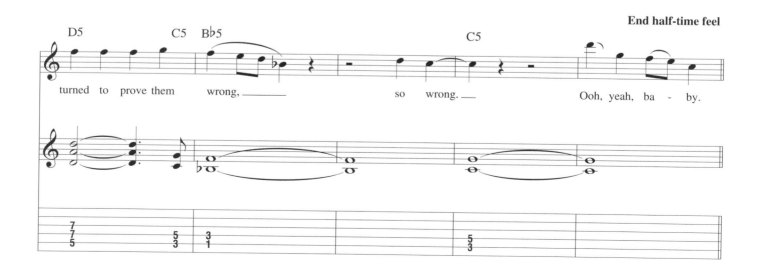

turned to prove them wrong, _____ so wrong. _____ Ooh, yeah, ba-by.

End half-time feel

Guitar Solo

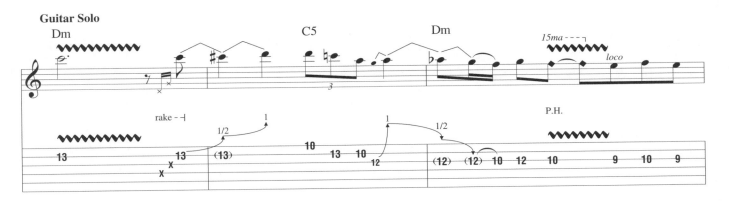

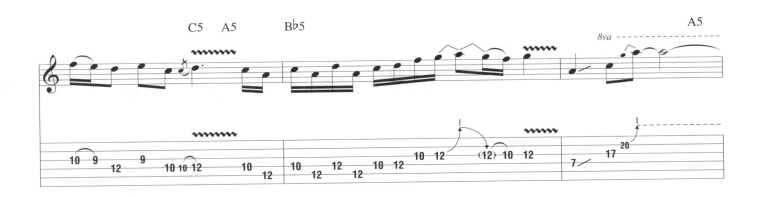

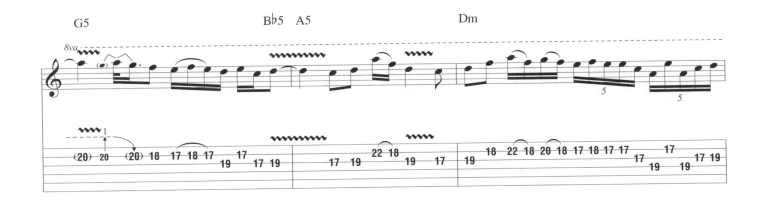

Pitch: C

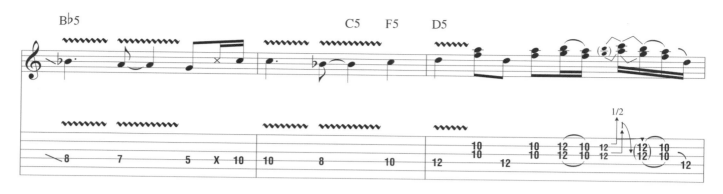

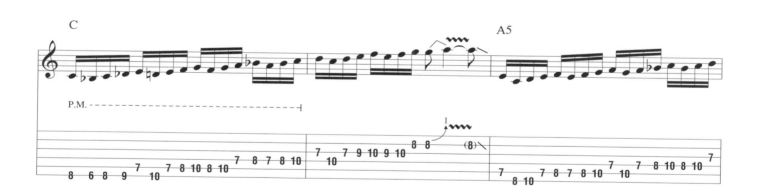

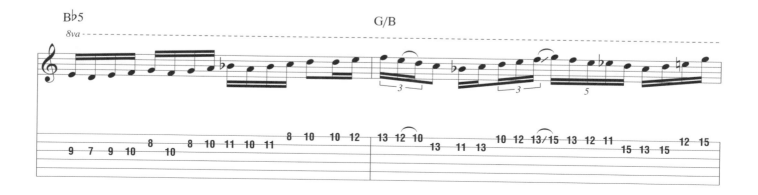

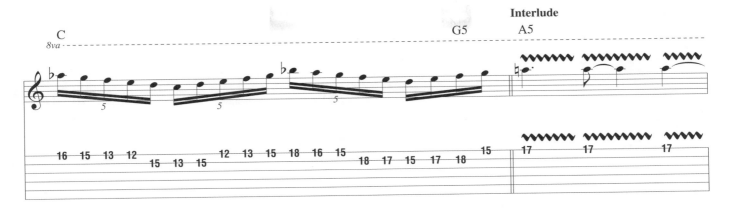

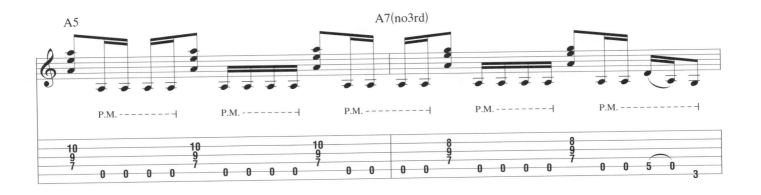

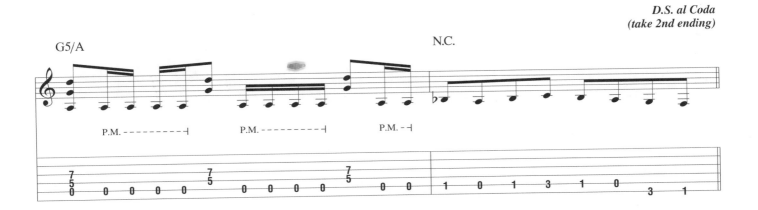

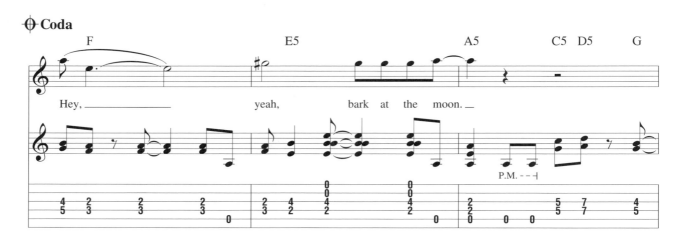

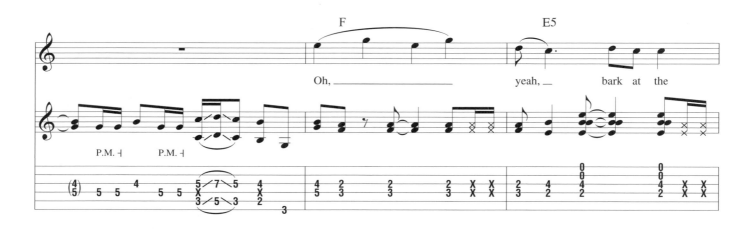

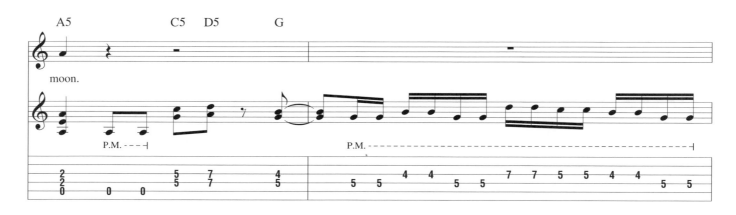

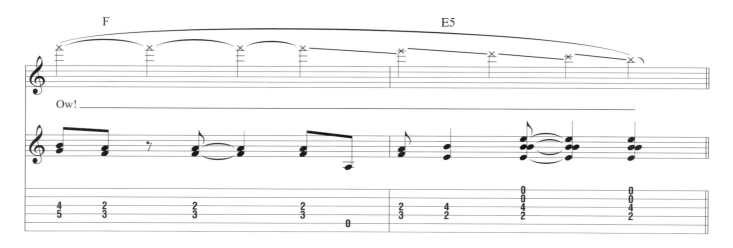

Outro

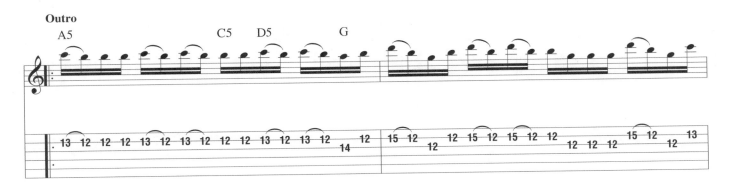

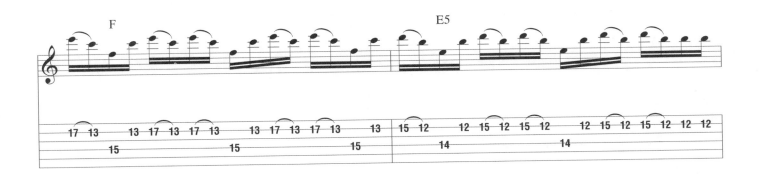

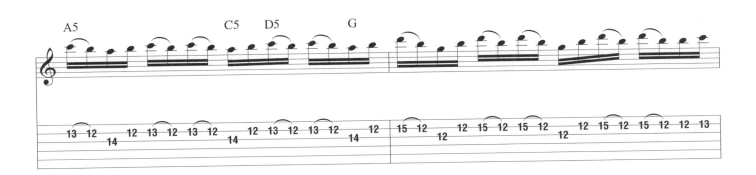

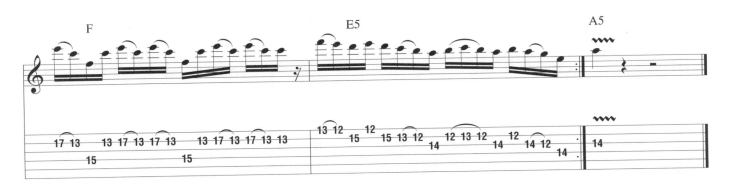

Additional Lyrics

2. Years spent in torment.
    Buried in a nameless grave.
    Now he has risen.
    Miracles would have to save.

3. Howling in shadows.
    Living in a lunar spell.
    He finds his heaven
    Spewing from the mouth of hell.

Brain Damage

Words and Music by Roger Waters

E/D   A7

fac - es   to ___ the   floor, ___   and   ev - 'ry - day ___   the   pa - per - boy ___ brings

D   Dsus2   D7   D7sus2

more.

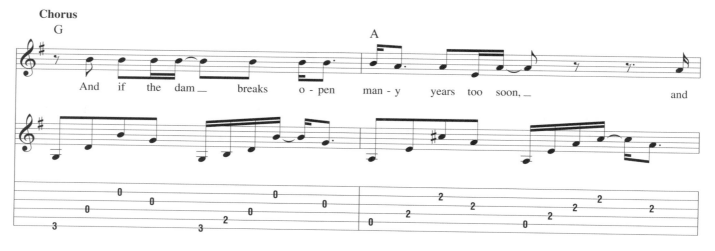

Chorus
G   A

And   if   the   dam ___   breaks   o - pen   man - y   years   too   soon, ___   and

C   G

if   there   is   no   room   up - on ___   the   hill. ___

head.   You raise __ the blade, __

you make __ the change. __   You re - ar - range __ me 'til I'm sane. __

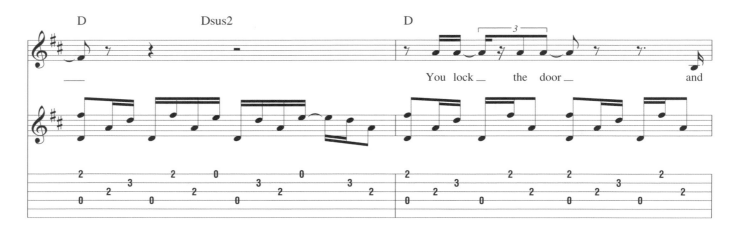

__   You lock __ the door __   and

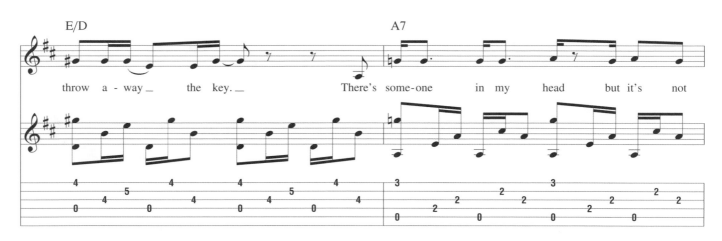

throw a - way __ the key. __   There's some-one   in my   head   but it's   not

Breaking the Chains

Words and Music by Don Dokken, George Lynch and Mick Brown

Intro
Moderate Rock ♩ = 125

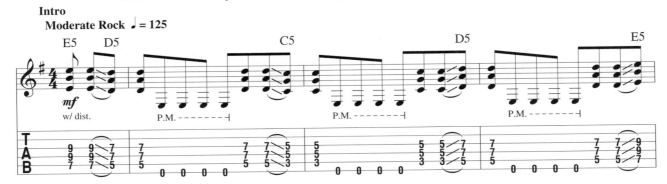

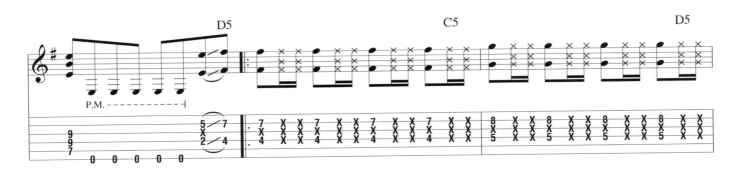

𝄋 Verse
3rd time, substitute Fill 1

1. Sit there   think-in'
2., 3. *See additional lyrics*

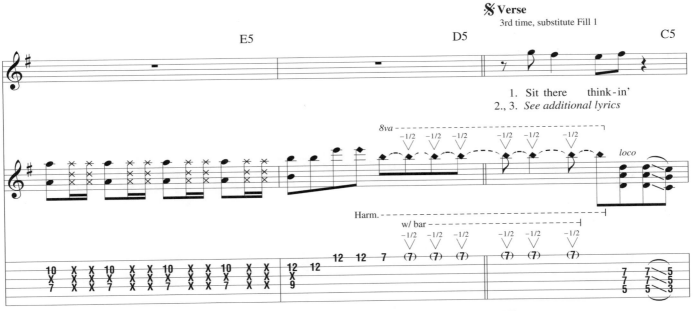

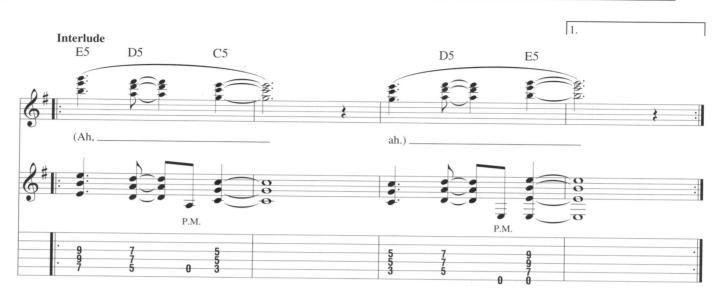

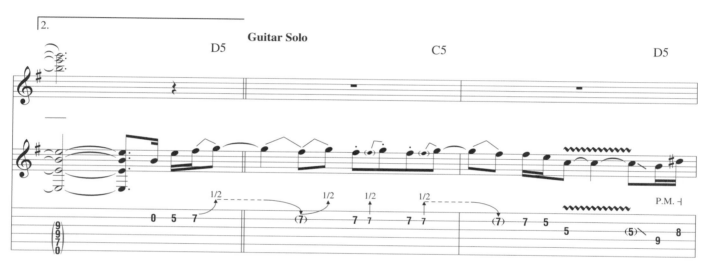

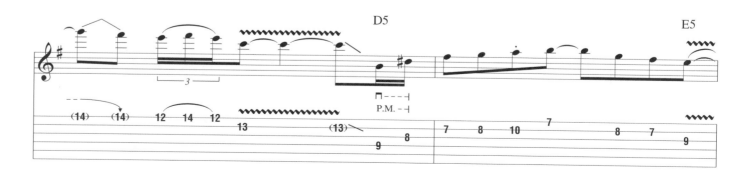

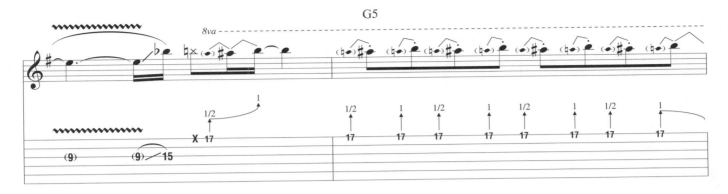

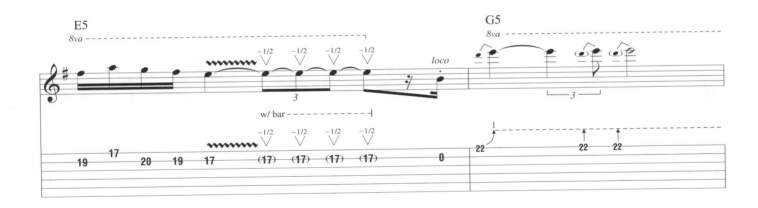

D.S. al Coda

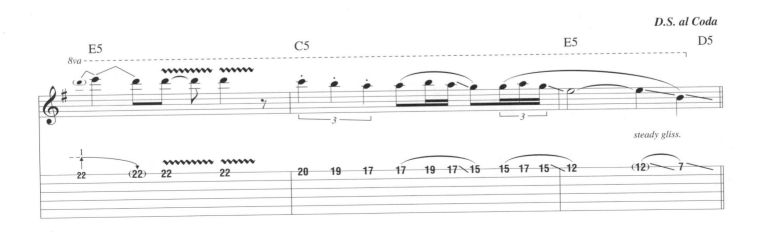

⊕ Coda

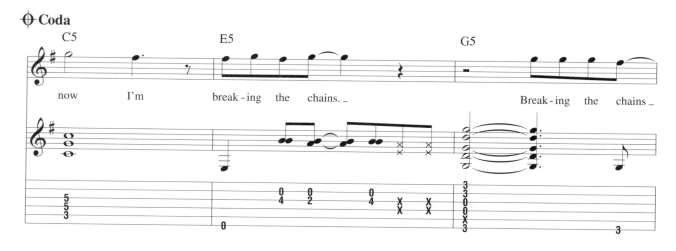

now   I'm   break-ing the chains. _   Break-ing the chains _

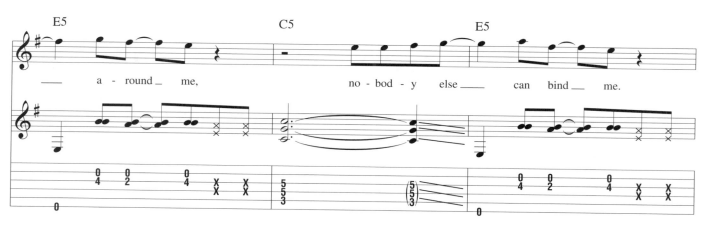

— a - round _ me,   no - bod - y else ___ can bind _ me.

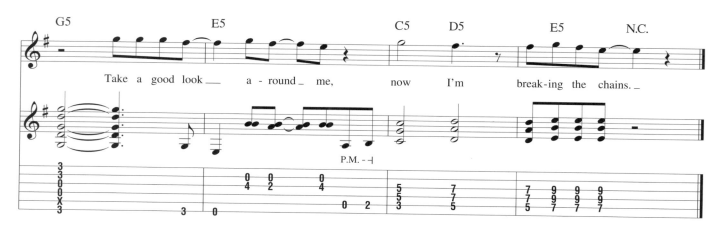

Take a good look ___ a - round _ me,   now   I'm   break-ing the chains. _

Additional Lyrics

2. Got this letter, came today,
   From my baby who left me yesterday.
   Said she loves me, she'll come back.
   She wants to try.
   I won't let her, she'll be upset.
   I know it's better than something I'll regret.
   She'd been dishonest and insincere.
   I lost my mind twenty times a year.

3. Woke up today, I'm alone.
   I look around but, baby, you are gone.
   But I don't mind and I don't worry,
   I will survive.
   I'm alone, now that you're gone.
   Don't need nobody to hold or tie me down.
   I broke the chains, so let me be.
   I've gotta be free.

Carry on Wayward Son

Words and Music by Kerry Livgren

Intro
Moderate Rock ♩ = 124

N.C.

Car - ry   on   my   way - ward   son. _____

There'll   be   peace   when   you ____ are   done. ____   Lay   your   wear - y   head ____

_____ to   rest. _____   Don't   you   cry   no ____ more.

w/ dist.

Em7

steady gliss.

Guitar Solo

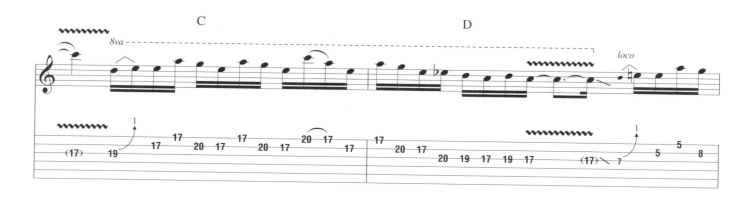

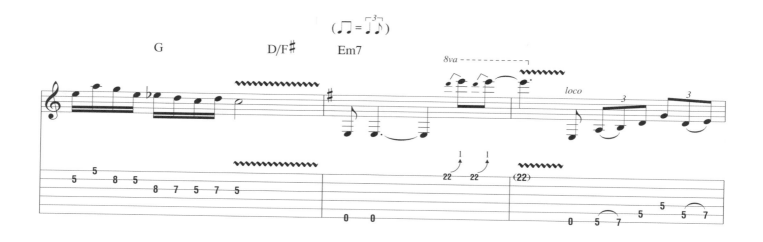

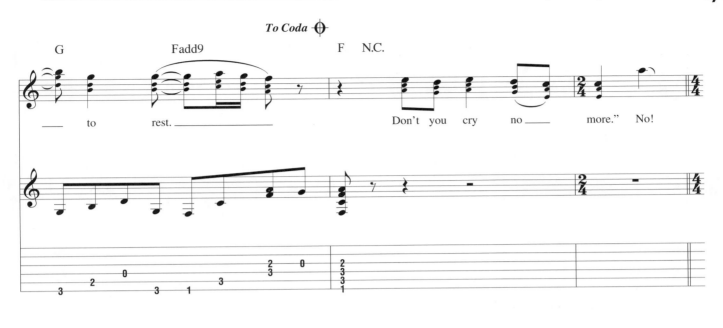

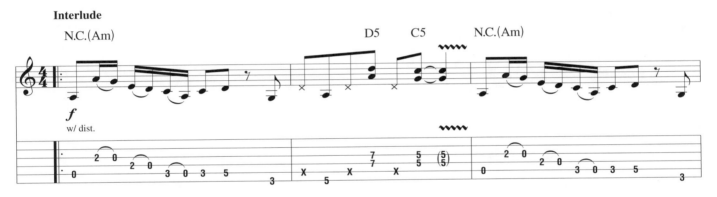

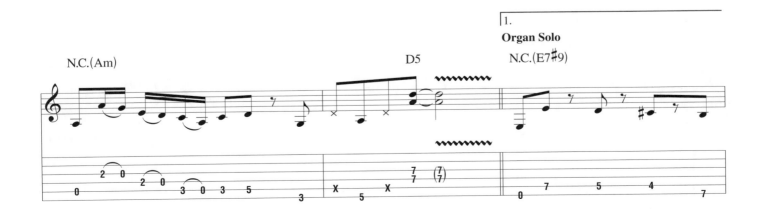

2.

Guitar Solo

N.C.(E7♯9)

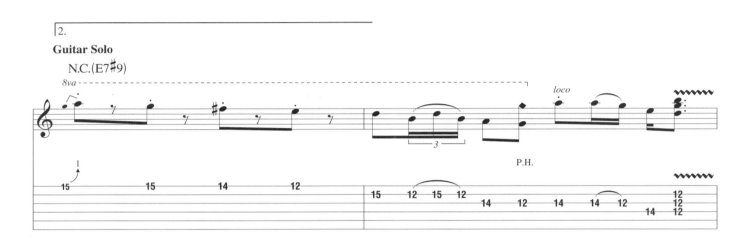

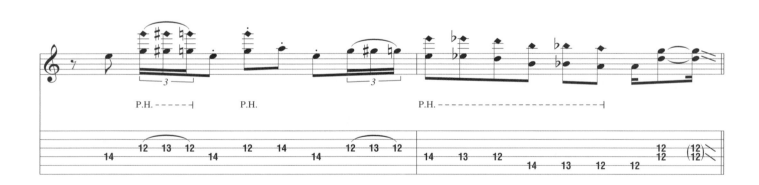

Interlude

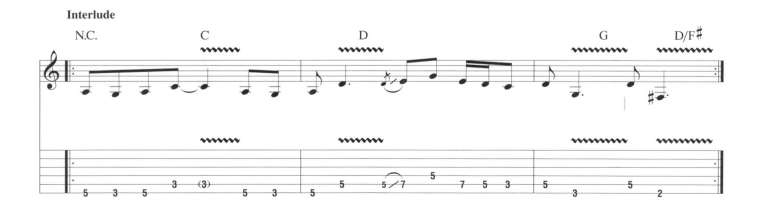

Bridge

Car - ry on, you will al - ways re - mem - ber.____

Car - ry on, noth - ing e - quals the splen - dor. Now your life's no lon - ger

D.S. al Coda

emp - ty.___ Sure - ly, heav-en waits for___ you._____

dist. off

Coda

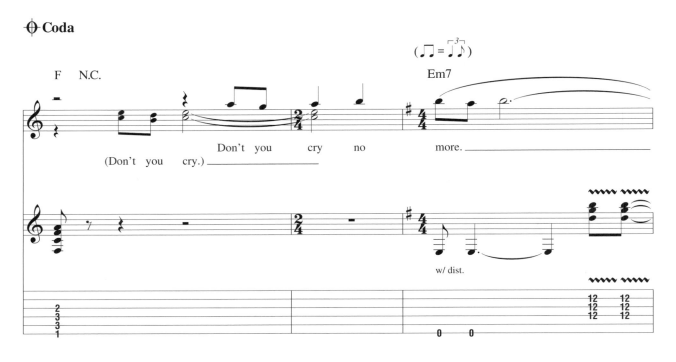

(Don't you   cry.) _____

Don't   you   cry   no   more. _____

w/ dist.

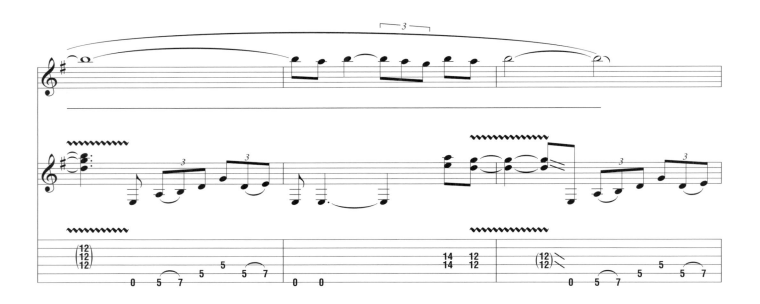

steady gliss.

Guitar Solo

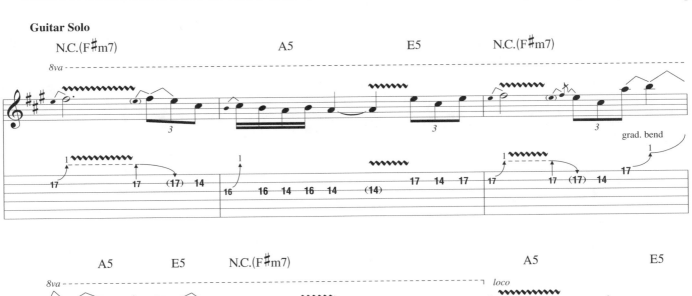

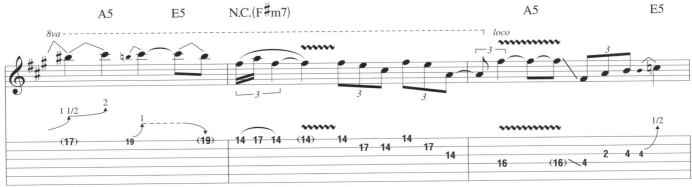

Outro

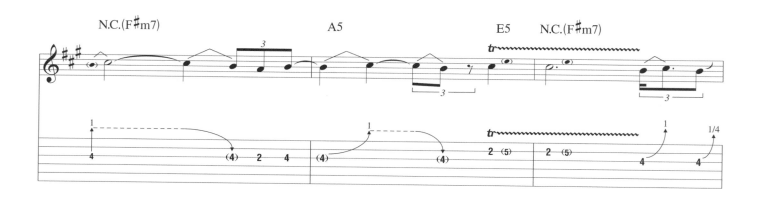

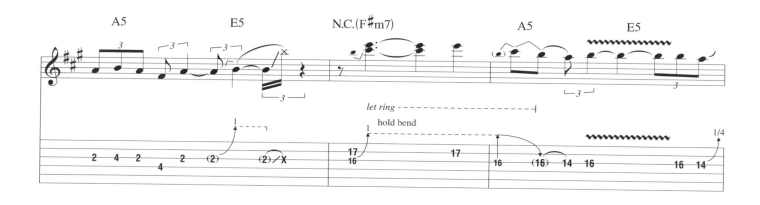

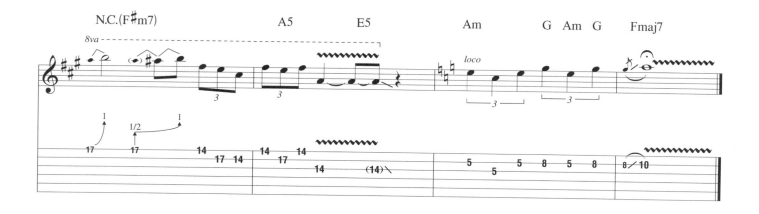

Cold Gin

Words and Music by Ace Frehley

Tune down 1/2 step:
(low to high) E♭-A♭-D♭-G♭-B♭-E♭

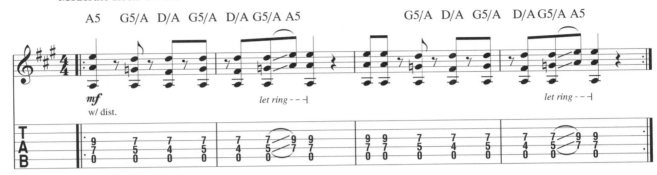

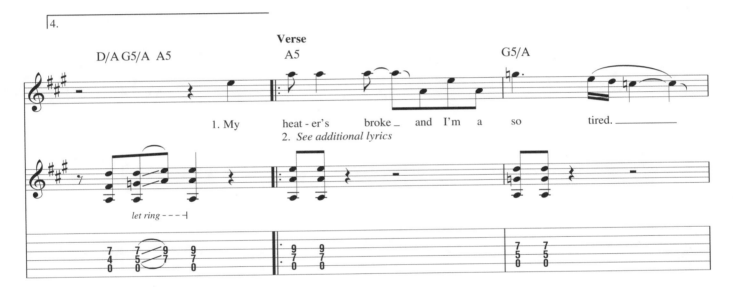

Interlude

To Coda ⊕

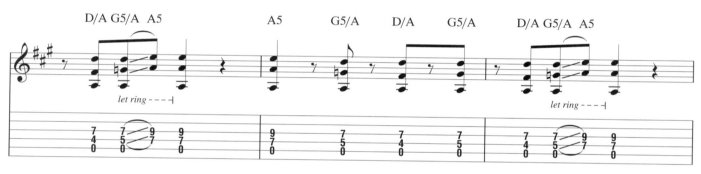

Interlude

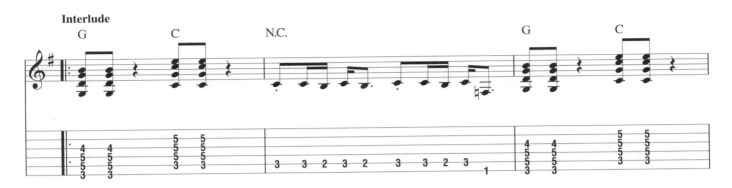

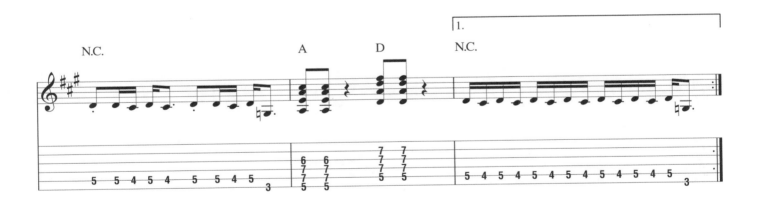

 Coda

Additional Lyrics

2. It's time to leave and get another quart
   Around the corner at the liquor store.
   The cheapest stuff is all I need
   To get me back on my feet again.

Cult of Personality

Words and Music by William Calhoun, Corey Glover, Muzz Skillings and Vernon Reid

Spoken: "And during the few moments that we have left, we want to talk right down to earth in a language that everybody here can easily understand."

*Key signature denotes G Dorian.

Bridge

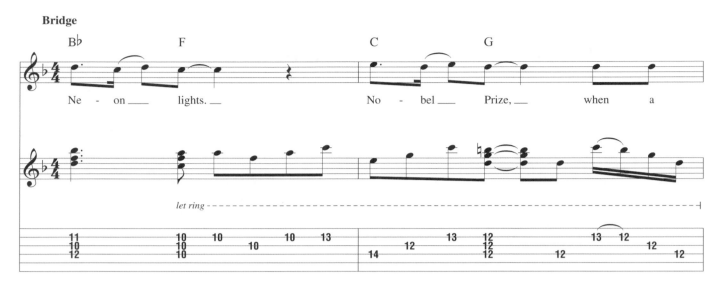

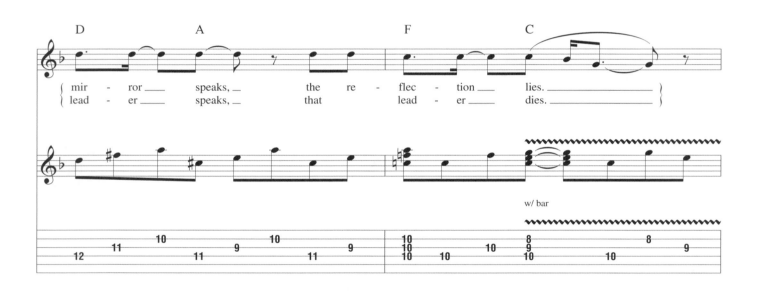

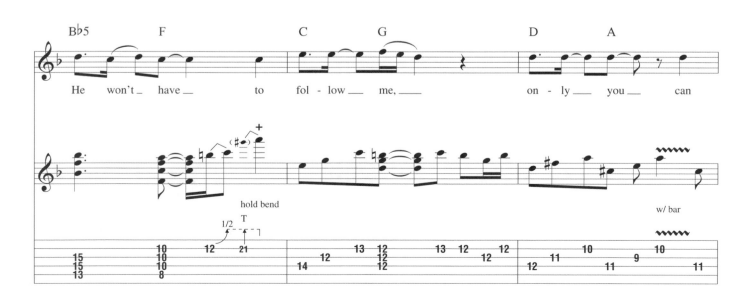

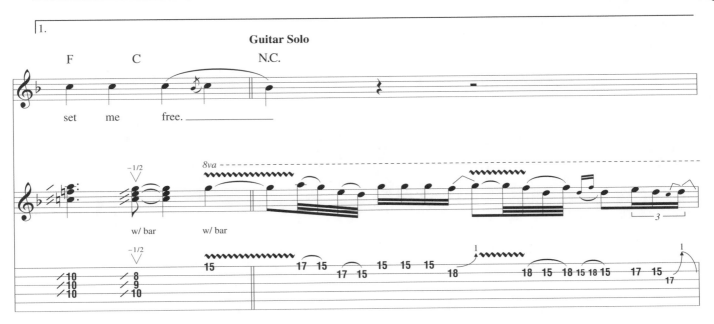

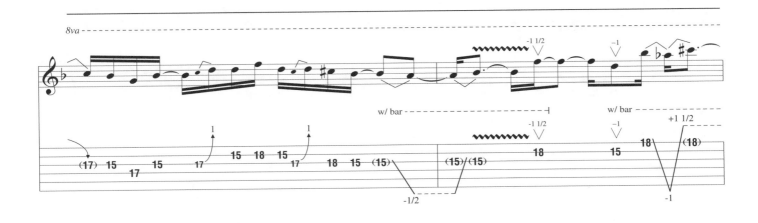

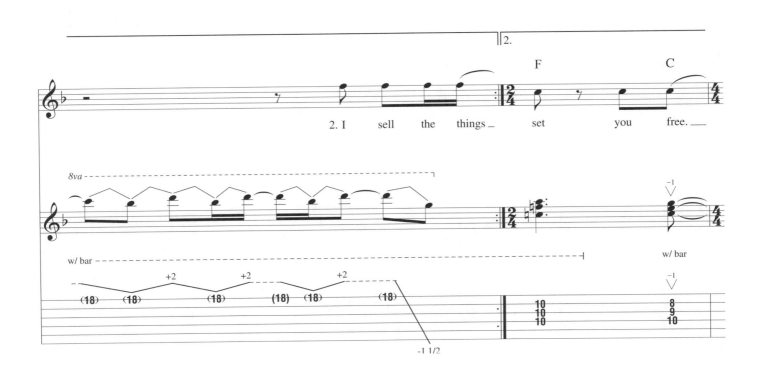

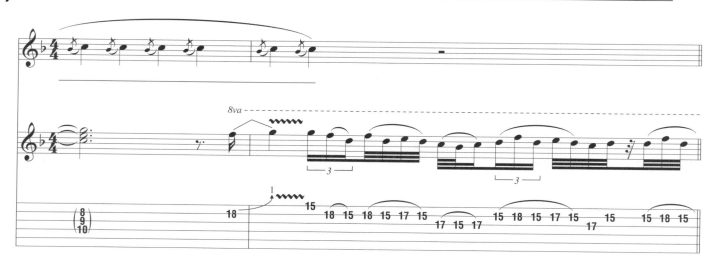

Guitar Solo

N.C.

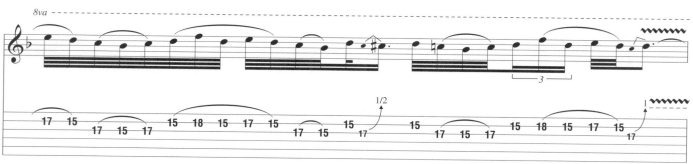

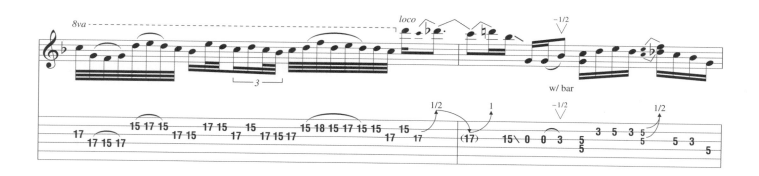

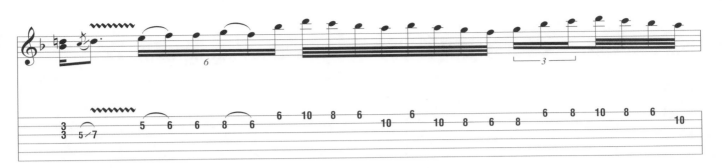

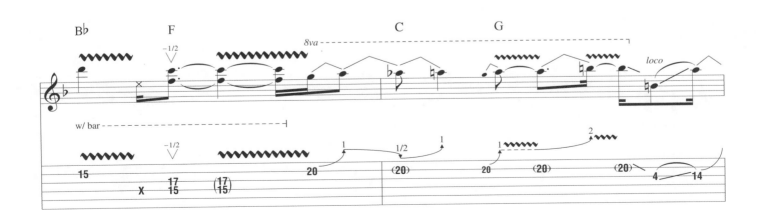

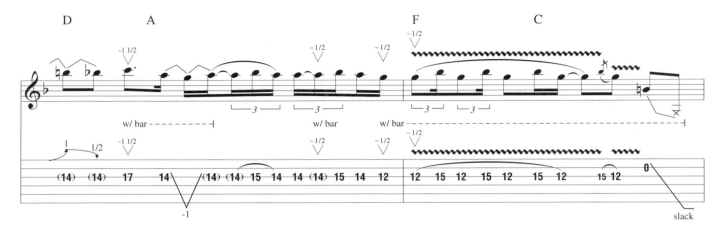

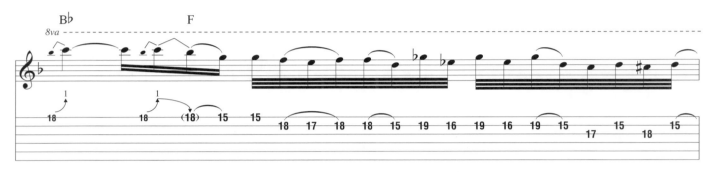

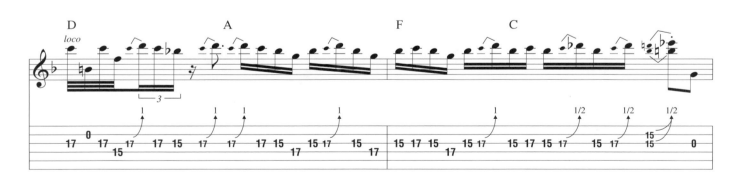

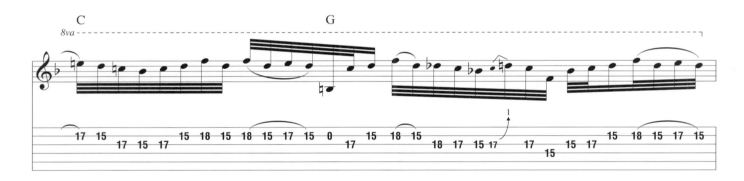

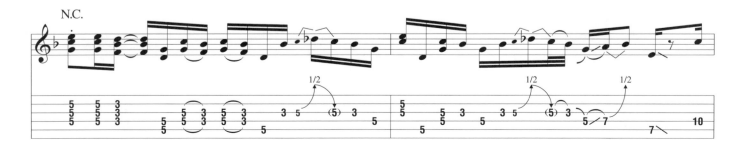

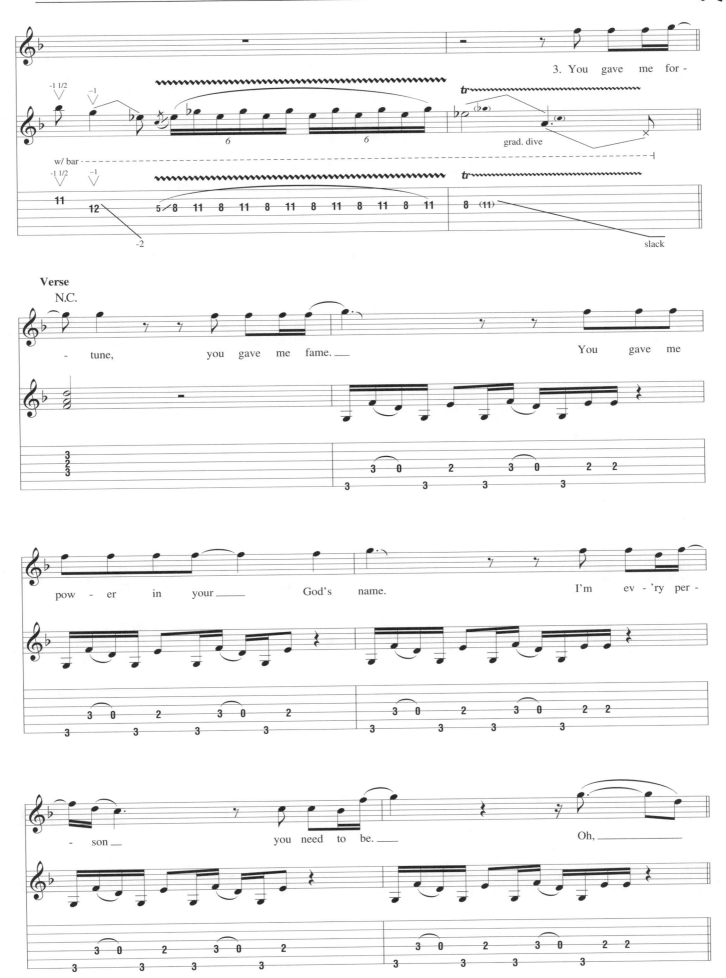

Outro
Double-time feel
N.C.

not what your coun - try can do for you..."

Spoken: *"The only thing we have to fear, is fear itself."*

Additional Lyrics

2. I sell the things you need to be,
   I'm the smilin' face on your TV.
   Oh, I'm the cult of personality.
   I exploit you, still you love me.
   I tell you one and one makes three.
   Oh, I'm the cult of personality.
   Like Joseph Stalin and Gandhi,
   Oh, I'm the cult of personality,
   The cult of personality,
   The cult of personality.

Decadence Dance

Words and Music by Nuno Bettencourt and Gary Cherone

Tune down 1/2 step:
(low to high) Eb-Ab-Db-Gb-Bb-Eb

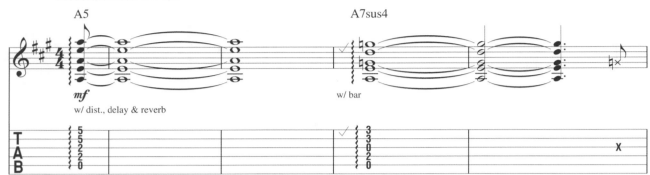

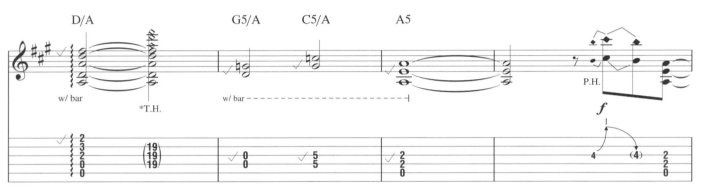

*Touch harmonic produced by lightly touching strings
w/ right hand while previous chord is still ringing.

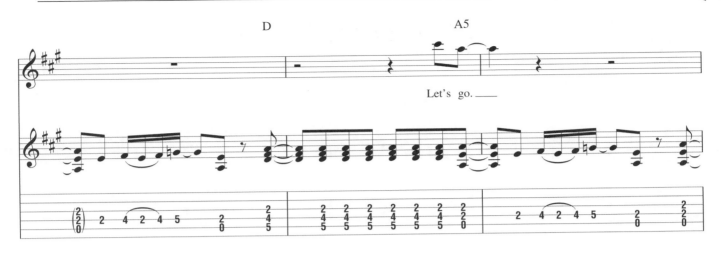

*Pick behind nut.

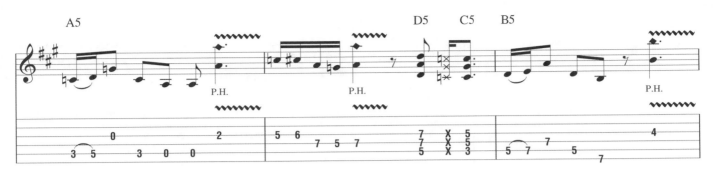

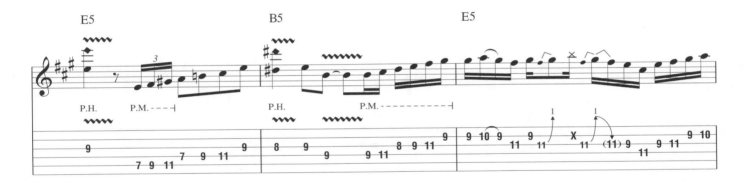

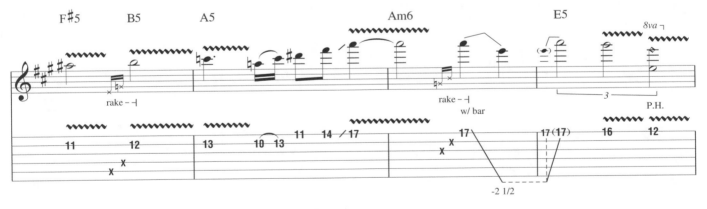

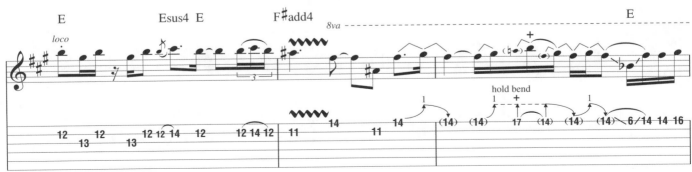

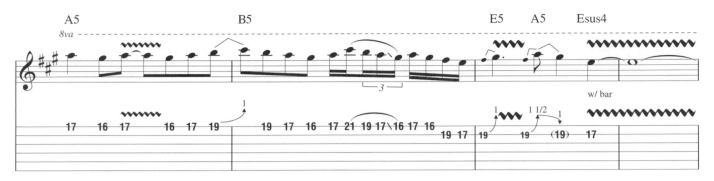

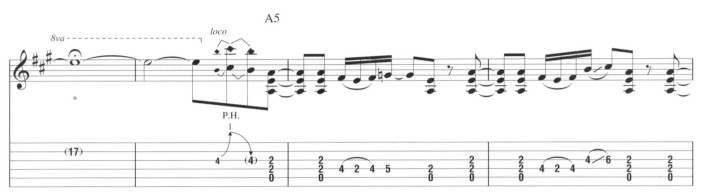

*Improvise over sustained note using feedback, whammy bar, glissandos and pick noises.

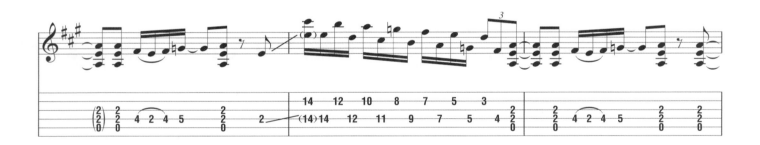

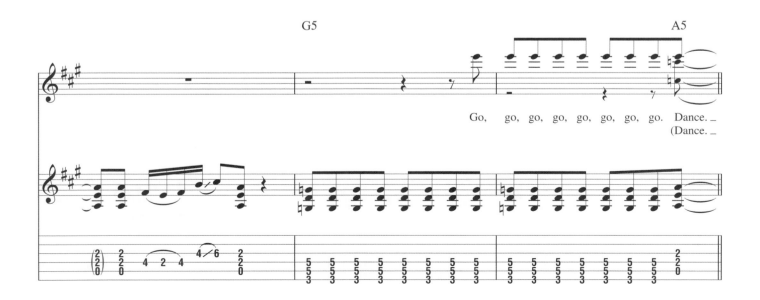

Go, go, go, go, go, go, go, go. Dance. _
(Dance. _

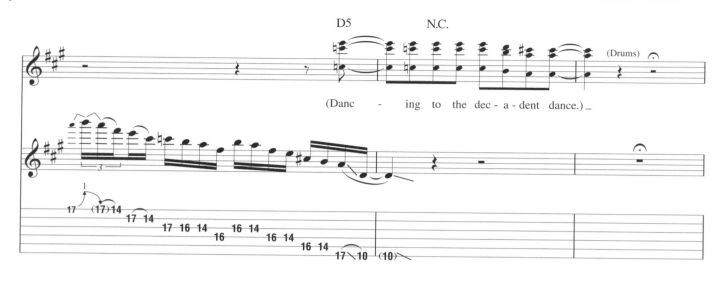

(Danc - ing to the dec - a - dent dance.)

Huh.

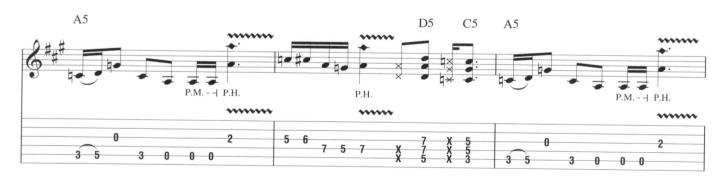

Pitch: E

Don't Treat Me Bad

Words and Music by Carl Snare, Bill Leverty, Michael Foster and Cosby Ellis

Tune down 1/2 step:
(low to high) Eb-Ab-Db-Gb-Bb-Eb

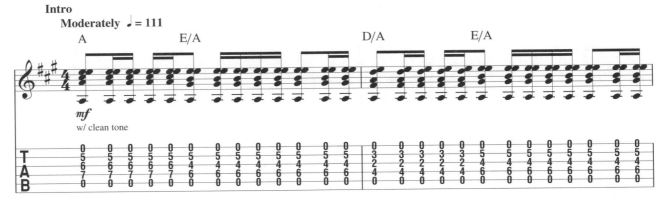

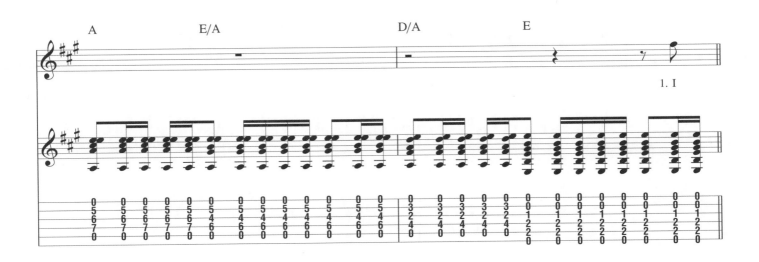

Verse

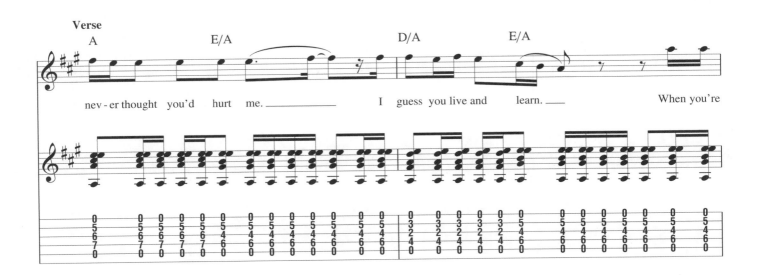

nev-er thought you'd hurt me. _____ I guess you live and learn. _____ When you're

*Rub edge of pick down the string, producing a scratchy sound.

Interlude

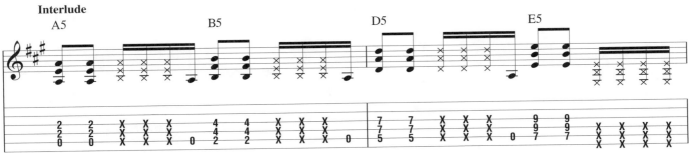

D.S. al Coda 2

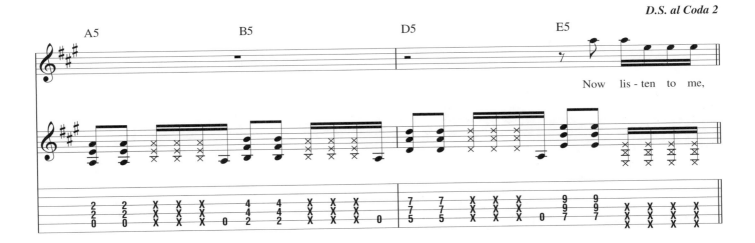

Coda 2

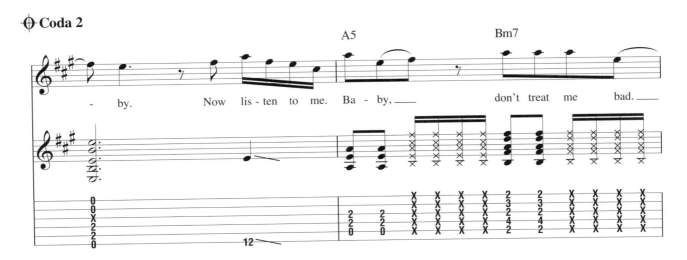

Down Boys

Words and Music by Jani Lane, Joey Allen, Jerry Dixon, Steven Sweet and Erik Turner

Tune down 1/2 step:
(low to high) Eb-Ab-Db-Gb-Bb-Eb

Intro
Moderate Rock ♩ = 112

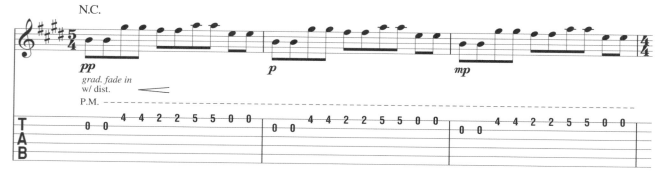

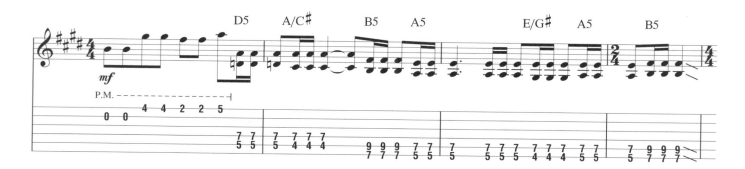

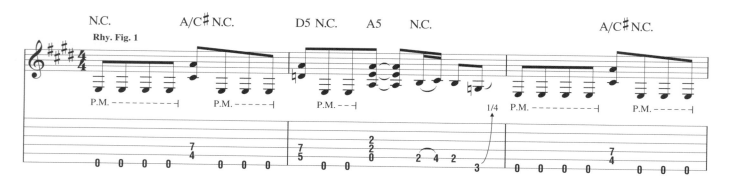

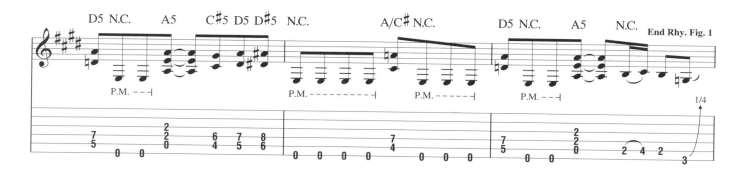

*Strike note while bar is still depressed.

D.S. al Coda

**Strike harmonic while bar is still depressed.

Additional Lyrics

3. You comb your hair, put on your shades,
   You look real cool.
   You're giving me the runaround, make me feel like a fool.
   Got a lot of nerve to call me cheap, even though it's true.
   Now I don't care where we go tonight, take me along with you.

4. Some things you do really make me mad,
   I must confess.
   The way the streetlight silhouettes your thighs,
   Inside your dress,
   Oo, yeah.

Empire

Words and Music by Geoff Tate and Michael Wilton

Intro
Moderately slow Rock ♩ = 80

Next message, saved, Saturday at 9:24 P.M. "Sorry, I'm just...it's starting to hit me like a, um, um, two ton heavy thing."

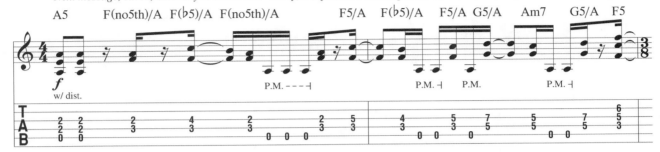

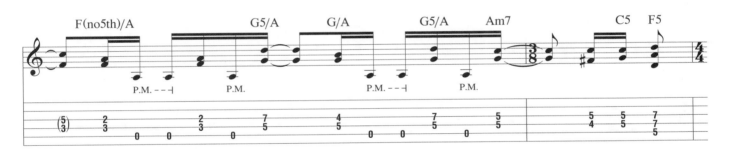

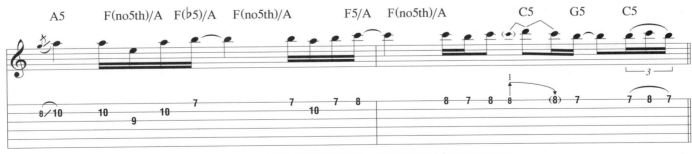

Verse

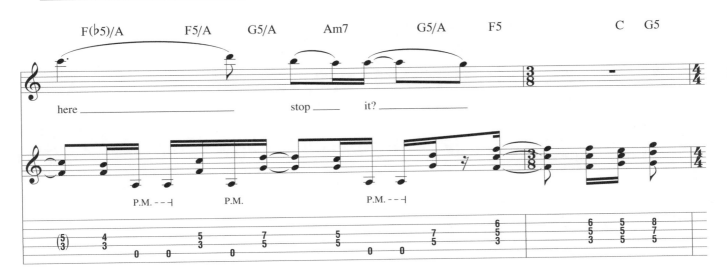

here _____ stop _____ it? _____

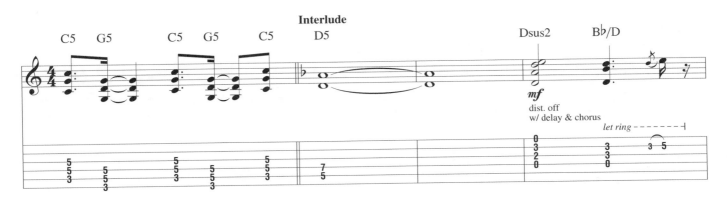

Interlude

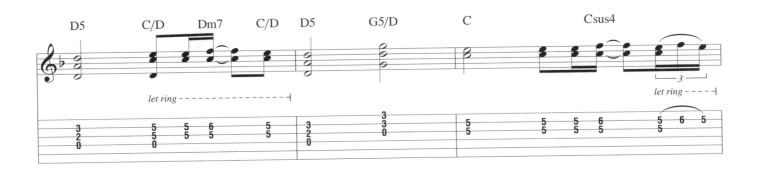

Spoken:
In fiscal year 1986 to '87 the local, state, and federal governments spent a combined total of 60.6 million dollars on law enforcement.

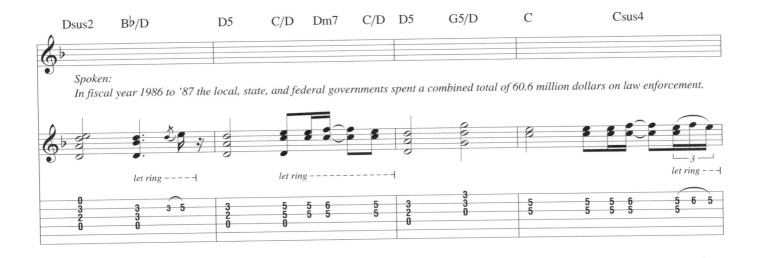

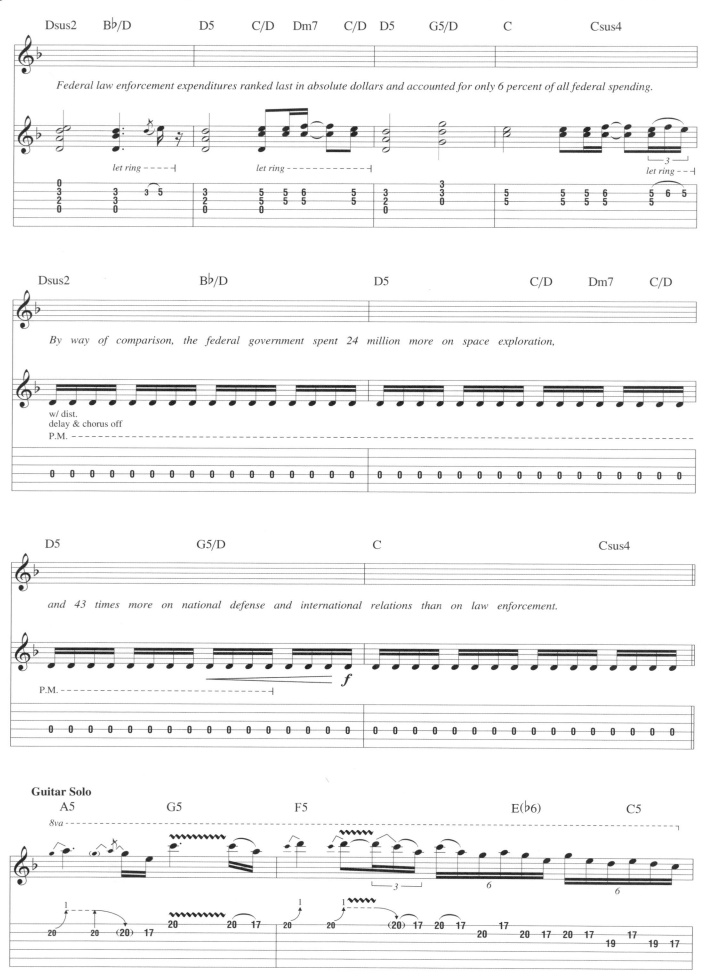

Federal law enforcement expenditures ranked last in absolute dollars and accounted for only 6 percent of all federal spending.

By way of comparison, the federal government spent 24 million more on space exploration,

and 43 times more on national defense and international relations than on law enforcement.

Guitar Solo

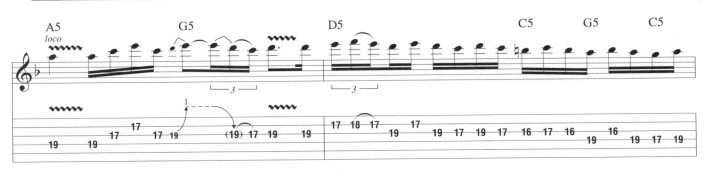

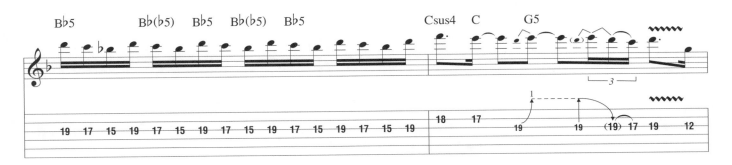

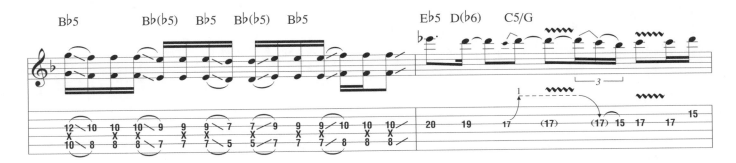

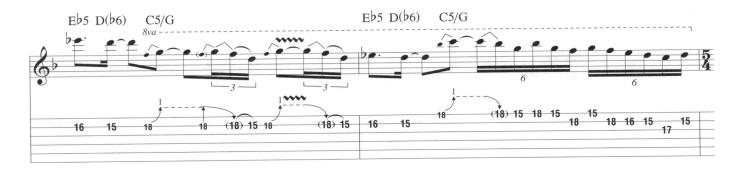

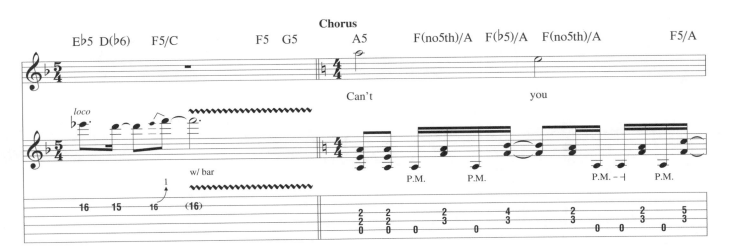

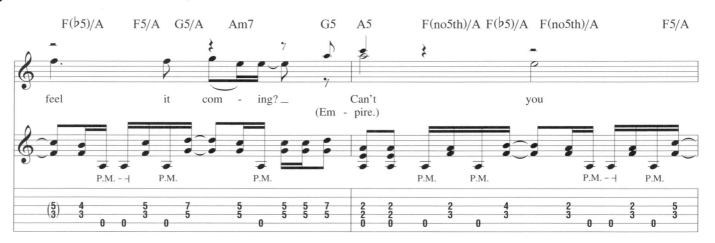

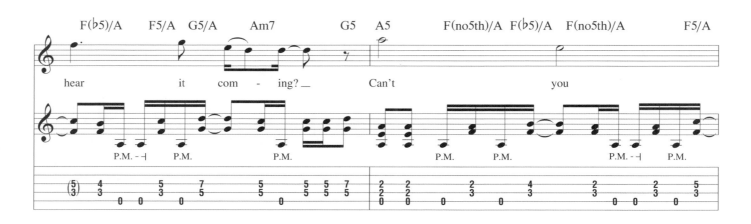

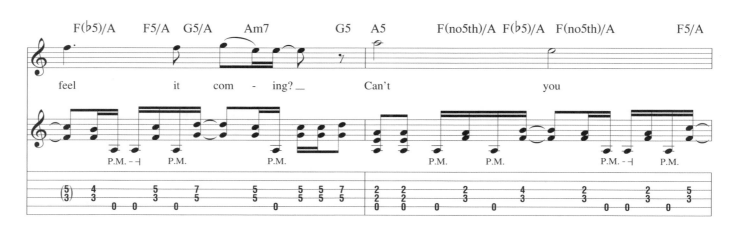

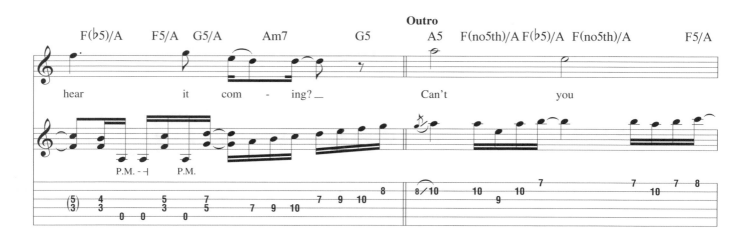

Here I Go Again

Words and Music by Bernie Marsden and David Coverdale

And I've made up my mind, ___   I ain't wast - in' no more   time. ___

Verse

3. I'm just an - oth - er heart in ___ need of res - cue, ___

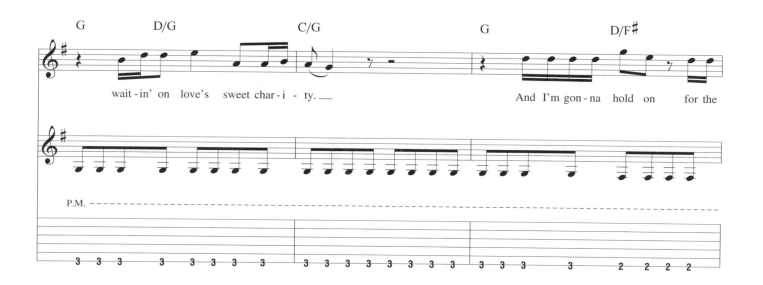

wait - in' on love's sweet char - i - ty. ___   And I'm gon - na hold on   for the

Pre-Chorus

C/E   C5   G/B   Am7   D

rest of my days. ___   'Cause I know what it means ___   to

Am7   D5   C5   D5

walk a - long ___ the lone - ly street ___ of dreams. ___   And

Chorus

G5   C   D   C   D   G5   C

here I go a - gain ___ on my own, ___   go - in' down the on - ly road ___ I've ev - er known. ___

Like a drift-er I___ was born___ to walk a-lone.___

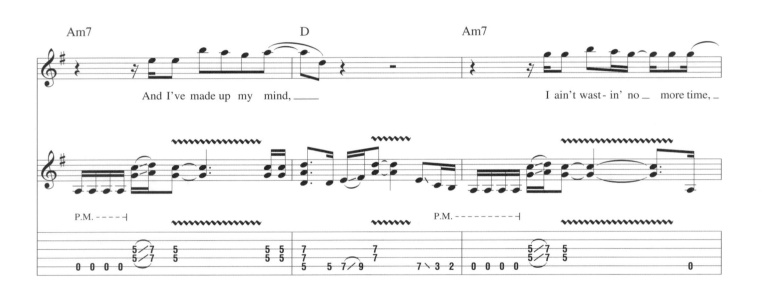

And I've made up my mind,___

I ain't wast-in' no__ more time,_

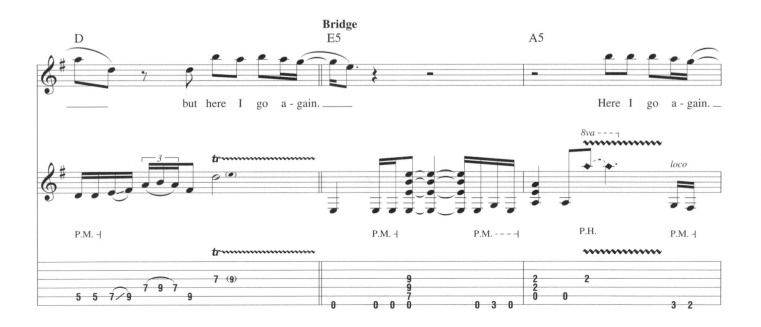

___ but here I go a-gain.___

Here I go a-gain.___

Bridge

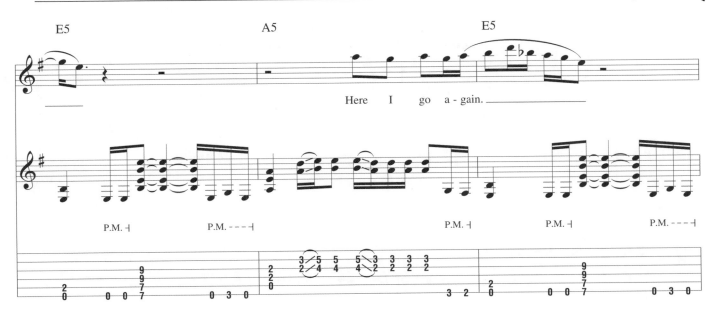

Here I go a - gain.

Here I go.

Guitar Solo

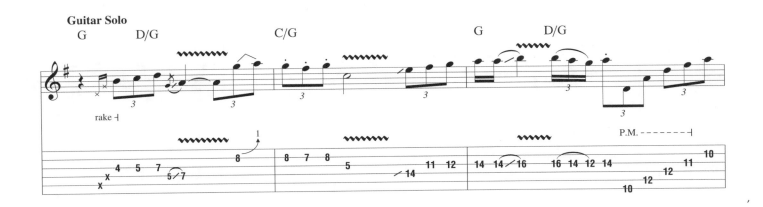

Chorus

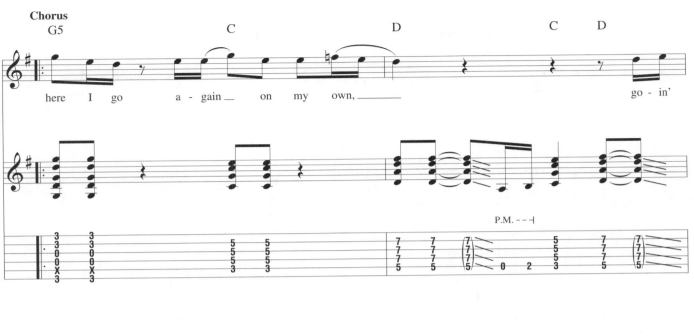

here I go a - gain on my own, go - in'

down the on - ly road I've ev-er known. Like a drift-er I was born to walk a-lone.

And I've made up my mind,
'Cause I know what it means to

Holy Diver

Words and Music by Ronnie James Dio

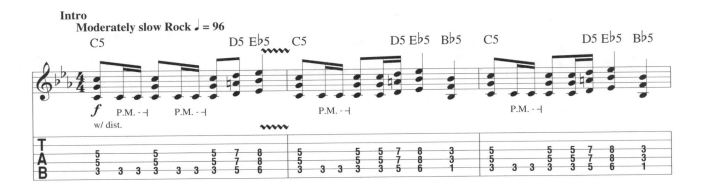

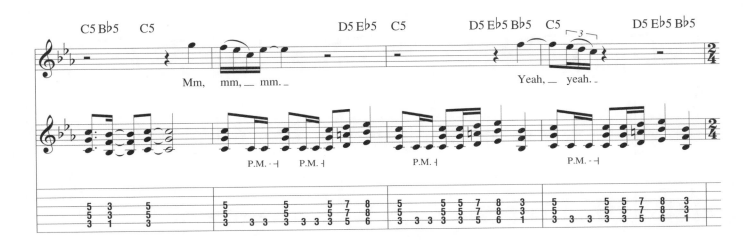

𝄋 Verse
2nd time, substitute Fill 1

shin - y di - 'monds   like the eyes of a cat in the black and   blue.
4. *See additional lyrics*

Some-thing is com - ing for you.   Look out!   Race for the morn-ing.   You can

hide in the sun till you see the light.   Oh, we will pray ___ it's al - right.

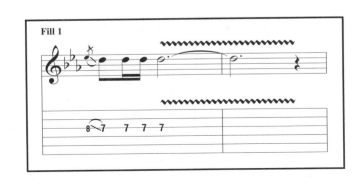

Fill 1

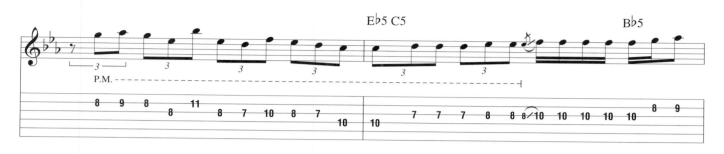

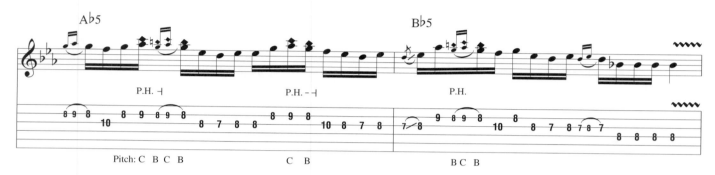

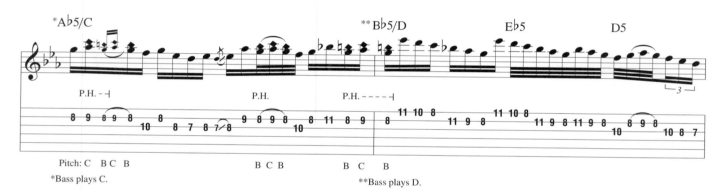

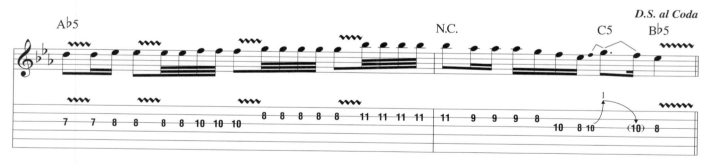

Additional Lyrics

4. Holy diver, you've been down too long in the midnight sea.
   Oh, what's becoming of me? No! No!
   Ride the tiger. You could see his stripes but you know he's clean.
   Oh, don't you see what I mean?
   Gotta get away, get away.

Iron Man

Words and Music by Frank Iommi, John Osbourne, WIlliam Ward and Terence Butler

Intro
Slow Rock ♩ = 69
N.C.(Em)

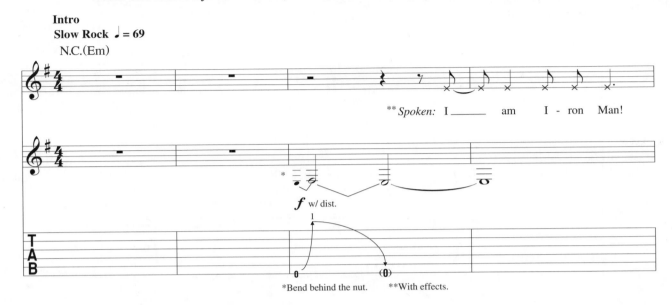

** *Spoken:* I _____ am I - ron Man!

𝆑 w/ dist.

*Bend behind the nut.   **With effects.

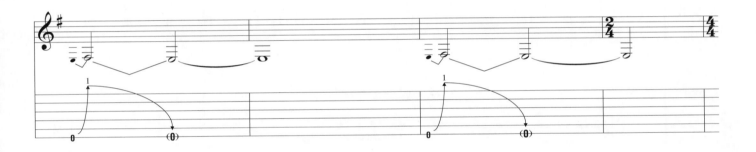

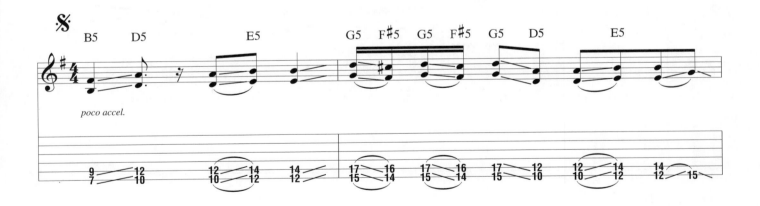

B5   D5   E5   G5   F#5   G5   F#5   G5   D5   E5

poco accel.

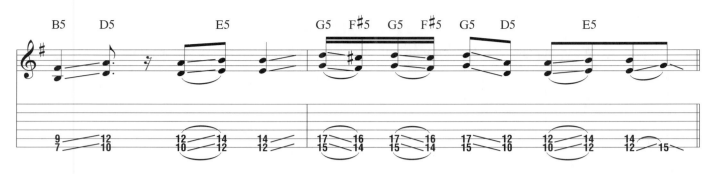

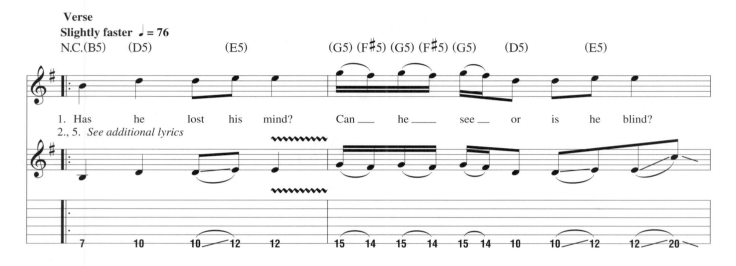

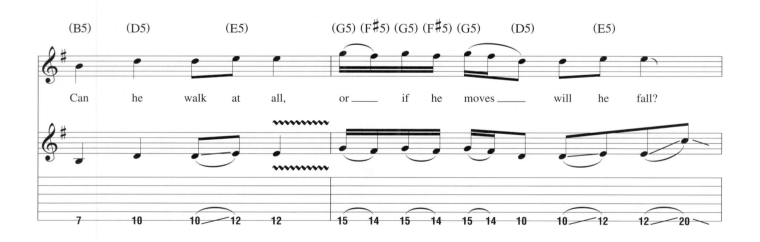

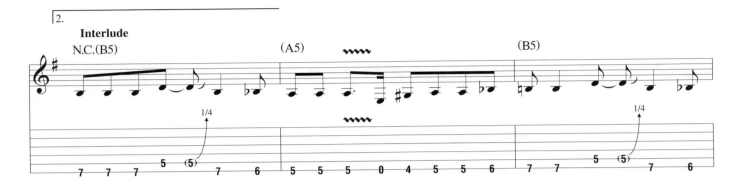

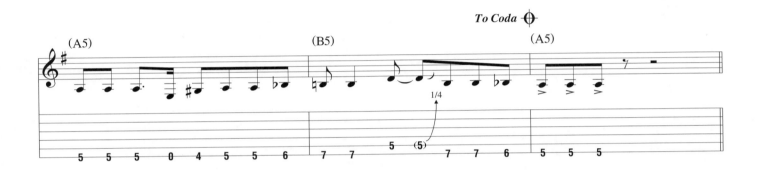

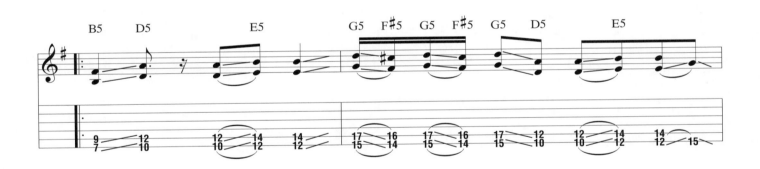

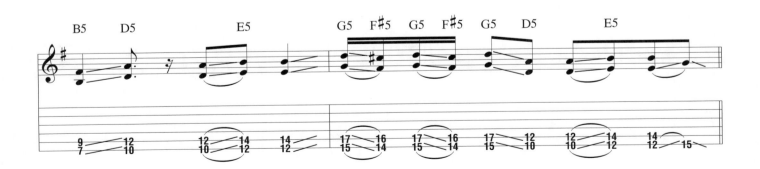

Verse

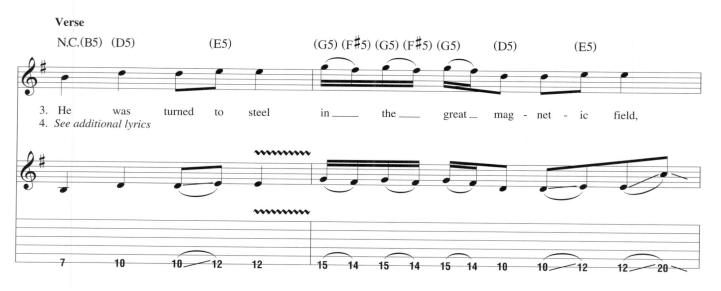

3. He was turned to steel in ___ the ___ great ___ mag - net - ic field,
4. *See additional lyrics*

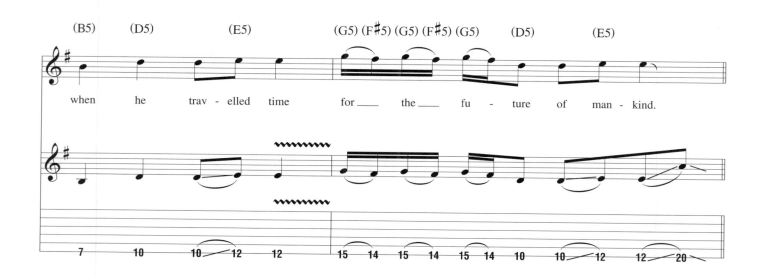

when he trav - elled time for ___ the ___ fu - ture of man - kind.

Bridge

No-bod- y wants ___ him, _ he just stares _ at the world. _
See additional lyrics

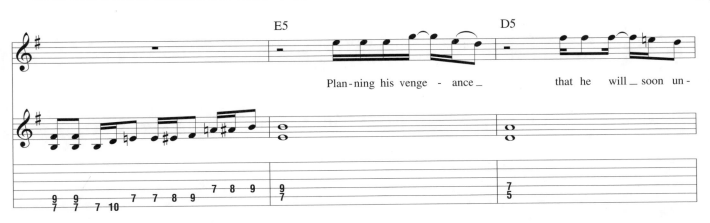

Plan-ning his venge - ance _ that he will _ soon un -

furl. _

Interlude
Double-time ♩ = 164
N.C.(C#m)

Guitar Solo
N.C.(C#m)

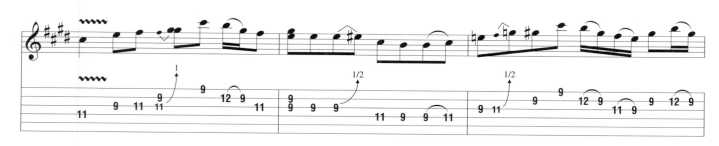

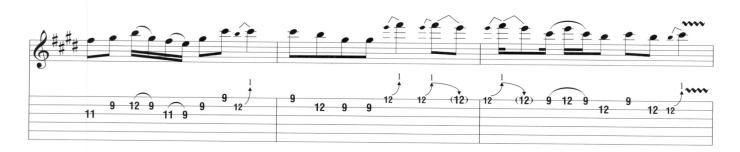

D.S. al Coda
(take 2nd ending)

Coda

Double-time ♩ = 164

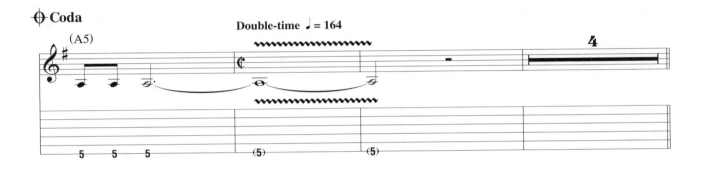

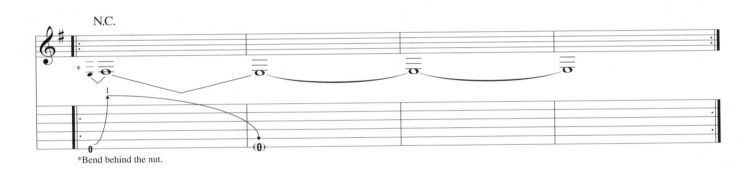

Bend behind the nut.

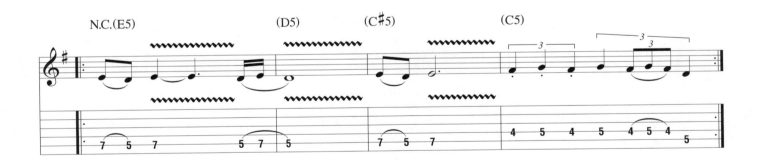

Guitar Solo

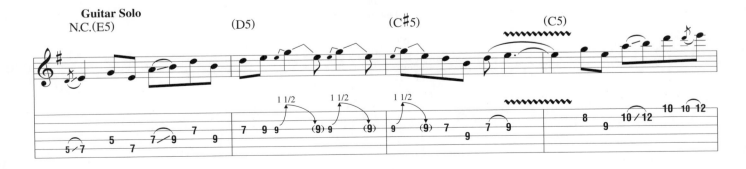

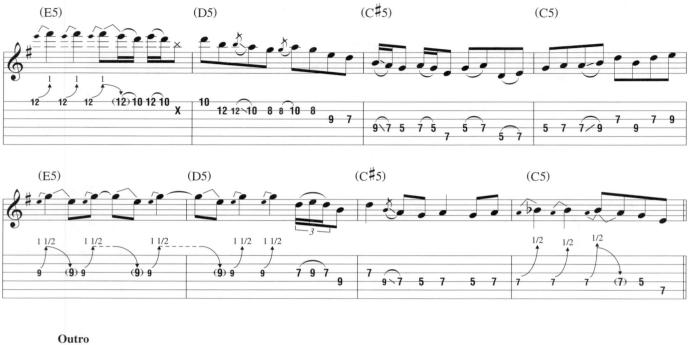

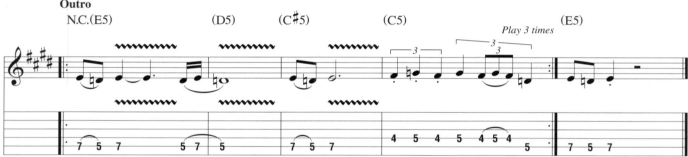

Additional Lyrics

2. Is he live or dead?
I see thoughts within his head.
We'll just pass him there.
Why should we even care?

4. Now the time is here
For Iron Man to spread fear.
Vengeance from the grave,
Kills the people he once saved.

Bridge Nobody wants him,
They just turn their heads.
Nobody helps him,
Now he has his revenge.

5. Heavy boots of lead,
Fills his victims full of dread,
Running as fast as they can;
Iron Man lives again.

Lights Out

Words and Music by Michael Schenker, Phil Mogg, Andy Parker and Pete Way

Intro
Moderately fast Rock ♩ = 152

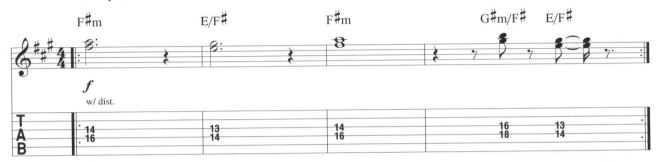

Verse

1. Wind blows back and the bat-tle's charg-in', it winds all the way.
2. *See additional lyrics*

*Chord symbols reflect overall harmony.

Up to the butt of my gun.

May - be now   your time ___   has come. ___

𝄋 Chorus

2nd time, substitute Fill 1

Lights   out,   lights ___ out ___ in Lon - don.   Hold on   tight   till ___

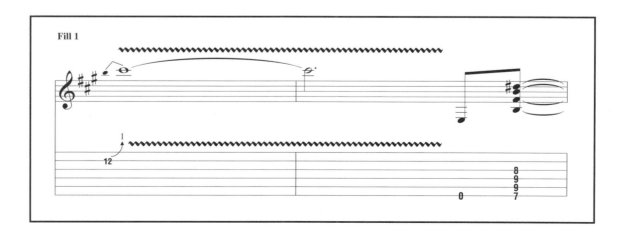

Fill 1

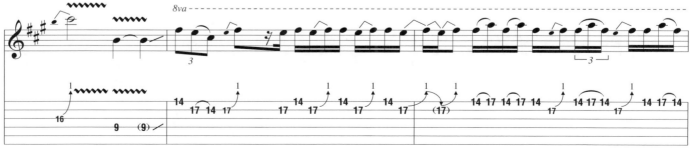

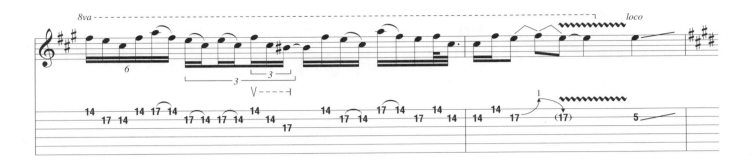

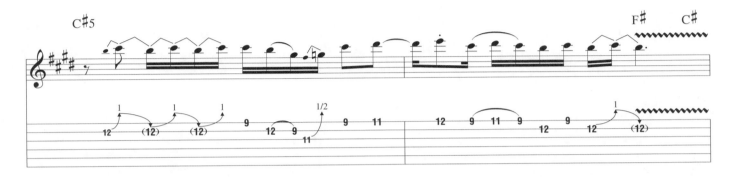

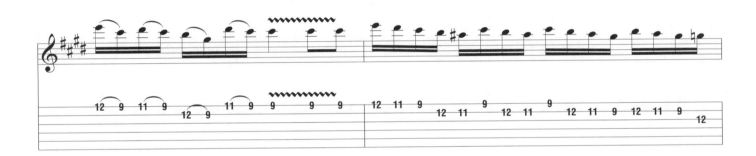

Outro-Guitar Solo

Lights out, lights out in Lon - don.

Additional Lyrics

2. From the back streets
   Thereís a rumblin';
   Smell of anarchy.
   No more nice time,
   Bright boy shoe shines;
   Pie-in-the-sky dreams.

4. You keep comin',
   There's no runnin';
   Tried a thousand times.
   Under your feet,
   Grass is growin'.
   Time we said goodbye.

Livin' on a Prayer

Words and Music by Jon Bon Jovi, Ritchie Sambora and Desmond Child

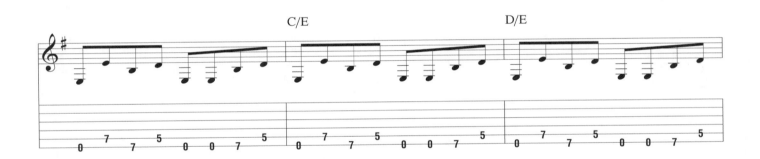

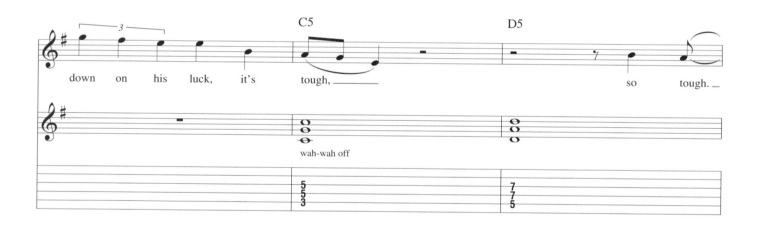

Pre-Chorus

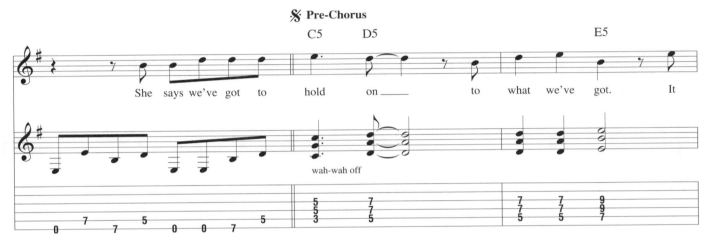

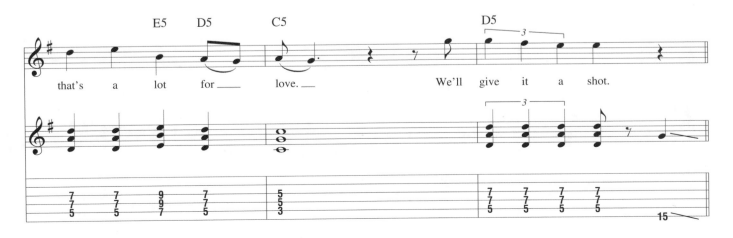

D.S. al Coda

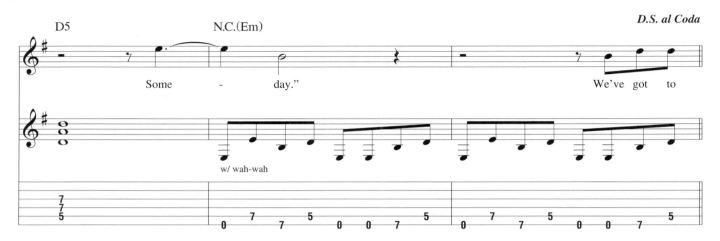

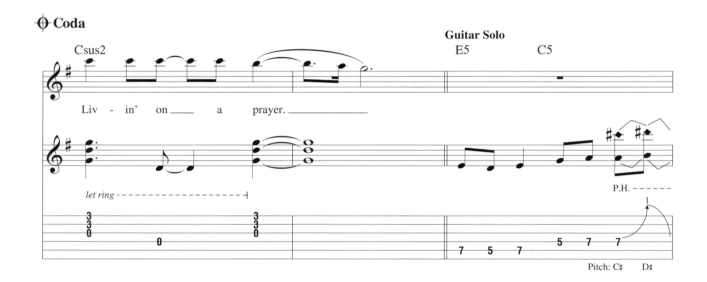

Coda

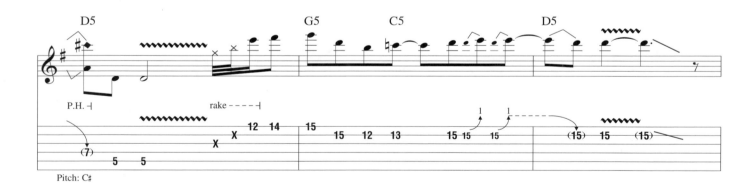

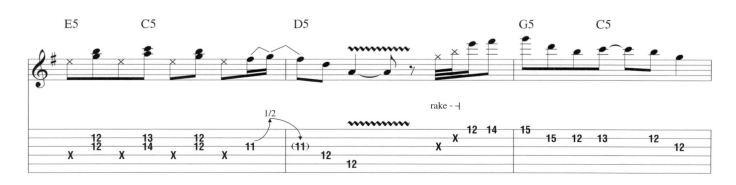

Living After Midnight

Words and Music by Glenn Tipton, Rob Halford and K.K. Downing

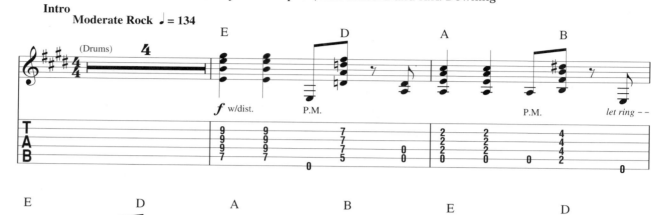

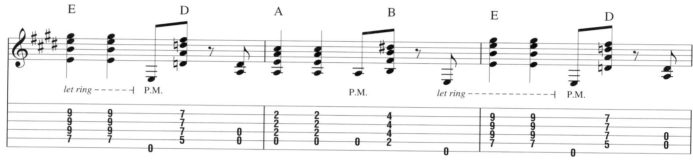

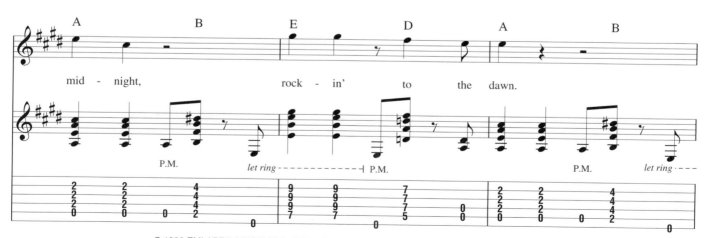

Lov - in' till the morn - in', then I'm gone. ___ I'm gone. ___

% Verse

1. I took the cit - y 'bout a one A. M. ___ Load -
2., 3. *See additional lyrics*

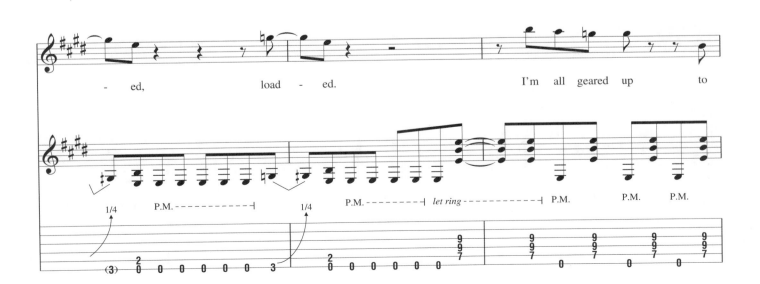

- ed, load - ed. I'm all geared up to

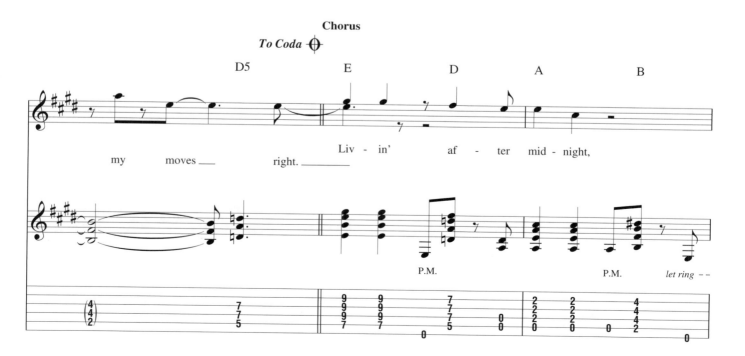

rock - in' to the dawn. Lov - in' till the

morn - in', then I'm gone, ___ I'm gone. ___

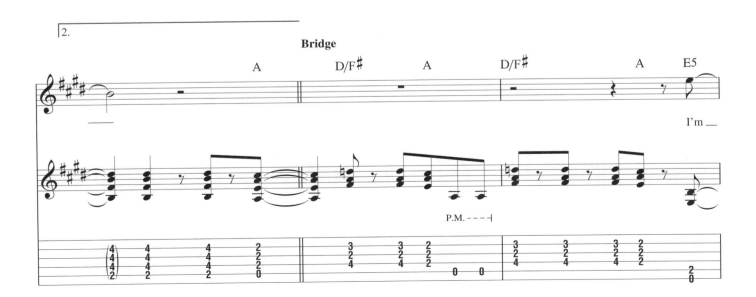

I'm __

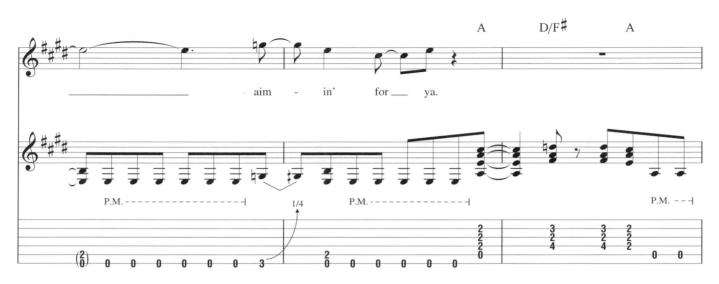

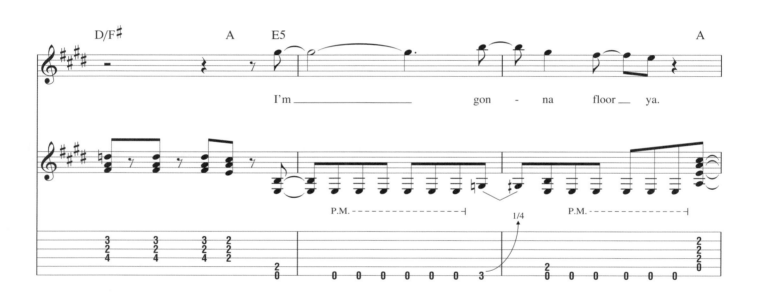

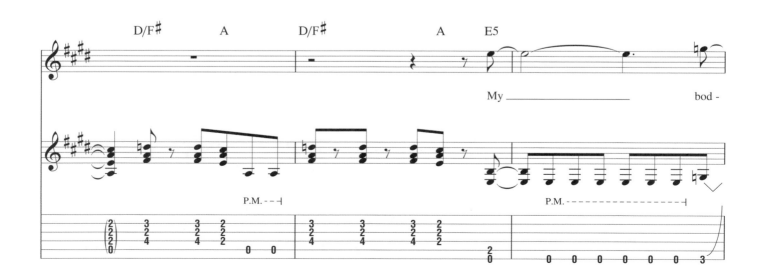

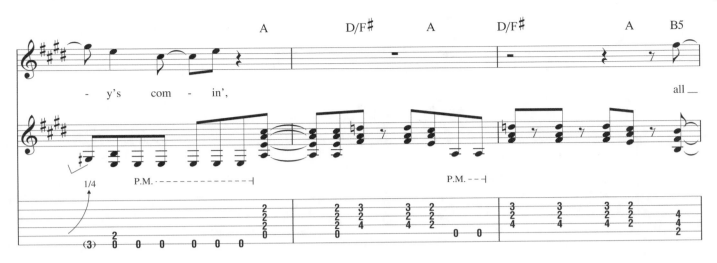

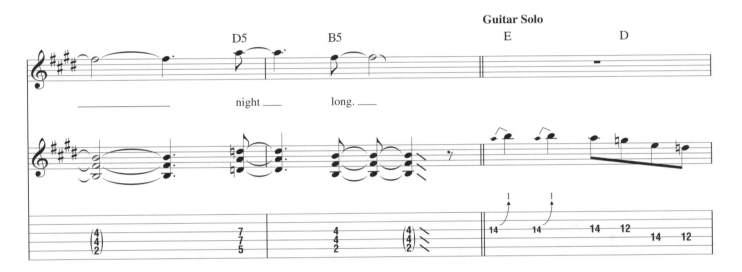

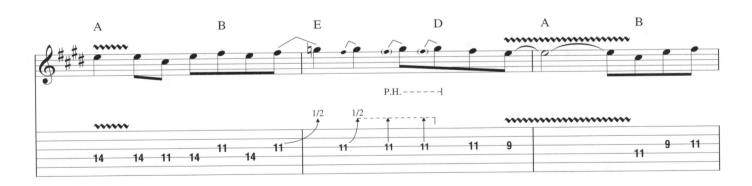

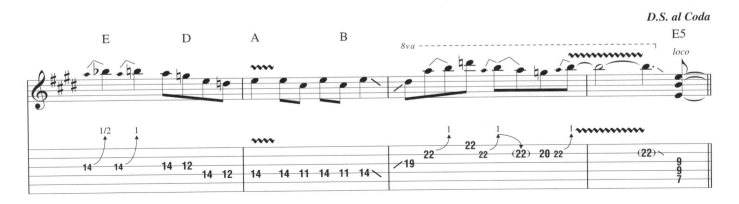

Additional Lyrics

2. Got gleamin' chrome reflecting feel.
   Loaded, loaded.
   Ready to take on ev'ry deal.
   Loaded, loaded.

Pre-Chorus 2. My pulse is racin', hot to take.
   But this motor's revved up, fit to break.

3. The air's electric, sparkin' power.
   Loaded, loaded.
   I'm gettin' harder by the hour.
   Loaded, loaded.

Pre-Chorus 3. I set my sights and then home in.
   The joints start fly'n' when I begin.

Performance Notes

Am I Evil? (page 6)

Of course you are — you're a rock guitarist! This musical question asked by Metallica was originally posed by the British heavy metal band Diamond Head, which was a big influence on the big M in the early days. This cover version of the epic tale of death and revenge was first recorded for the *Kill 'Em All* album (1983) and revived on *Garage Inc.* (1998). Kirk Hammett plays the shredding lead and James Hetfield chunks out the rhythm.

Classical Gas

Fans of the symphony might recognize the intro — it's loosely based on the "Mars" theme of *The Planets* suite by Gustav Holst. It's also based on *power chords* with the occasional *palm mute*. Wherever you see "P.M.," lay the palm of your picking hand on the affected strings at the guitar's bridge, and press down — but not too hard — just enough to get a chunky sound without changing the pitch. The intro pattern calls for three "chunks" and a wide-open (unmuted) E5.

Hammer Time

The classical intro breaks down to a "very fast" section of neoclassical *hammer-ons*. Pick the open B string once for every group of three notes, then "hammer" the following fretted notes with your left-hand index and pinky fingers. Then comes a group of *harmonics*—see the notation legend for the lowdown on them.

The "meat" of the song is based on more *palm mutes* and *power chords*, in a faster version of the intro. You can do this with all *downstrokes* until the super-fast section, which calls for fast *alternate picking* on the palm mutes.

Guitar Solo

If you possess the evil chops required for the solo, brush up on your *bends, vibrato, slides, hammer-ons* and *pull-offs,* plus *two-handed tapping* — combining the left and right hands on the fretboard for twice the evil. Notice the refrain of the neoclassical hammer licks from the intro.

The outro has more *hammer-ons* and their best friend, the *pull-off.* The song closes with a variation on the intro pattern, punctuated by a couple strums across fully muted strings — just lay your fretting hand on the strings so you get nothing but an evil "chick, chick."

Bark at the Moon (page 18)

The band of Ozzy Osbourne has been a breeding ground for some of rock's greatest guitarists. One of Ozzy's early shredding spawn was Jake E. Lee, who filled the shoes of the late Randy Rhoads on Osbourne's third solo release, *Bark at the Moon* (1983). The title track showcases Jake's command of the fretboard in two solos and a frenzied main riff.

The Pickup

"Bark at the Moon" starts with a *pickup measure,* which has less than four beats; start out counting, "1–and–2–and–3–and–4," and hit the first chord on the "and" of beat 4.

Pickin' 'n' Mutin'

The main riff bounces between three-note *power chords* with chunky *palm mutes*, played in a frenzy of *alternate picking*. Pick the palm-muted notes "down–up–down–up," and the upper chords as downstrokes. Take it slowly at first and make sure your chords are clean. The pre-chorus chords are played with a quick "down–up" swipe in between, then some quick palm-muted riffing with, of course, alternate picking.

Air Raid!

At the end of the verse, and throughout the rest of the tune, Jake throws some *dive bombs* with his whammy bar. To dive as Jake did, you'll need a durable vibrato bar/bridge system (ideally, a "floating" one) with a locking nut. Otherwise, your guitar will emerge from the dive completely out of tune. See the Guitar Notation Legend for the lowdown on whammy divin'.

Slippery Octaves

When you play one note on the A string and another two frets higher on the G string, you have *octaves* — two of the same note in different ranges. The D string in between gets dampened with the edge of a finger, so you only hear the two notes. On the chorus, Jake plays a pair of octaves and slides them up two frets, then back down — a classic jazz guitar technique that translates easily into rock.

Pinch Me!

The squealing sounds of the bridge are a result of *pinch harmonics.* Wherever you see "P.H.", turn the pick sideways and let the side of your picking thumb graze the string to produce the squawk of a hungry wolf pup. Try moving the pick to different places along the string to get different tones.

Rake Like Jake

If you dare to take on the master solo and outro licks, know that they require you to rake across the strings, *bend* at different intervals, *pinch, slide, vibrato, pull off,* and *riff* at an unholy fast pace. Godspeed!

Brain Damage *(page 28)*

Is it hard rock or prog-rock? No matter, because Pink Floyd's 1973 lunatic theme from the classic *Dark Side of the Moon* stands beside "Iron Man" and "Unchained" as required curriculum for the well-rounded rock guitarist. Not only that, it makes a great primer for *hybrid picking.* The legendary sci-fi blues texturalist, David Gilmour, does the pickin' (grinnin' optional).

Country Rock?

The technique in question is a variation on what's known as *Travis picking,* a style named after the country and western legend Merle Travis (who was never a member of Pink Floyd). Merle discovered a bouncy way to play two or more parts on the guitar at the same time. It might sound like acrobatics—and sometimes it is — but not in "Brain Damage," which is more song than flash. Traditionally, only fingers do the picking, but Gilmour hangs onto his plectrum (hence the direction *w/pick & fingers*).

Neo-Travis Picking 101

Put your left hand in a D chord (the first chord of the song) and leave it there. Now try playing just the "bass" part from the first measure with your pick; bounce it between the D and G strings in straight eighth notes. When you've got this down, start adding the finger of your choice (the middle works well) on the high E and B strings. Notice that your pick and finger pluck together at the start of each two-beat phrase. Keep playing measure 1, over and over, until your neighbors start complaining.

Now you can move your other hand! The chord positions shift around, and the picking pattern stays pretty much the same all through the verses but changes strings accordingly, as on the A7 chord. Sometimes a few extra notes are thrown in between vocal lines, as on the Dsus2 and D7sus2. Take it very slowly at first, and work it up to speed when you have all the chord changes down.

Arpeggios à la Floyd

You can give your right-hand finger a rest during the arpeggiated chorus. Just switch the chords and pick 'em one note at a time, noting that the Bm7 is a barre.

Congratulations; you are now one song closer to being a versatile hard-rock jack of all techniques!

Breaking the Chains (page 35)

The "rokken" band Dokken broke the mainstream in 1983 thanks to this song, the title track from their first major-label record. The tune broke them into the Top 40 and MTV charts, establishing lead guitarist George Lynch and his two-tone hairdo as forces to be reckoned with. "Breaking the Chains" features King George's lead over singer Don Dokken's rhythm.

The Pickup

We start with a *pickup measure,* which has less than four beats; start out counting, "1–and–2–and–3," and nail the first power chord on the "and" of beat 3.

Slippery Power Chords

The intro and verse pattern is a repeated sequence of *slides* (diagonal lines) and *palm mutes* (P.M.). Don't pick where you see the slides — instead, keep holding the chord shape while you slide it down (or up) two frets. Pick the next chord, then play the open E with enough of a palm mute to make it sound chunky (but not out of tune!). You'll notice that it's the same pattern repeated: "pick–pick–slide–pick (chunk–chunk–chunk–chunk–) — repeat."

Every Trick in the Book

When you play a note on the D string along with a note three frets higher on the B string, you have *octaves* — two of the same note in different ranges. But you must completely mute the G string in between! It's easier than it sounds — just position your hand so that one of the fretting fingers naturally touches that middle string and keeps it quiet. There's also some fully *muted* pick scratchin' in between the octaves; just mute all the strings with the hand of your choice while you pick. Then come the *harmonics* — lightly touch the high E string at fret 12, then fret 7, and if you have a vibrato bar, *dip* it!

Lynch Your Guitar

The solo, in the E minor scale, is a tasteful collection of the techniques above, plus *string bends, slurs,* and some palm-muted *rakes.* The tricky part is to keep your bends in tune — especially when you push up from the seventeenth fret and "rock" between half- and whole-step bends. Just listen for the right pitches, and with practice your hand will "remember" how hard to push.

Carry on Wayward Son (page 41)

Kansas was one of few American bands to take the prog-rock path in the 1970s. Known for classically-based arrangements and introspective lyrics, they also knew how to get their riffs out in tunes like this, penned by guitarist/songwriter Kerry Livgren for the 1976 album *Leftoverture.* A #11 single, the song has become a rock classic, covered by everyone from Yngwie Malmsteen to the Oak Ridge Boys!

Riffs Galore

The main intro riff shifts between a couple positions of the A minor pentatonic scale, anchored at fret 3, then 7 (notice the *slide* that connects them). At the E7 chord, cover three strings at fret 12 with one finger, and shake it lightly for *vibrato.* You can repeat the intro patterns through the first solo, or...

Solo!

Solo 1 has a series of sextuplet *pull-offs* (see the "6" above the notes), played by picking the first note (fretted with your pinky), pulling off to the second (fretted with your index finger), then pulling off to the open string — all in a millisecond — then repeat.

A New Big Word

Turn off your distortion for the verse and chorus, and play *arpeggios* (chords played one note at a time) based on some basic chord shapes. Just look at the chord symbols, put your hands in those shapes, play the individual notes, then tell all your friends you know how to *arpeggiate!*

More Riffs

Kick the distortion back in for the interlude. *Pull off* to the open notes, then play the *muted clicks* (Xs) by touching the strings just enough to dampen them. Bar the D5 and C5 with one finger each. Under the organ solo, the offbeat notes (with *eighth rests* between them) are best played with upstrokes to stay in the groove.

More Solos!

Solo 2 has more tasty techniques: *staccato* notes (played by damping the string right after you play it) and *pinch harmonics* — turn your pick sideways and let the edge of your thumb graze the string just right, and you'll get a screeching overtone like a soul in torment.

Dangerous Bends

The next pair of solos have *bends with vibrato* — push the string upward and shake lightly (just your fingers, not you whole body!) — then a gradual bend that goes up *two whole steps.* In both cases, accuracy is the key; listen carefully to the note you're hitting — if it's off you might be ducking beer bottles!

Cold Gin *(page 53)*

No hard rock collection would be complete without a sampling of New York's original kings of kabuki makeup and classic guitar licks. Kiss lead guitarist Ace Frehley's paean to a potent potable, "Cold Gin" was the riffiest track on their 1974 debut album. Paul Stanley plays rhythm to the Space Ace's slovenly lead.

Rock Tuning

This song is in an alternative standard tuning used by rock bands who like to make life difficult for guitar teachers. Each string is tuned down a half step lower than standard, making it easier to bend strings and belt out high vocals. Open strings, low to high, are E♭–A♭–D♭–G♭–B♭–E♭, but you don't need to tune down unless you plan to play with the recording.

The main intro/verse pattern is played with an open A string underneath moving two-note chords. The trick is to stop the chords at the right time. It helps to have your picking hand moving down and up in imaginary *eighth notes*, and slap it lightly on the strings to keep them quiet in between strums. Also know when to *slide* your chord up from fret 5 to 7.

Chorus Fills

The chorus is three-note power chords and "chicken scratches" (where you see the Xs, mute the strings and scratch away), then a transitional *fill* to take you back to the main pattern. Ace plays three different fills in the song:

✔ An expanded *unison bend*; put your first finger over the high E and B strings, and let another finger push the G string up from fret 14 while you play all three strings.

✔ Fill 1: a run down the scale with *hammer-ons* and *pull-offs*; the same move repeated on different pairs of strings.

✔ Fill 2: bar fret 12 again, and this time walk up the G string, one finger at a time, while you rake your pick across the strings one at a time.

Pickin' 'n' Riffin'

The interlude has some fancy pickwork. Alternate pick the single-note lines, and wherever you see the staccato dot, play the note and quickly lift your fret-hand finger off the fret (but not off the string) just enough to stop the sound and make the note short (literally, staccato).

Cult of Personality (page 59)

The sampled voice of Malcolm X opens this kicking tune by the New York band Living Colour. Guitarist Vernon Reid, founder of the Black Rock Coalition, is a versatile monster musician who showed his rock chops on this track, a Top 10 hit and GRAMMY® Award winner from the band's 1988 debut album *Vivid*.

Preferred Fingers

You begin with the wicked main riff, a combo of picked notes and *pull-offs*. Put your middle finger on the E string, fret 3, and leave it there (for now). Use your ring finger to *pull off* the D string from fret 3 to open position; follow with the index finger on fret 2. Do this with *alternate picking*: down on the low E string; up on the D. When the riff climbs, you have to shift your hand and use the often-neglected pinky on fret 5. At the end of the verse, all your fretting fingers get involved as the riff climbs higher.

Arpeggios 101

To play a chord one note at a time is to *arpeggiate*, and Vernon does just that on the chorus. Follow the tab, understanding that most of the notes are held chord positions that you pick selectively.

Bend, Tap, Shake, and Dip

The chorus also has a *bent* and *tapped* note (marked "T"), along with a whammy-bar *dip*. Then comes the first twisted solo, based mainly on the G minor pentatonic and blues scales with lots of *vibrato, pull-offs,* and more *dips*. Stay rooted at fret 15 and you can't go wrong. The same is true in the next solo, until it drops down an octave to root on fret 3 and climbs up from there. One of Reid's favorite devices is to bend a string up half a step, drop it back down, then push it up higher — this is a "feel thing" that can only be developed with practice. Another is the whammy-bar *dip* and *dive,* best achieved with a locking-nut vibrato bar system (so your strings don't pop off the bridge).

Decadence Dance (page 70)

The opening track from *Extreme II: Pornograffitti* (1990), the second and biggest album from the Boston band Extreme, is a lesson in funky metal riffs and blistering technique from the Portuguese-born guitarist Nuno Bettencourt.

Rock Tuning

See "Cold Gin" for the lowdown on tuning down half a step to better rock the world.

The Pickup

If you're counting beats, notice that the first chord of "Decadence Dance" starts before beat 1. We show this with a *pickup measure*, which shows the first chord on beat 3 1/2. In other words, start out counting, "1–and–2–and–3," start playing on the "and" of beat 3.

The first few chords are strummed slowly from the low E to the high E string, with the edge of the pick to get that "frrrang" effect. If you have a vibrato bar, *dip* it down slightly before hitting the chord, and release it as you strum.

If You Pinch It, They Will Scream

Nuno relies heavily on *pinch harmonics* (P.H.), turning his pick sideways to make the string scream in pain. Wouldn't you scream if you were pinched? This is combined with a full-step *bend and release* at the beginning of the main riff and throughout the song. That riff also includes *hammer-ons* and *pull-offs, slides,* and the bending of two strings at once — use your ring finger on both strings.

In the verse, riffs between vocals feature sliding mini-chords known as *parallel 4ths* (technically they're not always 4th intervals, but don't worry about that). Play these with two fingers roughly parallel to each other on the D and B strings. (Watch for more of these on different strings all over the song.) "Pick behind nut" means this: reach your pick hand over to the end of the neck, where the strings go to the tuning pegs, and pick them to get a metallic sound similar to a car starting up.

Flashy!

Fills and solos in this song showcase Nuno's command of these techniques:

- ✔ *Dips, dives,* and *vibrato* "w/bar" – all of which require a good locking-nut vibrato bar that won't pull your tuning out of whack.

- ✔ *Two-handed tapping* – as if you don't have enough notes, using a right-hand finger to tap the neck (where you see a "plus" sign) and extend your reach on the frets.

- ✔ *Tremolo picking* in a "steady gliss" – alternate picking at blazing speed while your left hand slides up the A string from fret 2 to 17.

- ✔ Other techniques as discussed above and in the Guitar Notation Legend. Have fun!

Don't Treat Me Bad *(page 85)*

A band that prospered at the tail end of the "glam rock" era and lived on to tell about it, FireHouse are not members of the firefighters' union, but makers of power ballads and anthems like "Don't Treat Me Bad," the second single from their self-titled, double-platinum debut album in 1990. Guitarist Bill Leverty juggles acoustic and electric.

Rock Tuning

Open strings, low to high, are tuned down a half step for this song — see "Cold Gin" for details.

The intro and first verse have strummed chords over an open A-string *pedal point* — a static bass note that drones under the chords. Strum this with constant alternating down- and upstrokes, missing the strings strategically on the longer notes. The slightly jazzy F#m7 and C#m7 chords are played as full barres (the first finger *bars*, or covers all the strings on one fret).

Chicken Scratching and Palm Muting

After kicking in the distortion, play the chorus with fully dampened scratches (Xs) in between the chords; simply lay your picking hand lightly over the strings and pick, "chick-a chick-a." The end of the chorus has moving two-note *power chords* with *palm mutes* in between; keep your picking hand close to the bridge, so that you can push it on the strings wherever you see "P.M."

Song Arrangement for Dummies

The second verse is strummed spaciously on a clean electric for a nice taste of variety. Here you have what the classical maestros call "theme and variation." Brav-eau.

Happy Pull-Offs

The guitar solo starts in A *major pentatonic* position at fret 14, then moves up for a series of major-scale *pull-offs* over a mini-barre at fret 17: lay your first finger over the B and high E strings at that fret, and pull the other notes off with other fingers. Then play another variation of this by holding the B string at fret 19 (with the middle finger) and the high E string at fret 17 (with the first finger), and pulling off the notes above with whatever fingers you have left.

The solo ends with rock's greatest noise, the *pick scrape* — do it very slowly, so you don't run out of string before the interlude!

Down Boys *(page 94)*

Pounding out the glam rock with finesse, the L.A. band Warrant hit it big with their smash debut album, *Dirty Rotten Filthy Stinking Rich* (1989). The Top Ten release spewed out hit after hit, including this rock anthem — a showcase for the licks and riffs of guitarists Joey Allen and Erik Turner.

Rock Tuning

As in "Cold Gin," this song is tuned down a half step below standard tuning. Open strings, low to high, are E♭–A♭–D♭–G♭–B♭–E♭, but you don't need to tune down unless you plan to play with the recording.

Time Warp

The intro (and outro) is in a *5/4 time signature,* in which each measure has five quarter notes instead of four. You can think of this as ten *palm-muted* notes in each of the first three measures. Then the first power chords come in, and a measure of *2/4* connects them to the main verse pattern.

That pattern combines power chords with palm muted open notes, and tasty licks in between with *quarter-step bends* — pull the low E string very slightly downward after you pick. The glam guitarist's favorite toy, the *vibrato bar,* is used for *dips* and *dives* throughout. Review *pinch harmonics* in the Guitar Notation Legend, and notice the *arpeggios* (chords played one note at a time) in between vocal lines.

Harmonic Insurgence

The pre-chorus is straight chords, except for the harmonic at fret 5. Lightly touch the G string above the fifth fret, pick, and push that whammy bar!

Solo Techniques

Played mostly in E *minor pentatonic* and *blues scales* rooted at fret 12, the solo is chock full of the aforementioned *pinch harmonics,* plus:

✔ *Bends with vibrato* – pushing a string up a full step and giving it just the right wiggle — a "feel thing" that can only be perfected with practice

✔ *Raking* up muted strings with the pick

✔ *Sliding* a pair of notes up and down in 5ths (with one finger barring the high E and B strings)

✔ Lots of *vibrato bar* — in one case, striking a *harmonic* while the bar is pushed down, and letting it up slowly for a police-siren effect

Empire *(page 101)*

Seattle's Queensrÿche are the first band to put an *umlaut* over the letter Y — how do you pronounce that? They're also a "thinking person's hard rock band," creating concept albums and story songs with their own metallic edge. Case in point: the title track from their success-ful fourth album, Empire (1990). Guitarists Michael Wilton and Chris DeGarmo perform their duties with power and taste.

Let's Do the Time Warp Again

Notice that the intro has a couple odd measures of 3/8 time. Queensrÿche often does this, adding a little breathing space between patterns (and making the transcriber's life difficult). You'll also see a measure of 5/4 in the pre-chorus (more breathing space) and one of 2/4 at the end of the first chorus. If you know how the song sounds, you can just "feel it" without all that counting.

The intro and chorus patterns are built on *dyads* (two-note chords) with a palm-muted open A string in between. Think of most of the dyads as *upstrokes,* and *alternate pick* the open string.

Mind Your Bends!

The slow intro solo has some long-sustaining *string bends* that have got to be accurate, so make sure you know how far to bend to be on pitch. The same goes for the *pre-bend* toward the end of the intro — bend the string before picking it, then slowly release it.

The verse is mostly *power chords,* with occasional *octaves.* Mute the D string in between the notes by letting a finger touch it lightly. The pre-chorus is more power chords, but with *slides* in between — just hold the chord position and let it slide to the next. Kick off your distortion for the interlude, and note the sparse *hammer-ons* and *pull-offs* between chords. The buildup to the solo is on one *palm-muted* open string — very convenient if you need to use your left hand to take a drink or blow your nose.

Solo

The guitar solo takes place in A *minor pentatonic* position, rooted mostly on fret 17 with some added minor notes. Again, mind your bends! Some highlights:

- *Backpedaling* in *scale segments* – starting at fret 20, run down three notes of the minor pen-tatonic scale, then do the same from fret 17, and so on — like taking three steps forward and one back.

- *Following the chord changes* – at the B♭5 chord, the notes change to accommodate the change. Tasty!

- More octaves, now *slid,* and some tasteful *vibrato* with the whammy bar.

Here I Go Again *(page 112)*

This hair-metal soliloquy from Whitesnake was a remake of their own song, originally recorded in 1982 on *Saints & Sinners.* This 1987 version was a #1 hit and MTV staple from the smash album *Whitesnake.* One of many guitarists in David Coverdale's revolving door of musicians, Adrian Vandenburg plays the melodic solo.

Take Five

While the keyboard player plays the intro and first two verses, you can read a book or make a phone call. Just make sure you're ready to come in with the fifth- and seventh-fret *barre chords* that usher in the chorus.

The playing here is stylish, with *slides* and *palm muting* in between the full chords. Practice the chords first, then you can throw in the frills. A *half-step bend* before the Am7 chord should be accurate and clean — pull the A string *downward* (toward your feet) to raise the pitch (down is up!). Then comes a series of *double stops* on adjacent strings, that should be barred with one finger on both strings.

Give the Riffs a Rest

You know what to do on the verse: Be the supportive guitarist who's content backing up the vocals with palm-muted single notes. Never play over the singer — or you'll be fired from Whitesnake.

Two Kinds of Harmonics

The bridge calls for more dynamic *palm mutes,* and a *pinch harmonic* played by turning your pick sideways to coax a scream from the G string. Add vibrato, and the string wails. *Natural harmonics* (marked "Harm.") and a tasty series of *pull-offs* follow.

Tongue Twister

The solo follows a C major scale (which you could look at as A minor), shifting positions upward as it progresses. Pay attention to the way it's articulated, with staccato notes alternating with *legato slides* and *bends.*

Your challenge is to play the blistering run of *thirty-second notes* that closes the solo. This is built on *a sequence of scale segments* — if you can say that three times fast, you can play it. The first segment climbs up frets 8–10–12, then your hand shifts up to play 10–12–14. Repeat that on the next string, then shift up to 12–14–15, and so on. By the end of the solo, you will have *sequenced* eight *segments* of the C major scale — a fine exercise for the aspiring shredder.

Holy Diver (page 121)

Any album whose cover depicts a demon tormenting a drowning priest is bound to make a splash (huh huh). 1983's "Holy Diver" was the first album and single from the band of ex-Rainbow and Black Sabbath frontman Ronnie James Dio. This metal classic features the chunk of guitar god Vivian Campbell, who has gotten around the rock world quite a bit since then.

The chunky, plodding rhythm of "Holy Diver" is perfect for moderate-tempo headbanging with minimal neck trauma. It's also a great exercise in *power chords* and *palm muting.* Make sure you *alternate pick,* "down, down–up, down, down–up, down, down, down" for the first measure, and continue in the same sixteenth-note pattern.

No Major 3rds Allowed!

Every chord in this song is a power chord of some sort — even if it doesn't look like one. Consider the *unmuted* A♭5 chord stabs in the verse. That A♭5 is played as if it's a full, first-position major *barre* chord — but with the G string fully *muted* instead of fretted, removing what musicians call the *major 3rd* and making it an expanded power chord. But don't sweat the theory; simply leave your middle finger touching the G string and resist the urge to push it down — or else it will sound way too happy!

The bridge is built of more — that's right — power chords, this time played as stabs with empty space (quarter-note rests) in between.

Triplets, Hammers, Pulls, and Pinches

Begin the guitar solo in box 1 of C *minor pentatonic* (rooted on fret 8), with a bent *double-stop* (two adjacent strings played together) that can be pulled down or pushed up depending on your mood, then released and *pulled off.* Navigating around the boxes, Vivian spices his licks with *pinch harmonics* and *triplets* galore — wherever you see eighth notes beamed together with a "3" below, that means you're fitting three notes in a space that would normally fit two, for an expressive, stumbling effect. The climax comes with a series of minor-scale *hammer-on/pull-off* licks combined with precise pinch harmonics. Hint: Hitting fret 7 on the G string during this flurry usually requires a quick shift of your hand, down a fret and back up again. Godspeed!

Iron Man *(page 129)*

"[Traveling] time for the future of mankind" may include mild but irreversible side effects, such as being "turned to steel in a great magnetic field." Such is the fate of "Iron Man," as told by Birmingham metal pioneers Black Sabbath on this classic from their second album, *Paranoid*. This is perhaps the most famous metal song of all time, thanks in no small part to the timeless power chords of Tony Iommi.

The Immortal Intro

If your guitar does NOT have a locking nut, you can play the intro as Tony did. Pick the open low E string. Reach your left hand up past the frets to the headstock, where the strings go over the nut to the tuners. Push the string slowly, release it, then utter the magic words, "I am Iron Man."

Then come the power chords. This is just one two-note chord shape, slid around the neck to different positions. Don't lift your fretting hand; let the slides be your guide. When the vocals come in, break it down to single notes, and notice the *pull-off* from fret 15 to 14.

Chromatic Blues from the Underworld

King of evil blues riffs, Iommi plays the bridges and interludes with notes from the *minor pentatonic* and blues scales, rife with *chromatic* notes (played one fret at a time). These riffs sit mostly in "box" positions, between frets 5 and 7 or 7 and 10. Think "one finger per fret," and you'll have no worries. Some details:

- The first interlude has a *quarter-step bend* played by pulling (with your first finger) ever-so-slightly downward (toward the underworld), SLOWLY, just before you release the note.

- At the bridge, anchor your first finger at fret 7 for the ascending riff.

- The second interlude shifts between a couple of box positions: start anchored at fret 9, and shift to 7. Stop the strings in between the up beat notes, and alternate pick: "down–up, up, up, up, up–down (hammer) down."

The Solos

For the equally bluesy solos, consider that you're shifting between different positions of minor pentatonic scales, with all the requisite blues techniques: *unison bends,* legato playing (*hammer-ons, pull-offs,* and *slides*), and in the final solo, extra-wide step-and-a-half bends — best executed on light strings.

Lights Out *(page 137)*

This title track from the British band UFO's sixth (and biggest) album in 1977 helped establish German guitar legend Michael Schenker, also an on-and-off member of the Scorpions, as an international phenomenon. Schenker's lead is supported by rhythm guitarist/keyboardist Paul Raymond in this galloping epic.

Chords That Aren't Chords

Dryads are mythical forest-dwelling tree nymphs — not to be confused with *dyads,* clusters of two notes that can imply major or minor chords. That's what you hear in the intro, played over a driving F♯ bass note to become *inversions* or *slash chords,* like E/F♯ and G♯m/F♯. Whether or not they're really chords, they sure sound cool.

The Galloping Gourmet

The verse is a collection of *power chords* and open notes, best played in a "down, down–up, down, up–down–up" pattern. Notice the *eighth-note* rest, where you should quickly pick your fret hand off the frets (but not off the strings) for a split second of silence. Notice that when there are no vocals, Schenker "opens it up" and plays the pattern without the rest. But in between, there's a full E *barre chord* alternating with *palm muted* open notes. Consider this an alternate picking pattern (see "Holy Diver" for details) played at hyperspeed.

The chorus gallops along with the same sort of palm muting, plus full major chords that sometimes fall on *upbeats* — the "and" of beat 4 — and should be picked as *upstrokes.*

Modulate Your Blues!

The first guitar solo begins in box 1 of the F♯ *minor pentatonic scale* (rooted at fret 14) and is a great collection of blues-rock licks for the aspiring bender. *Bending* with *vibrato* is a "feel thing," honed by lots of practice at making sure the bent note is on pitch. When the G string is bent a half step from fret 16, you get a *blue note,* a "flatted 5th" that is outside your regular scale to add a touch of evil.

But wait! The solo *modulates* (changes keys) to C♯ and Schenker moves his pentatonic anchor to fret 9, where he stays until the solo eases back into the chorus. The same thing happens in the second guitar solo, which ends up riding boxes 1 and 4 of the C♯ *minor pentatonic scale* (with added minor notes) until fadeout (or lights out).

Livin' on a Prayer *(page 147)*

Bon Jovi was one of few bands to emerge from the eighties "hair band" scene to become an enduring force in rock music — with help from a good barber and strong pop/rock songs. This #1 single from the 1986 album *Slippery When Wet* features the slippery guitar licks of Richie Sambora.

Talking Guitars

Sambora's guitar grunts like a pig with the help of a couple devices: a *talk box* and an *octaver* (or *harmonizer*). The talk box has a tube you actually talk into while playing, and the guitar sound follows your voice. The octaver, as the name implies, adds an octave (in this case, a low one) to every note you play. But don't rush to your music store — you can get through this tune just fine without either device. You could even substitute a *wah-wah pedal* if you have one.

Richie's main riff draws from the E *minor pentatonic* scale. You can use one finger (preferably your third) on the low E and A strings, seventh fret, to make the quick note change — then use your first finger on fret 5. The pre-chorus and chorus are built on three-note *power chords,* with a *slide* down the E string in between. No sweat!

Slippery When Bent

The second verse has a couple fills:

- A whole-step bend of the G string from fret 14 — make sure it's on pitch! (To check this, compare the bent note to an unbent note two frets higher.)

- Another *bend,* this time with vibrato, followed by a whammy-bar *dive* all the way down to the "slack" realm where the string has no notes. Do this only if you have a decent vibrato bar with a locking nut.

Tasty Techniques

Navigating a couple positions of the E minor scale, Sambora flavors the tasty solo with a bent *pinch harmonic* (turning the pick sideways to get a high overtone from the string), *rakes* (preceding a fretted note by "raking" across a couple muted strings), and dashes of vibrato.

Key Change with a Time Warp

Lots of songwriters use *key changes* (also known as *modulations*) to add drama to their tunes. "Livin' on a Prayer" modulates up a step and a half in the outro-chorus, with a measure of *3/4 time* to confuse us more. The time change follows the vocals, so just "feel it" and don't sweat the numbers.

Living After Midnight (page 154)

Leather-clad metal gods Judas Priest were part of the New Wave of British Heavy Metal, colonizing the world with guitar firepower from Glenn Tipton and K.K. Downing. This bar-band classic came from their sixth album, *British Steel* (1980).

Happy Metal

The catchy main chorus pattern is played in full major (not power) chords. It's best to keep your picking hand moving down and up in imaginary *eighth notes*, so the *palm muted* (P.M.) notes end up on downstrokes, and offbeats are up. Keep the same thing going as you move into the verse, until after the third-fret *quarter-step bend* — pull the string downward slightly, and play the following *palm mutes* in downstrokes. Note that the pre-chorus chords, and many throughout this tune, fall on *upbeats*, in anticipation of the measures ahead (on the "and" of beat 3).

Blues Rocking

The bridge has more *palm mutes* and *quarter-step bends,* under a classic blues-rock chord pattern: bar the A chord with your first finger, and add fingers on frets 3 and 4 on top of that (to transform it to D/F♯) — then it's easy to shift back to A by picking up those extra fingers.

Two Scales in One

It's way cool, but not unheard of, that this guitar solo flips between minor and major pentatonic scales. This is a time-honoured blues-rock tradition that adds variety to solos. Start out anchored at fret 12, with a fourteenth-fret bend in E minor pentatonic position. Then there's a bend from fret 11, which guitarheads usually associate with E *major* pentatonic. Shift down and anchor your first finger at fret 9, and you're fully in major pentatonic position.

Screams and Slides

Pinch harmonics (marked "P.H.") are played by turning your pick sideways and letting the edge of your thumb touch the string and produce a high overtone that screams for mercy. Bends from the eleventh fret go from a half step (implying minor) to a whole step (major). After shifting back up to fret 12, *slide* up to 22 for the final bends: Use your third finger to push up the B string, and your pinky at the same fret on the (unbent) high E string.

No Excuses (page 184)

Seattle's Alice in Chains were the missing link between metal and grunge, with demonic blues licks and lyrical tunes provided by guitarist Jerry Cantrell. "No Excuses" was their biggest single at #1, an unusually mellow tune for the band from their 1994 EP *Jar of Flies*.

Rock Tuning

Tune all your strings down a half step if you plan to play this along with the original recording. If not, don't sweat it. (See "Cold Gin" for more about "rock tuning.")

No Distortion — Yet!

Put your left hand in the position that would normally be a full major barre chord in first position, but leave the high E and B strings open. Start at fret 5 and *slide* the whole chord up two frets. Suspending those open strings gives you some close intervals that sound best with a clean sound — so kindly leave your distortion off until the guitar solo. Otherwise, your chords turn to pure mud under the influence of overdrive.

Strumming Is Allowed in Hard Rock!

The two-measure strum pattern in the intro and verse should be played smoothly, "Down, down, down–up–down–up, up–down, down–up–down–up." Basically, keep your right hand moving up and down in imaginary eighth notes, and strategically miss the strings wherever there's a pause in the pattern (as shown by commas in the preceding pattern). The chorus is a variation of the same pattern; keep it steady and hypnotic.

Pentatonic Pizzazz

Now you can kick on the distortion. The solo is based on the B *minor pentatonic* scale, starting in the upper *box 2* (anchored at fret 10) and shifting between that and *box 1* (at fret 7). Cantrell draws on classic blues moves — *pull-offs, bends,* and *double stops* — for maximum grunge. The most classic move happens over the G6 chord: hold the high E string at fret 7 with your index finger, bend the G string up from fret 9 with your ring finger, and alternate between the two.

A gradually *bent double stop* is best played with one finger on both strings, pushed upward slowly. Adding *vibrato* once they're bent is an acquired technique mastered only by locking yourself in your garage and practicing until the proverbial cows come home.

Rock You Like a Hurricane *(page 188)*

Hannover, Germany spawned Deutschland's biggest and most enduring hard rock band, The Scorpions. "Rock You Like a Hurricane," from the 1984 album *Love at First Sting,* is considered one of the most influential rock anthems of all time. Power chords and stinging leads are brought to you by guitarmeisters Rudolph Schenker and Matthias Jabs.

The classic intro and chorus pattern is a blitz of three-note *power chords* — just move the one shape around the neck as shown, with a downward *slide* on the E5. The verse is more of the same power chords, now with *palm muting*; rest the edge of your picking hand on the strings near the bridge for an extra-chunky sound.

Plectrum Damage Control

Verse 1 ends with rock's greatest noise, the *pick scrape*. Unless your pick is made of some space-age material, this will put ridges in it. Use the back edge of it, away from the tip, so that when you play notes again, those ridges won't catch on the string and make another noise that doesn't rock.

Theme and Variations

The Scorps play a variation on the verse theme later on. This time, you approach the C5 from below in single notes from the major scale. This variation, followed by a slide of the E5 chord, makes for some *wunderbar* harmonic variety.

Matthias Jams

You won't get a free ride through the leads in this tune, but here are some of the special techniques employed by Herr Jabs throughout:

✔ *Segmented scale playing* – running down a scale (E minor) in "segments," that is, playing four notes downward, then backtracking to a note you just hit and beginning another four-note segment there, and continuing.

✔ *Two-handed tapping with slides* – the left hand plays a series of hammer-ons and pull-offs, and a right-hand finger (marked with a "plus" sign) taps a higher fret, then quickly *slides* upward.

✔ *Pinch harmonics* – turn the pick sideways and let the edge of your thumb graze the string as you pick, so you get a screaming overtone. Try this at different places on the string for different tones.

✔ *Bent double stops* – play two strings barred with one finger, and bend both at once (pull down or push up, depending on your mood).

School's Out (page 201)

Playing with snakes onstage can help make you a rock icon — don't try this at home, kids — and so can anti-authority rock songs like this one, the 1972 title track from shock-rocker Alice Cooper's fifth album. The Top Ten single from the #1 album features the guitars of Glenn Buxton and Michael Bruce.

Finger Tips

Here's one of the catchiest riffs in rock history, in E *minor pentatonic*: play a two-note power chord at fret 12 (with two *downstrokes*). Bar your ring finger over the D and G strings at fret 14 (an upstroke). Repeat the chord, then bar fret 12 with the index finger. This is a lot of string shifting, but you'll get used to it. After the vibrato at fret 12 comes a downward *slide*. Notice that when Alice starts singing in the verse, the guitar skips the slide to leave more space.

Power chords in the pre-chorus are played *staccato* (short). Lift your fretting hand off the frets (but not off the strings) for immediate silence right after you play the *dotted* chords.

Unison Bending and Feedback

The chorus opens up with a unison bend in G *minor pentatonic*. While you hold the B string down at fret 3, bend the G string up to meet the same pitch. Thick, isn't it? There's more unison bending in different positions throughout the song. *Feedback* happens when you're loud enough, distorted enough, and at the right position in front of your amp so that an "accidental" overtone is magically conjured from its speakers. Are your neighbors complaining yet?

Timeless Rock Licks

The guitar solo keeps riding the E *minor pentatonic* box 1 at fret 12 with more unison bends, then a cool trick straight out of the Chuck Berry school of proto-metal: *slid double stops,* barred with one finger over the B and high E strings. Those notes descend *chromatically* (one half-step note at a time), then you slide back into box 1 for a high bend that should be on pitch, because you have to hold it up and pick it again. (There's more of this later in the song, so get used to it!)

Did I say Chuck Berry? His spirit reappears in the last chorus, with another *unison bend* (downstroke) that alternates with a fretted high E-string note at fret 15 (upstroke). Class dismissed!

Seventeen (page 207)

The band Winger, featuring Kip Winger (formerly of Alice Cooper's band), had a 1988 debut album called, that's right, *Winger*. Their music was catchy as all get-out, but with plenty of chances for the group's monster players to shine. "Seventeen" was their first single, featuring the slick licks of guitarist Reb Beach.

Rock Tuning

This song is in that "slack" tuning first discussed in "Cold Gin" — but you don't need to tune down unless you plan to play along with Winger.

The Pickup

This tune starts with a *pickup measure,* which has less than four beats. Start out counting in sixteenth notes: "1–e–and–a–2–e–and–a–3–e–and–a–4–e–and," and nail the first power chord on the "a" of beat 4.

Riffs Riffs Riffs

Alternate picking is the key in the intro and chorus riff. These are second-position barre chords, with the third finger held over three strings at a time. Keep your picking hand close to the bridge, so you can *palm mute* on the downstroked open notes. Notice the fast picking of double notes under the C5 chord — start with middle and ring fingers on the fifth fret, and index finger on the G string, fret 4. Pick up the ring finger, then the others. Repeat. Viola! The verse riffs around an A tonality. Watch for the fully *muted* notes inside the G chord. Stops and *staccato* notes make for a tight arrangement with drums and vocals. Same deal on the pre-chorus, where *slid power chords* add spice in between *pull-offs*.

Super Flash Alert

The solo, a song in itself, is ushered in with *harmonics* and a whammy-bar *dive* bomb. We revolve around the B *minor pentatonic* position at fret 7, but with lots of extra spicy notes. When *tapping* time comes, you need three left-hand fingers and one right. Later comes a whammy-bar *scoop* and lots of legato madness — all of which can only be learnt with lots o' practice.

But Wait, There's More!

The interlude is another monster riff that will require all your fingers. With your first finger situated at fret 2, think "one finger per fret," and you can't go wrong. If that's not enough, the outro-solo is another flash extravaganza — this time in E, floating around fret 12 in assorted tonalities. As always, check the Guitar Notation Legend for symbol translation.

Shake Me *(page 218)*

This was the first single from one of Philadelphia's hairiest bands, Cinderella, who came to fame on an opening tour with Bon Jovi. From their MTV-friendly debut album *Night Songs* (1986), "Shake Me" has Tom Keifer and Jeff LaBar doing the guitar thang.

The intro and verse riff is built on *power chords* in both varieties: the moveable "closed" position, and open-position, which requires some *string muting* (where you see an "X" in the tab, lay a stray finger over that string to keep it from ringing). Most are played with an upstroke, after which you lay your picking hand across the strings for silence. The single notes on fret 3 and 4 are best played "up–down." As the verse builds, just add palm-muted downstrokes in between the wide-open chords.

More Picking Tips

Onward to the chorus, where alternate picking is the key to keeping things groovin'. Just think rhythmically: downbeats=downstrokes, and upbeats=you know what. That means under the first "all night" line, you could pick "up, up–down–up, up–down–up." On the bridge, slide from fret 2 to 4 on A string, then do the same on the low E string. Keep alternate picking!

A Solo

Here you get to try some of rock's tried-and-true lead techniques, including the whammy dive, requisite *hammer-ons* and *pull-offs,* plus one- and two-string *bends* — some of which should be pulled with one finger over two strings. See the Guitar Notation Legend for the lowdown.

Turn It Down!

The interlude brings it down a notch with *arpeggiated* power chords (played one note at a time) that outline the verse pattern. If you're amplified, turn your guitar's volume control down a couple notches, and your distorted sound will clean up just enough to hear the notes clearly and add some of what we eggheads call "dynamics." Crank it up again for the full power chords.

Another Solo

The outro-solo is full of *dyads* (two notes played together on adjacent strings), oft bent together for a down-and-dirty twang. This, with good doses of slides and vibrato, takes the song out in classic rock style.

Smokin' in the Boys Room *(page 227)*

One of many acts of delinquency promoted by Mötley Crüe is free use of the heavy-metal *umlaut* with reckless disregard for lïngüïstïc cönventïöns. Another is "Smokin' in the Boys Room," a cover of a 1973 hit by Brownsville Station. The Crüe version was their first Top 40 hit at #16, from the 1985 album *Theatre of Pain* — featuring Mick Mars, the Munsters' favorite guitarist.

Röck Tüning

A pact with the Devil stipulates that the Crüe tune their guitars a half step below standard tuning. Open strings are E♭–A♭–D♭–G♭–B♭–E♭, but you don't need to tune down unless you plan to play with the recording.

Swïng It!

When you play with a *shuffle* (or *swing*) *feel,* a pair of eighth notes turns into something completely different (see the tempo indicator at the start of the song). Think of it as playing more like a heartbeat. Unless you're a robot, your heart doesn't beat in straight eighth notes; it has a long beat and a short beat. When you strum or pick with a shuffle feel, the downstroke is usually longer than the upstroke. (Do this on the chorus.)

The Picküp

We start with a *pickup measure,* which has less than four beats; start out counting, "1–and–2–and–3–and–4," and nail the first slippery power chord on the "and" of beat 4.

The intro and verse pattern is built on three-note power chords that are *slid* to from one fret below. Hit the first chord, slide it up one fret, and repeat. The chorus is a blues pattern, played with *palm muting;* start with a two-note power chord, then place your fret-hand pinky up two frets and play again. Remember to swing it! (The same goes for the harmonica solo.)

Fills and Sölö

In between power chords in the chorus, Mars plays an assortment of bluesy fills, mostly in A and E *minor pentatonic* positions, and the guitar solo follows suit. His favored techniques:

- ✔ *Pinch* harmonics – played with the edge of the pick, so your pick-hand thumb grazes the string and makes it scream
- ✔ *Quarter-* and *half-step bends* – best played by pulling downward (toward the floor)
- ✔ *Chromatic* walking down the A and E strings – one fret at a time, one finger per fret
- ✔ Other Martian techniques as shown in the Guitar Notation Legend

Sweet Child o' Mine *(page 234)*

Guns N' Roses set the standards for a generation with their creative use o' apostrophes and immortal guitar riffs. A #1 hit from the enormous 1987 album *Appetite for Destruction,* "Sweet Child o' Mine" features the riff every aspiring rocker uses to test out amplifiers at the local guitar store, thanks to an accidental composition by lead guitarist Slash. He came up with the riff as a technical exercise, and whilst playing it at rehearsal, Izzy Stradlin' joined in with chords and a megahit was born!

Rock Tunin'

GN'R tuned a half step lower than standard. Open strings, low to high, are E♭–A♭–D♭–G♭–B♭–E♭, but you don't need to tune down unless you plan to play with the recording or join Guns N' Roses.

No Finger Left Behind

Anchor your first finger on fret 12 for the main riff. The usual rule is "one finger per fret," but you have other options here: When you see two fourteenth-fret notes in a row on the G and high E strings, you can use a pair of fingers, parallel to each other, so your ring finger doesn't have to do all the work on that fret. *Alternate pick* throughout.

Strum the verse in straight open-position chords, and note the spots where a D chord turns into a Dsus4 — simply a matter of adding the pinky on fret 3.

The chorus has more challenging variations on the main riff — this time outlining an A and C chord. Again, feel free to break the finger rule where necessary (but don't tell your guitar teacher I said that).

Solos Galore

Mini-solos at the end of the first and second chorus are played in a *major pentatonic* scale position with some added major-scale notes. Review your *pull-offs, pre-bends, held bends,* and *slides*.

After the third chorus comes another solo which is a song unto itself. Halfway through it comes the weepy sound of the *wah-wah pedal.* If you have one, kick it in — if not, hold your tears; you can get through without it.

Neck Trauma

The outro solo floats around the E *minor pentatonic scale* with *bends* and *pull-offs* galore. The final *dip* is done by pushing the back of the guitar neck with one hand while you hold the body of the guitar with the other. Don't push too hard, or your guitar will need a chiropractic adjustment!

Talk Dirty to Me (page 245)

This is the song that helped put Poison — hairspray, makeup, and all — on every teenage rocker's TV in 1987. It was the band's second single from *Look What the Cat Dragged In,* making them MTV's favorite feelgood rock band and launching their brief but explosive trip to the top. "Talk Dirty to Me" was written by the World's Blondest Guitarist, C.C. DeVille.

Rock Tuning

Poison tuned their guitars down a half step, so as to better rock the world. Open strings, low to high, are E♭–A♭–D♭–G♭–B♭–E♭, but you don't need to tune down unless you plan to play along with C.C.

Surfin' with C.C.

We begin with the catchy surf-style chorus pattern. Strum the first C5 chord, then pick your fret hand off the frets (but not off the strings) so you get a muted "click." Notice how the C5 *slides* into the D5 chord — just move the chord up without picking up your fret hand or strumming. Do the same between the F♯5 and G5 chords, to get that classic surf-punk sound. Then comes the *pick scrape,* the screeching sound of the edge of your pick digging into the lower guitar strings.

Power chords in the verse are played in all *downstrokes* with *palm mutes* — use the edge of your picking hand to push the strings at the bridge, just enough to get a chunky sound. Release the mute on the accented chords where you don't see "P.M."

What to Call These Licks

C.C. spices up the verses with a few fills:

- ✔ In verse 1, *sliding* under the D chord in what we call "parallel 4ths" (a kind of mini-chord played on parallel strings)
- ✔ Verse 2: bouncing between the open D string and *dyads* (two-note chords) that outline the D major scale
- ✔ Ending verse 2 and 3 with *harmonics* one the B and G string — barely touch the string above fret 7, reulting in a heavenly bell-like sound

"C.C., Pick Up That Guitar and..."

The solo begins with more dyads, outlining C, G, and D scales, then progresses to unison bends (fretting a note on one string and bending another string up to match it) and double pull-offs, then good ol' single-string bends and vibrato.

The Trooper (page 255)

Air-raid siren vocals. Intricate harmony guitar solos. Eddie the Head. Enough said. This is Iron Maiden, a group of London East Enders who crested the New Wave of British Heavy Metal in the early Eighties with their own brand of literary rock. This epic, based on a work of Nathaniel Hawthorne, is from their fourth studio album, *Piece of Mind* (1983), featuring the coordinated master licks of Dave Murray and Adrian Smith. *Everything* in this song is a "Champion Strategy!"

Ready for the Riffs?

The opening riff is one move, repeated in different positions. Play it starting at fret 7, move it to 5, then 3, and quickly slide your index finger up to play the fifth-fret notes on the A and D strings (that puts you in position to start the riff again). We're in the key of E minor, and the next riff could be looked at as box 4 of the E *minor pentatonic scale* (with an added minor 3rd note). The *trill* is a quick series of *hammer-ons* and *pull-offs* played with the index finger held and the middle finger doing the work.

The verse requires you to switch between power chords at blazing speed; use *alternate picking* to make it smooth. *Palm mute* the galloping chords in between those changes (in a rhythm similar to "Lights Out"). Your picking hand gets a slight rest with held chords in the chorus.

Two Lead Guitarists = Two Solos

Solo 1 starts in E *minor pentatonic box 1* at fret 12 (with some "blue notes"). Highlights:

- A *bend* of the G string followed by a hammer-on of the B string, repeated

- Alternating *pull-offs* in upper-position box 2 (anchored at fret 15)

- *Backpedaling* down the E minor scale from fret 19 to 20, to 17 to 19, and so on — for a stumbling effect

Solo 2 plays off the A *minor pentatonic,* starting in *box 1* (at fret 5), with:

- More *trills* that jump from string to string

- Decending *chromatically* with *pinch harmonics*

- A whammy-bar *dip,* and *bends* that jump around the strings

Turn Up the Radio (page 265)

The LA band Autograph made a splash in the mid-1980s with this headbanger's theme song from their first album, *Sign In Please* (1984) — a platinum effort achieved after they raised record company eyebrows while opening for Van Halen. Steve Lynch wields the fiery plectrum of death.

Tuning That Rocks

See "Cold Gin" for details on tuning down one half step.

Whammy Madness

The whammy-bar madness begins before the first chord is struck. Attempt this only if you have a decent vibrato bar system that won't yank everything out of tune — otherwise, you're of no use for most of the song. That said, here are your special whammy techniques:

- ✔ A *pre-dive* that ushers in the first power chords — push the bar down before you pick, play the first power chord, and slowly release.
- ✔ Various *dive bombs* — pick a *harmonic* or a fretted note and slowly push the bar down to the nether regions.
- ✔ *Dips* — quickly push the whammy down and release, for a fast drop and return to pitch.

Aside from that, your first job is to support the keyboard chords with *downstroked, palm muted* single notes and *accented* power chords. This pattern continues under the opening fills, which include a *glissando* played with the edge of the pick, some *two-handed tapping,* and that whammy madness — all optional.

The verse pattern is played in major *triads* (three-note chords) connected by a riff that you can play with one fret-hand finger over each pair of strings at frets 5 and 3. Then comes a nifty series of *harmonics* that outline the G chord at frets 5 and 12.

Rule of Thumb

The chorus is an exercise in full first- and second-position *barre chords,* played all over the neck. The Esus4 chord is just an E barre with your pinky added on the B string (it *suspends the 4th*). If you're not a barre-chord master, remember that it's best to keep your thumb on the back of the neck, directly behind the chord, as you play them.

Mixo-What?

There's no way to make the solo simple, but know that it revolves around the A *Mixolydian mode* — a kind of hybrid major and minor scale — until *two-handed tapping* time, when Steve's notes follow the chord changes. Consult the Guitar Notation Legend for special symbols, and be careful out there.

Unchained (page 273)

What book of hard rock songs would be complete without the man who popularized two-handed tapping and striped guitars? Eddie Van Halen's gonzo techniques set the standards for generations of guitar gods. "Unchained" was on the 1981 *Fair Warning* album by Van Halen the band (named after Eddie and his equally gonzo drummer brother, Alex).

The Pickup

Start with a *pickup measure,* which has less than four beats; start out counting, "1–and–2–and–3–and–4," and start playing on the "and" of beat 4.

Rock Tuning + Drop D + Flanger + Palm Muting = Rock

Not only is "Unchained" tuned down a half step (see "Cold Gin" for the lowdown), it's also in *drop D tuning* — the low E string is tuned down to D. On top of that, Eddie uses a *flanger* at strategic moments to get that slow helicopter-blade effect (optional), which goes hand in hand with *palm muting* on the open strings. On top of these chunky notes are full major barre chords, with the pinky added to create the sus4 chords.

Sync'd

The verse is a single-note variation of the intro/chorus pattern, with lots of *string bends, slides, vibrato,* and *pinch harmonics.* Then comes the pre-chorus, which is syncopated — it feels like something other than 4/4 time, but catches up with itself. Harmonics here are just the effect of picking while lifting your fingers off the frets (but not off the strings) between chord hits. Notice that drop D tuning lets you play power chords with one finger on the two lowest strings.

Shred Like Ed

The tastefully quirky solo follows the pre-chorus chord changes with *dives, two-handed tapping, pre-bends, pull-offs,* and so on. After Sir Edward came along, new notation had to be made up to symbolize some of these things! Consult the Guitar Notation Legend for details.

Pluck 'n' Tap

For the bridge, lower your volume, drop your pick, and pluck the *staccato* notes with your fingers. *Touch harmonics* (T.H.) are played with a tap 12 frets higher than the notes you're fretting. Now grab your pick, roll your volume up, and *palm mute* back into the chorus.

More soloing closes out the tune, with sliding *octaves* and more gonzo whammy-bar techniques. Don't attempt the deep dives unless you have a durable vibrato bar with a locking nut!

Up All Night (page 283)

This rock anthem for bats was the first single from Slaughter's first album, *Stick It To Ya*, in 1990. Coming into the hard-rock scene just as glam was dying out, the band's music had a Led Zeppelin-esque sophistication that kept it on the charts through the grunge revolution of the early nineties. "Up All Night" features the pickin' and riffin' of singer/guitarist Mark Slaughter and lead guitarist Tim Kelly.

Beyond Rock Tuning

Tuning down a half step didn't rock enough for Slaughter — they gave it the extra push off the cliff by dropping the strings *a whole step*. Open strings, low to high, are D–G–C–F–A–D.

Strum the opening Asus2 chord with your volume down to 0, then gradually increase *(swell)* it. Three slides down the low E string, and you're into the first riff over *palm muted* open notes. Note the octaves that usher in the verse — make sure the middle string is muted where you see the Xs.

Cardinal Twang

The pre-chorus is built on *arpeggios* — just hold the chords and play one note at a time. When you play these with your pick close to the bridge, you get an extra-clean twangy sound.

A Big Word for a Big Chord

The chorus chords are mostly the power variety, but the Dsus2 has an extra A note at the bottom. Technically, this is an *inversion* — a big word in jazz circles. All I know is that the low note makes your chord sound HUGE. Watch for the quarter-step bends (to be pulled downward) and hammer-ons in the following riff.

Pinch It!

Mr. Kelly has a thing for *pinch harmonics* — turning the pick sideways so the thumb grazes the string and makes it scream. This happens in the first interlude, along with a two-step bend (facilitated by low tuning) and blazing *hammer-ons* and *pull-offs.* Same deal with the second interlude, which plays off a *pedal point* (a single open G string repeated in between moving notes). The solo, another song in and of itself, has more of the same, wiggled ad infinitum with wide *vibrato.* Tim's fast *legato* licks are the result of strong hammering and pulling combined with *slides* — a fine workout for the left hand.

Wait (page 290)

The 1980s school of hairspray and spandex produced its share of noteworthy music from top-class guitarists, including Vito Bratta of White Lion. Bratta was best known for melodic and humanly impossible guitar solos, as on this Top 10 single from WL's second album *Pride* (1987).

Fingerpickin' Great

Put your pick between your teeth, or wherever you won't lose it, for the *fingerpicked* intro. Find the first D chord position, and hold it while your thumb plucks the D string and your fingers *arpeggiate* in order: ring–middle–index. Repeat the pattern as you shift, skipping a note at the end of each measure.

Down Is Up

Use whatever acrobatics you see fit to hit the following power chord, grab your pick, and use it to *arpeggiate* some more on the verse. Generally, use downsrokes as you arpeggiate "upward," and upstrokes as you go down the chord (pitchwise).

Arpeggios Parmigiano

The interlude and verse bounce between two-and three-note chords, *palm muted* notes, and even more magic arpeggios (I just like to say that word). Rest your picking hand close to the bridge, so you can mute with it when the "chunk" is called for — same goes for the pre-chorus.

Guess what the chorus is based on? *Palm-muted arpeggios!* Just don't push down too hard, or you'll confuse the lead singer when your chords go sharp.

Ah, the Solo!

Vito's mellifluous solo begins with a cool move: with the G string fretted at fret 2, *tap fret* 14 (up an octave) with your pick hand, middle finger, then *bend* your original note underneath it, release, slide the tapped note up to fret 21, and add *vibrato* with your left hand. The two hands keep working together like this throughout. "T.H." means that your right hand touches the string at fret 22, just enough to coax a high, singing harmonic note. Later comes a series of *taps and slides,* in which your left hand slips about the neck between taps of a single note at fret 15. Finally, the right hand is left to pick while the left does a series of *pull-offs* and — guess what — *arpeggios!*

We're Not Gonna Take It (page 299)

Dee Snyder, Twisted Sister's sharp-toothed frontman, wrote this song of rebellion with inspiration from Slade, the Sex Pistols, and a Christmas carol ("Oh Come, All Ye Faithful"). This 1984 anthem from the album *Stay Hungry* was an MTV smash for the makeup-clad horror/glam outfit from New York, driven by guitarist Jay Jay French.

Essential Gestures

The intro is mostly guitarless, so your very important job is to hold up one or both hands in the "heavy metal salute" (a fist with the index and pinky finger extended) while your singer belts out the main hook. Then it's a descending line on the A string and power chords galore.

I–IV–V

Said power chords follow what teachers call a *I–IV–V progression,* the universal three-chord formula for everything from blues to punk. Why the numerals? The chords' root notes are the first, fourth, and fifth notes of the scale or key of the song. Be sure to dampen the strings for silence where you see the *eighth-note rest* at the last measure of the progression.

The chorus is more of the same, plus a sustained swipe of the open B and high E strings for a little space. Notice in the bridge how the *palm muted* chords include an A/C♯ — the transcriber's way of saying, just move the bottom note of the previous D5 down a fret.

Bouncy Bouncy

If you want to play the guitar solo just as Jay Jay did, you need a durable vibrato bar (ideally, a "floating" one) with a locking nut. Anything less, and all these bouncing *dips* and *dives* will send your guitar out of tune, if not to the luthier's boneyard!

Having said that, the solo follows the verse melody in a position of the major scale rooted at fret 9, with slides, a whammy-dipped twelfth-fret *harmonic,* and the aforementioned vibrato-bar madness.

You know what to do on the breakdown-chorus: Give the audience the proverbial salute (tongue wagging optional).

Yankee Rose (page 307)

David Lee Roth, the first of many singers to exit Van Halen (or be shown the door), made a big solo comeback on his 1986 album *Eat 'Em and Smile.* Roth's band featured some of the monster musicians of shred-rock, including the celebrated guitar maniac Steve Vai. Stevie plays some of his most "spanking" riffs in "Yankee Rose." I could write a book on this song alone, but I'll stick to describing select techniques as they appear.

Super Whammy Bar Alert

If you want to play everything just as Vai did, you need a durable vibrato bar (ideally, a "floating" one) with a locking nut. Anything less, and you'll have strings and springs flying off your broken guitar.

Feel free to skip over the intro "banter" and jump right into the verse. Playing around an open G5 chord, palm mute the first low lick. After the B♭ chord, bend the G string up in mini-steps until you get up to a whole step, then release and *pull off* as shown. More whammy licks follow, and at the end of the verse is a flurry of notes using every technique imaginable.

The pre-chorus has *pinch harmonics* played on two notes at once — turn your pick sideways and push, so the edge of your thumb against the string creates squawky overtones.

The chorus involves more palm mutes, some slides, and a bending lick played with more *pinch harmonics.* Pull the A string at fret 3 *downward* a whole step, release, *pull off* to fret 1, and continue.

The bridge has a refreshing clean guitar part, picked with each note held out to the next so that they all ring out. Then it kicks in to "straight" power chords, ending with a D7♯9 chord, sliding down each time you hit it.

Legendary Licks

Outro licks of interest:

- ✔ Sliding *power chords,* followed by a whammy *dive* and *pull-offs*
- ✔ *Two-handed tapping* with left-hand notes moving below the right
- ✔ A good old-fashioned unison bend between frets 15 and 18
- ✔ All manner of over-the-top techniques that have created the need for new guitar notation symbols — consult the Guitar Notation Legend for details

You Shook Me All Night Long *(page 319)*

The importance of keeping one's "motor clean" cannot be overstated, especially in hard rock songs. AC/DC has been rocking the world since their formation in 1973 in Sydney, Australia by guitarist-brothers Angus and Malcolm Young. Their 1980 album *Back in Black* spawned hit after decadent hit, including this classic, made immortal by aspiring Anguses everywhere.

Bending and Fretting Down Under

Put on your schoolboy uniform! The slow intro shifts between two partial open-position chords (G5 and D5) with embellishments including a *quarter-step* bend — pull the string slightly downward — and a bluesy slide. The main chord pattern is all open-position chords. Tip: fret the first G5 chord with your third finger on the low E string, so you can quickly shift to a C without rearranging your fingers.

The chorus opens things up with a full G5 chord (*mute* the A string so it doesn't ring out), and *arpeggiation* on the "all night long" part. Just find the chord positions, hold 'em, and play one note at a time as shown on the tab. (Then remind your friends that you know how to *arpeggiate*.)

Caffeinated Guitar Solo

Angus begins this superblues solo in a standard G *minor pentatonic* position, but in true rock fashion he adds some major notes and shifts up the neck over the course of the solo (see the scale diagram for reference). Remember, *whole-step bends* should be pushed upward (especially when they're *held bends*), and *quarter-step bends* are usually pulled down. Watch for *pre-bends* and *palm mutes* as well, plus the occasional *slide* — all discussed in the Guitar Notation Legend. The most distinctive part of the Angus style is a super-fast, shaky *vibrato* that might or might not be achieved with massive caffeine consumption.

No Excuses

Words and Music by Jerry Cantrell

Tune down 1/2 step:
(low to high) E♭-A♭-D♭-G♭-B♭-E♭

Intro
Moderately ♩ = 114

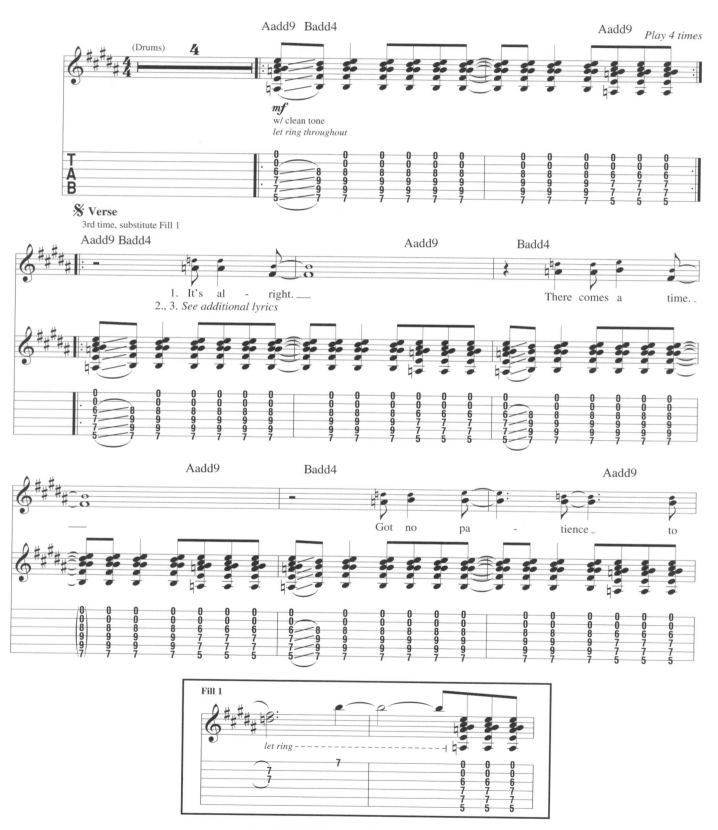

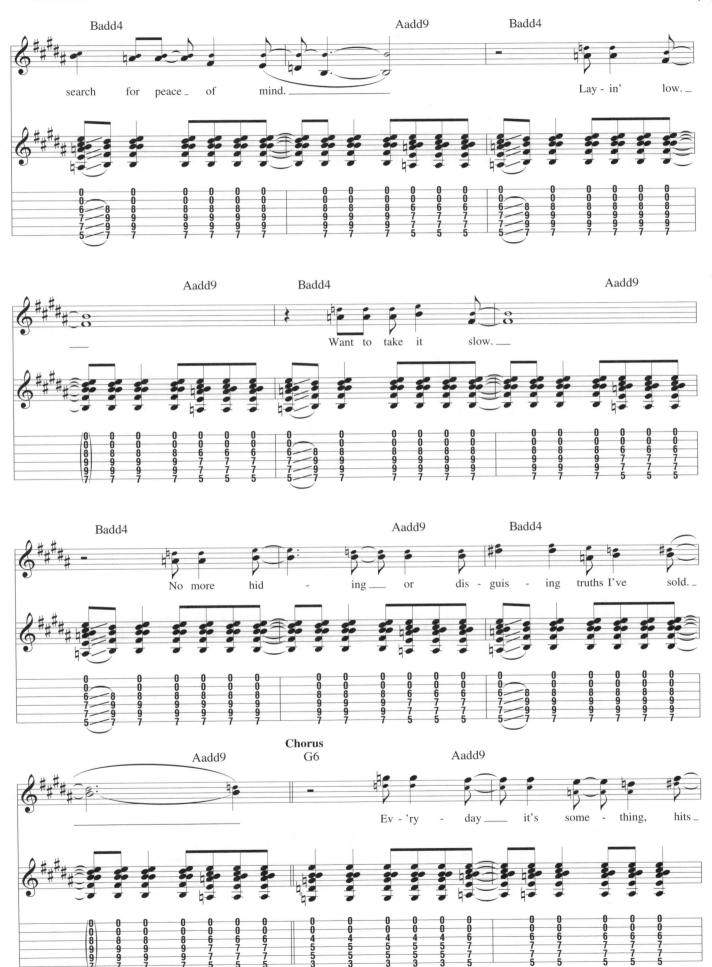

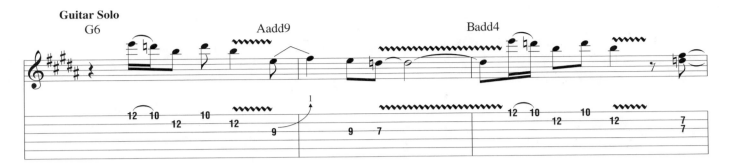

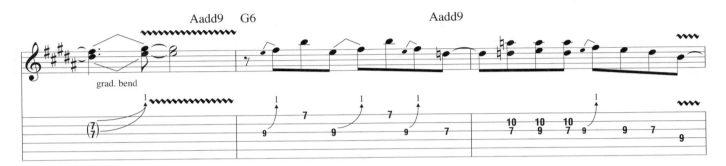

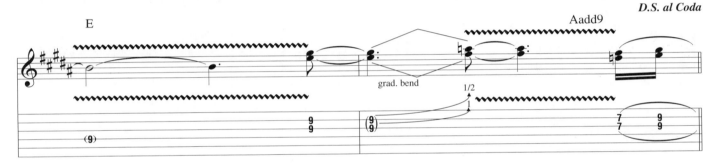

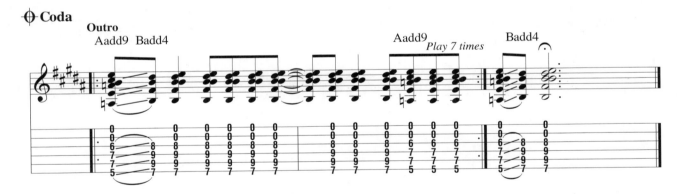

Additional Lyrics

2. It's okay. Had a bad day.
   Hands are bruised from breaking rocks all day.
   Drained and blue, I bleed for you.
   You think it's funny, well, you're drowning in it too.

3. Yeah, it's fine. We'll walk down the line.
   Leave our rain, a cold trade for warm sunshine.
   You, my friend, I will defend.
   And if we change, well, I love you anyway.

Rock You Like a Hurricane

Words and Music by Herman Rarebell, Klaus Meine and Rudolf Schenker

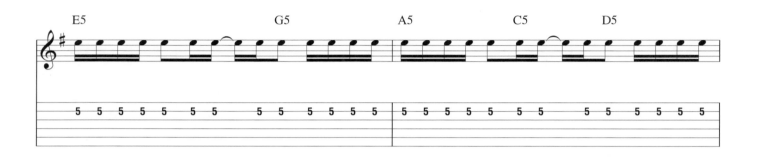

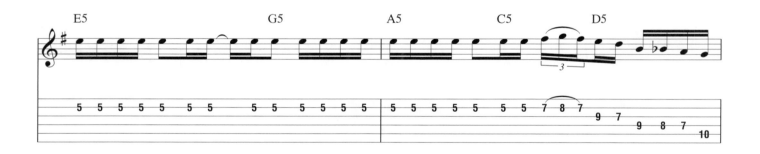

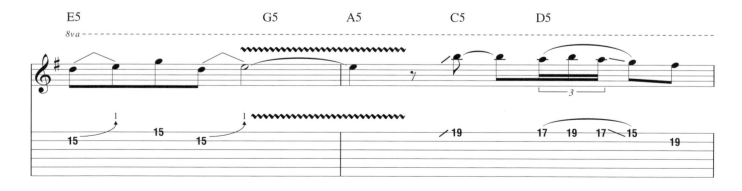

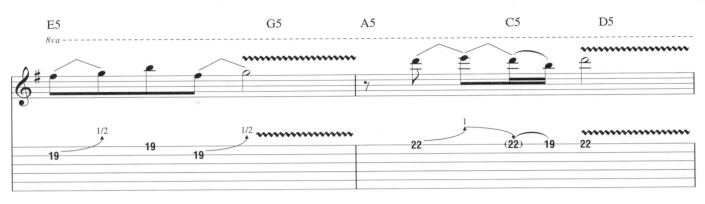

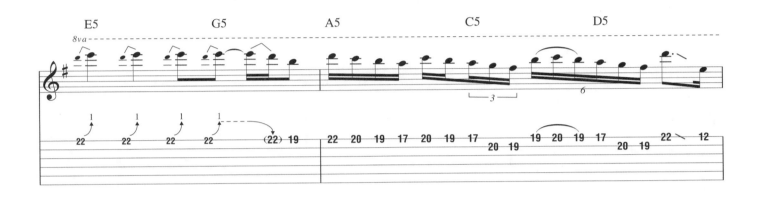

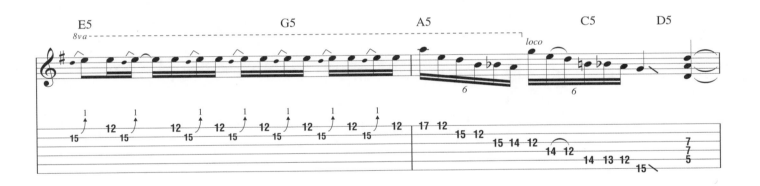

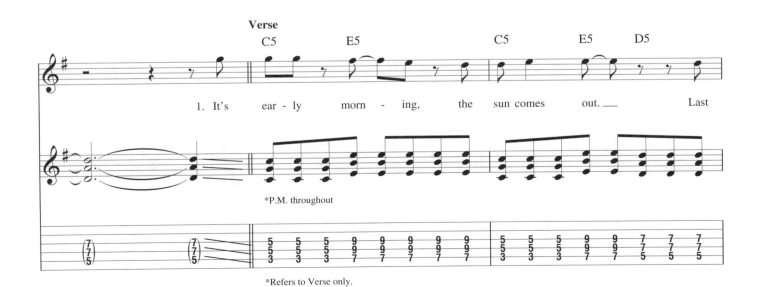

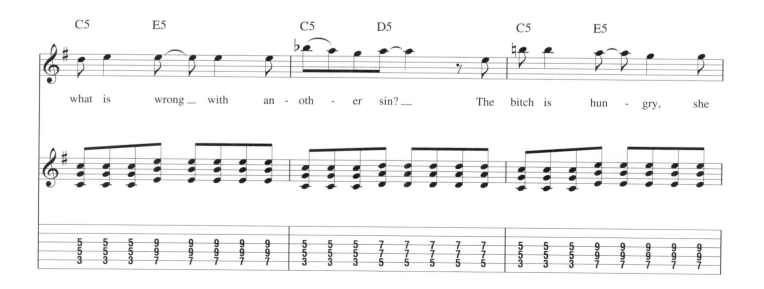

needs to tell, ___ so give her inch - es and feed her well. ___ More

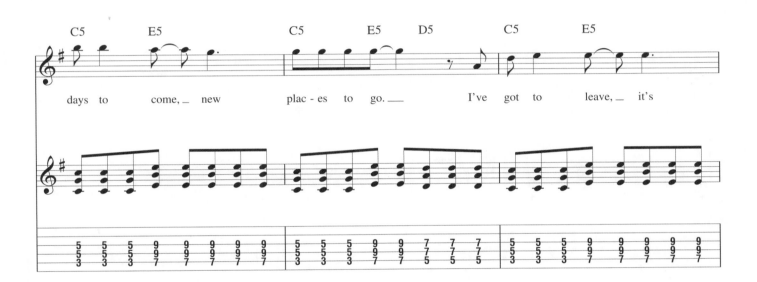

days to come, ___ new plac - es to go. ___ I've got to leave, ___ it's

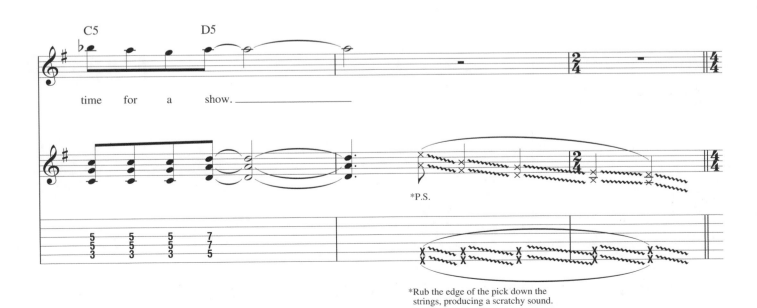

time for a show. _____

*P.S.

*Rub the edge of the pick down the
strings, producing a scratchy sound.

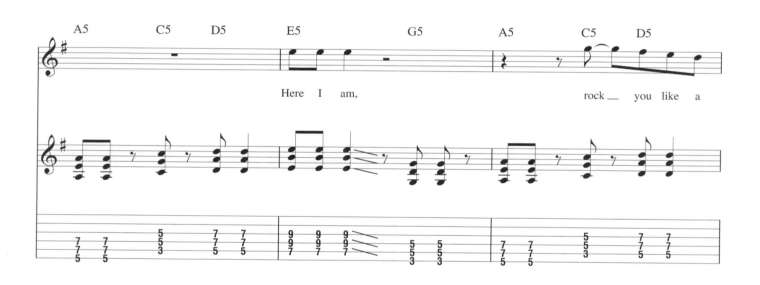

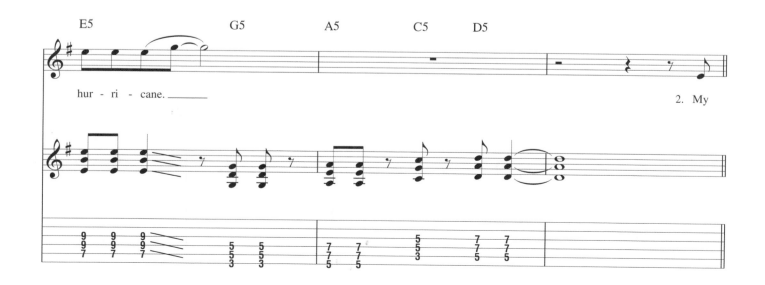

Verse
2nd time, Gtr. tacet, next 7 meas.

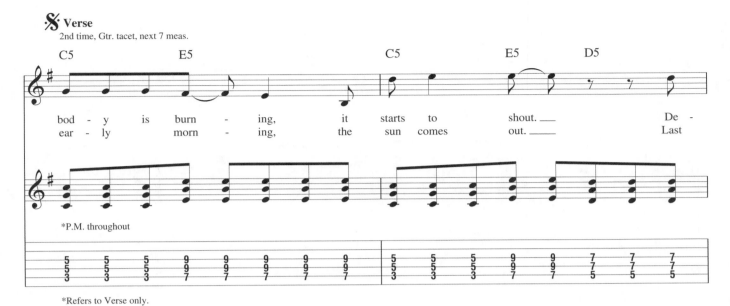

bod - y is burn - ing, it starts to shout. ___ De -
ear - ly morn - ing, the sun comes out. ___ Last

*P.M. throughout

*Refers to Verse only.

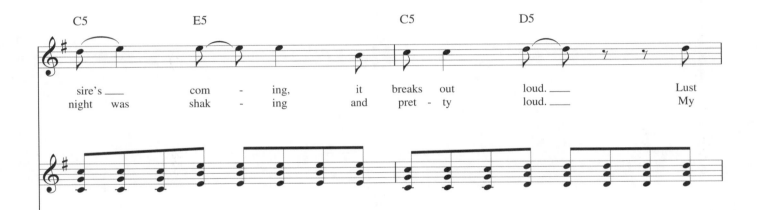

sire's ___ com - ing, it breaks out loud. ___ Lust
night was shak - ing it and pret - ty loud. ___ My

is in cag - es, 'til storm breaks loose. ___ Just
cat is pur - ring, it scratched my skin. ___ So,

hunt to - night __ for love at first sting. ____

Chorus

Here I am, rock __ you like a hur - ri - cane.

To Coda ⊕

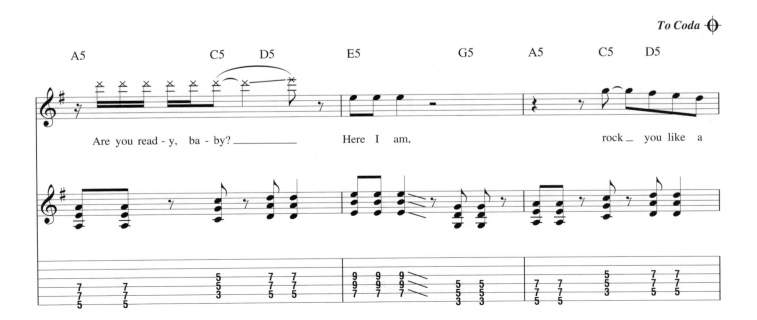

Are you read - y, ba - by? ____ Here I am, rock __ you like a

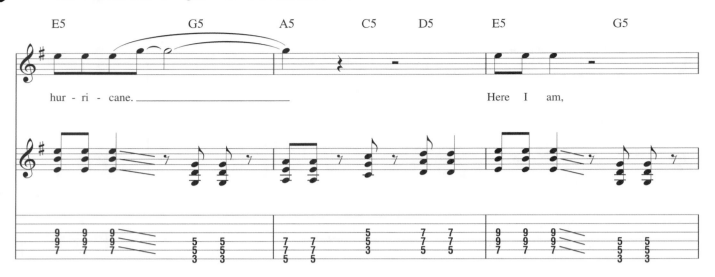

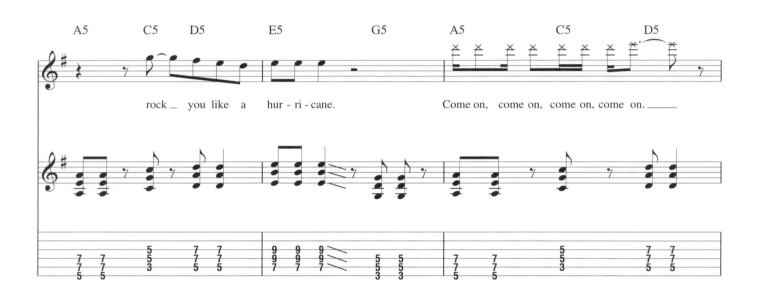

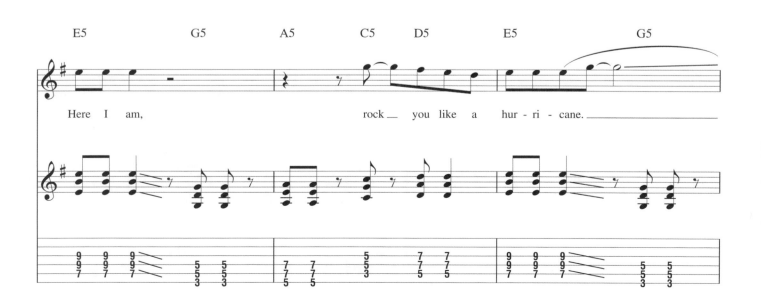

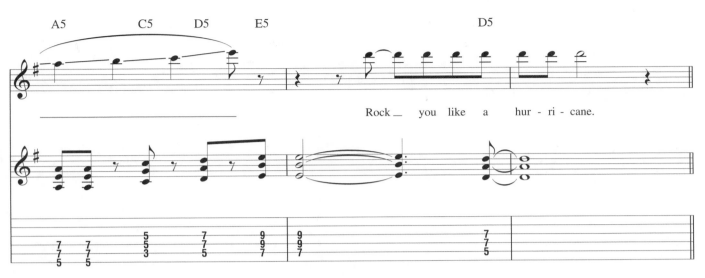

Rock __ you like a hur - ri - cane.

Guitar Solo

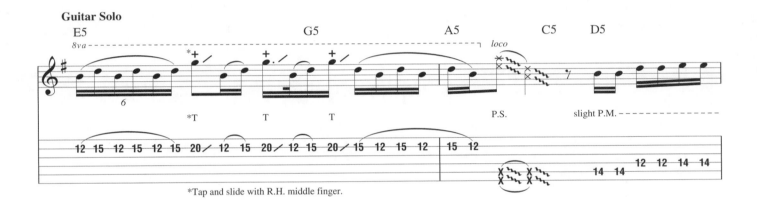

*Tap and slide with R.H. middle finger.

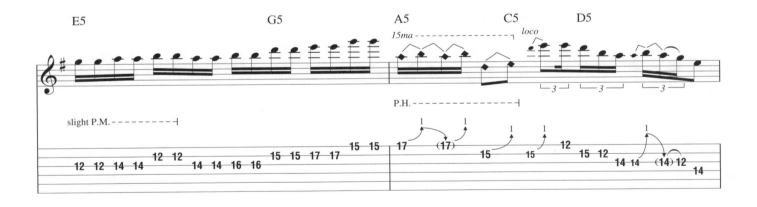

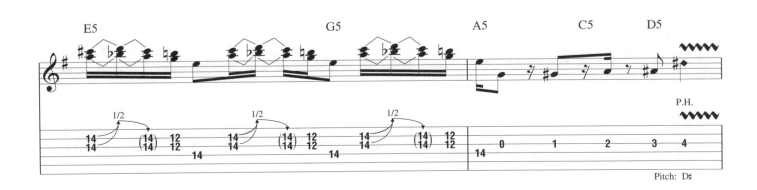

Pitch: D#

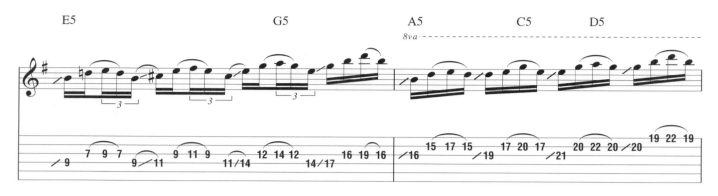

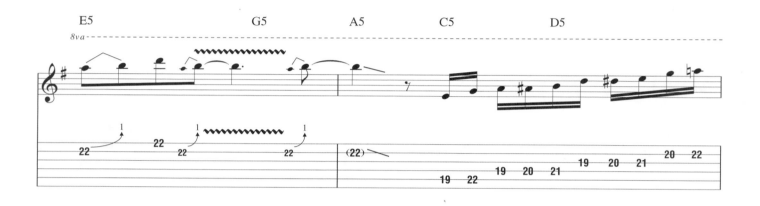

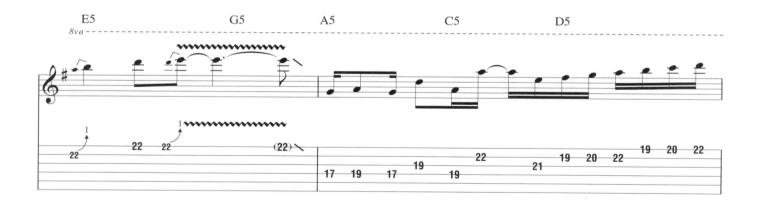

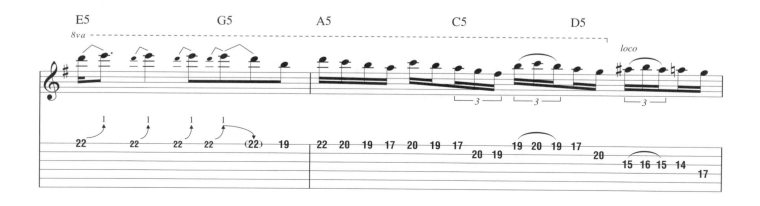

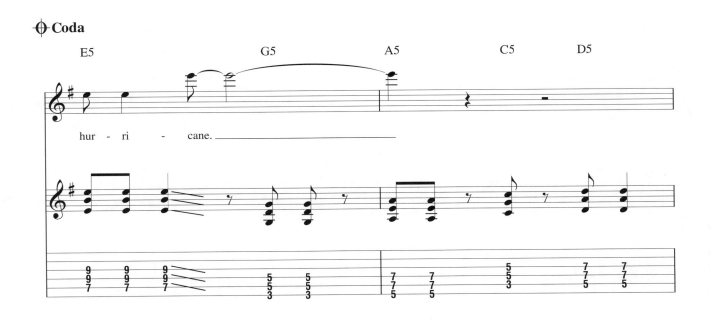

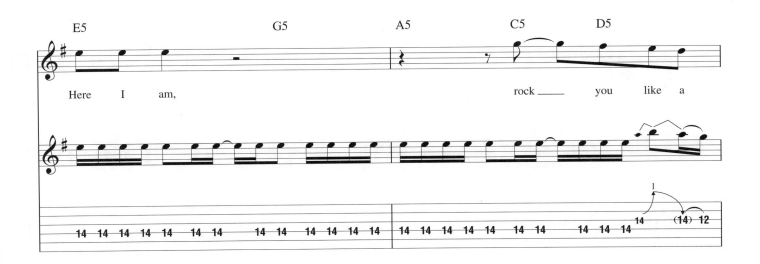

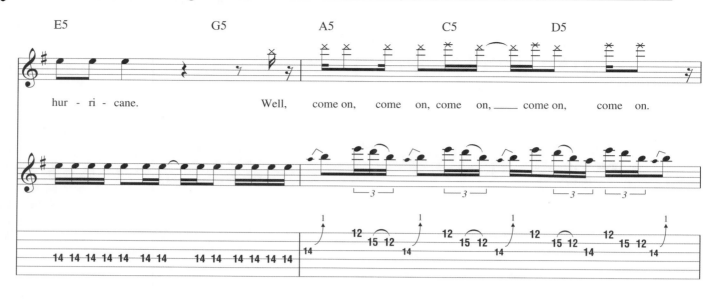

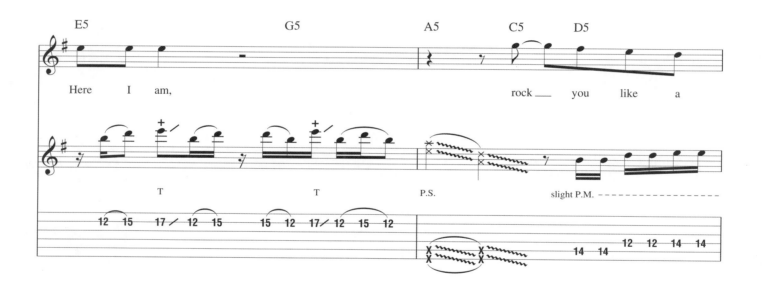

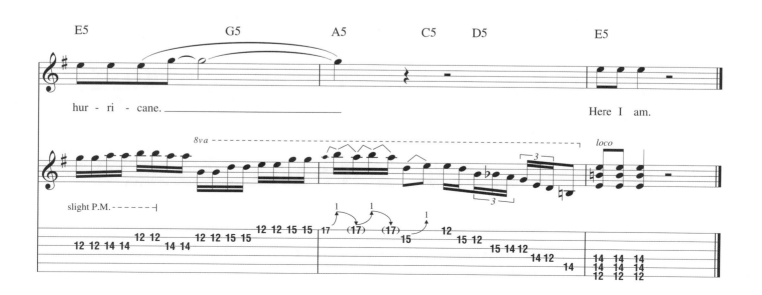

School's Out

Words and Music by Alice Cooper and Michael Bruce

Seventeen

Words and Music by Kip Winger, Reb Beach and Beau Hill

Tune down 1/2 step:
(low to high) Eb-Ab-Db-Gb-Bb-Eb

Intro
Moderate Rock ♩ = 96

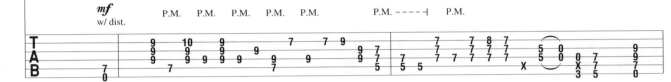

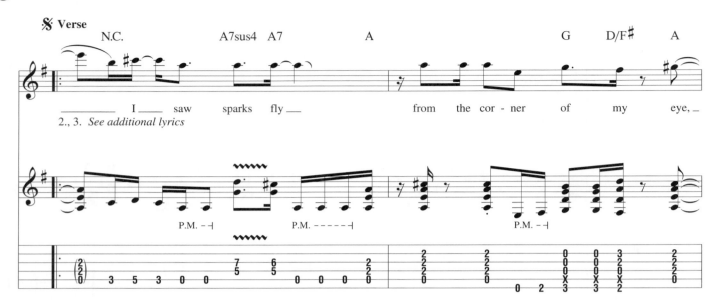

I ____ saw sparks fly ____ from the cor - ner of my eye, ____

2., 3. See additional lyrics

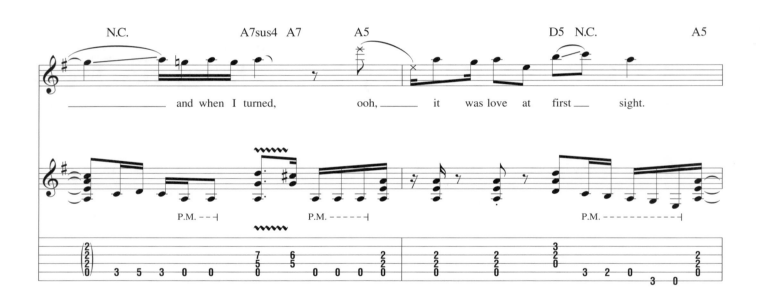

____ and when I turned, ooh, ____ it was love at first ____ sight.

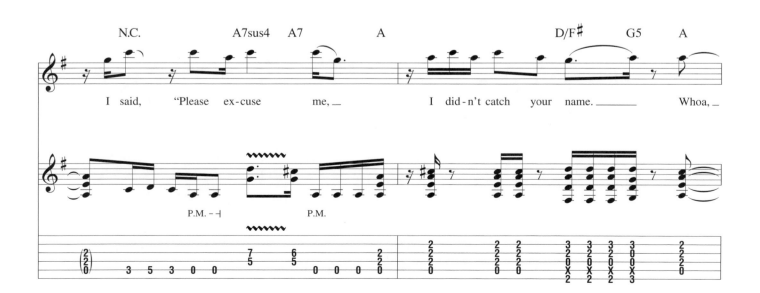

I said, "Please ex-cuse me, ____ I did-n't catch your name. ____ Whoa, ____

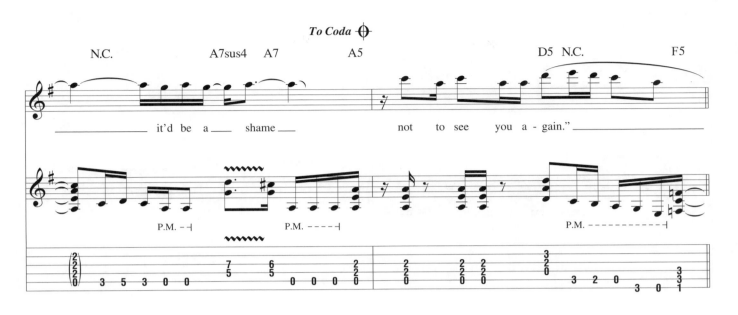

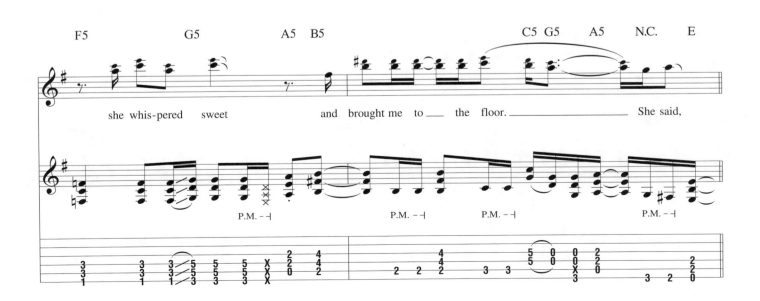

Chorus

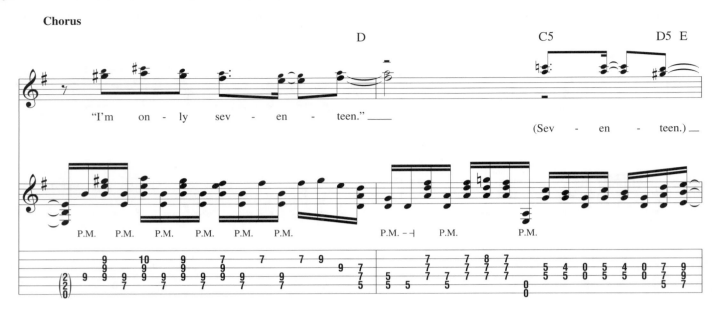

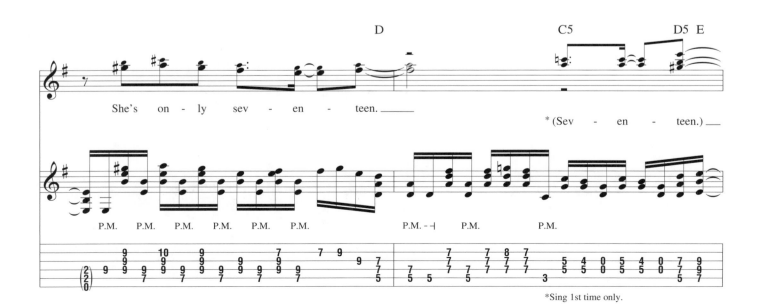

*Sing 1st time only.

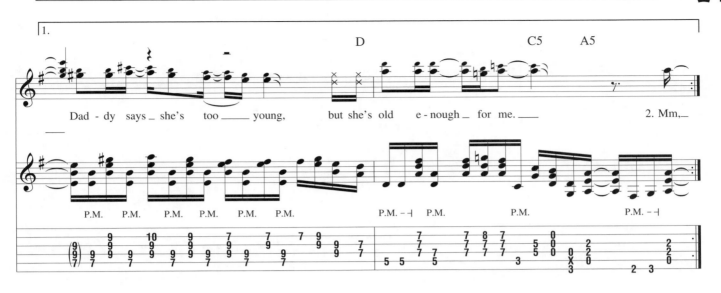

Dad - dy says _ she's too ___ young, but she's old e - nough _ for me. ___ 2. Mm,_

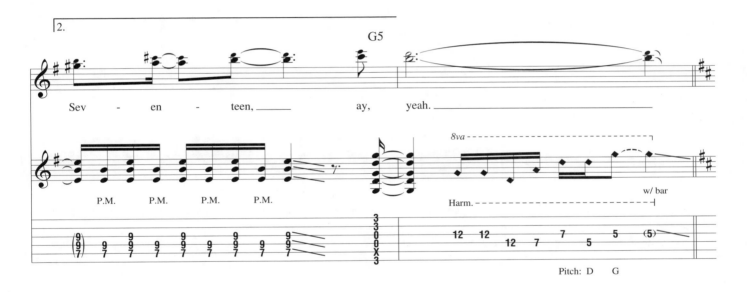

Sev - en - teen, ___ ay, yeah. ___

Pitch: D   G

Guitar Solo

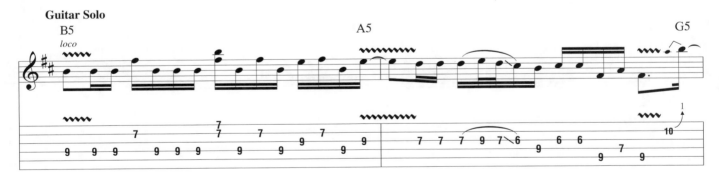

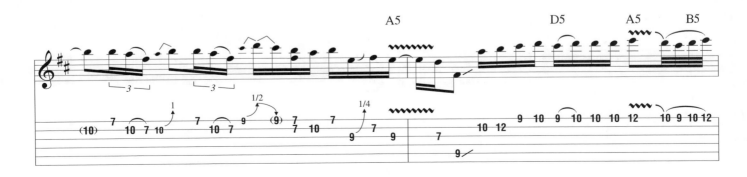

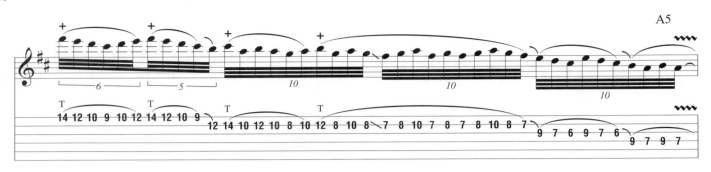

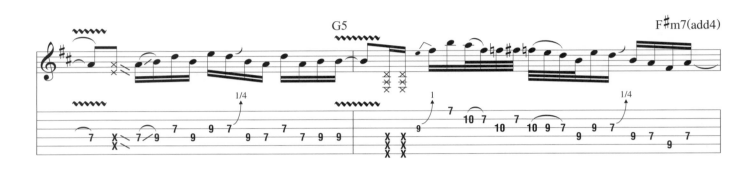

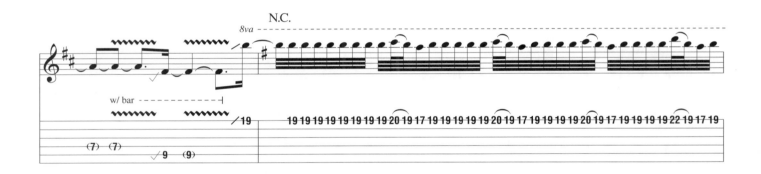

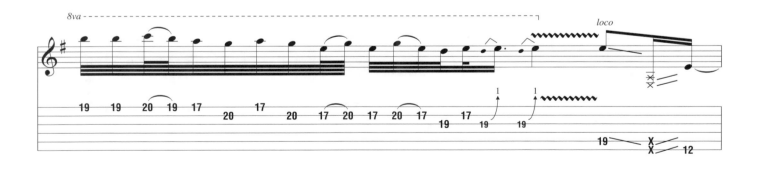

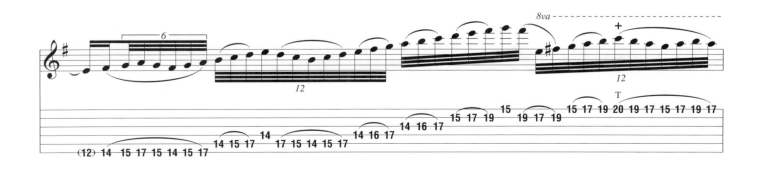

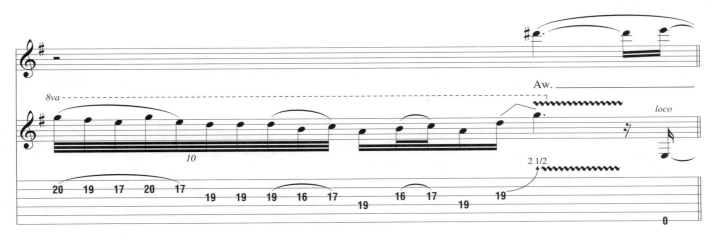

Interlude

D.S. al Coda

Coda

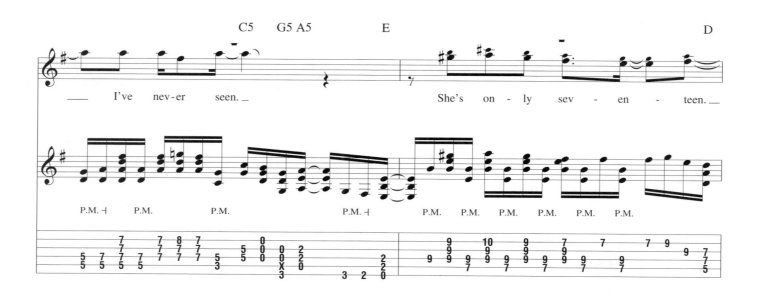

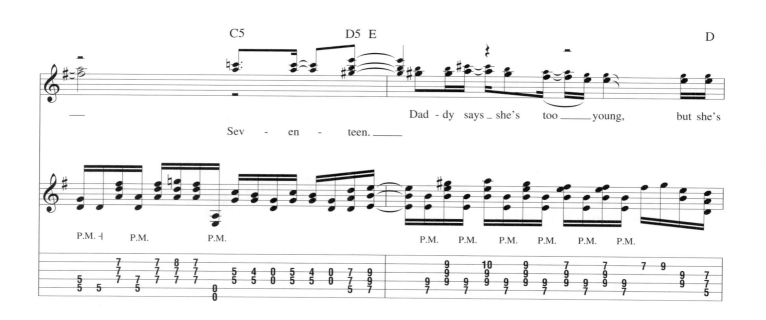

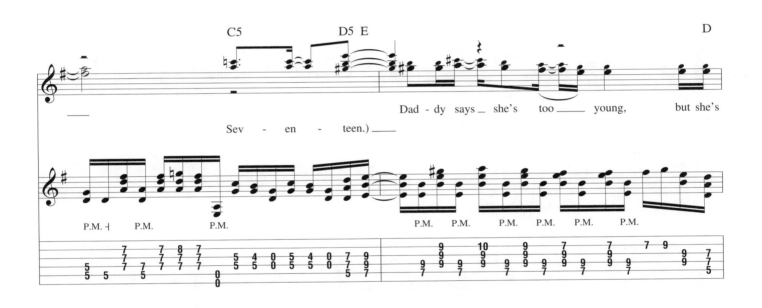

Outro-Guitar Solo

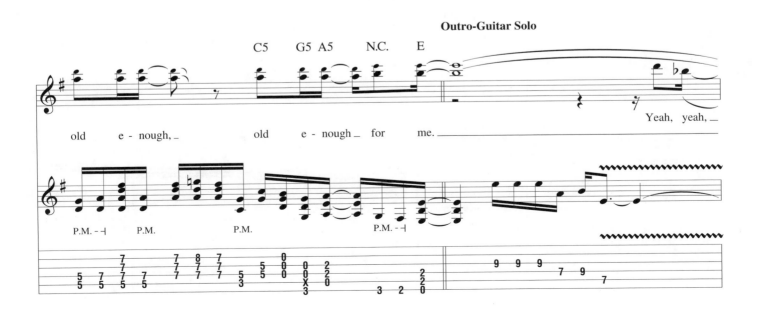

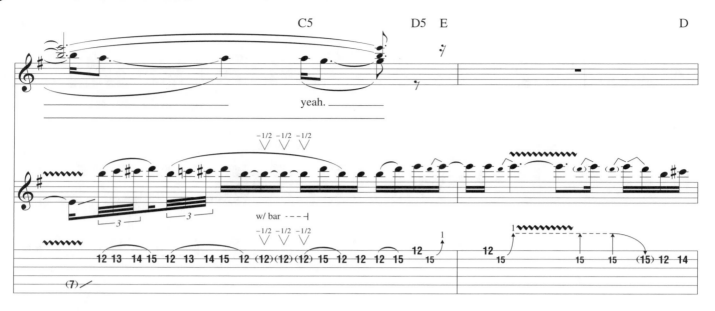

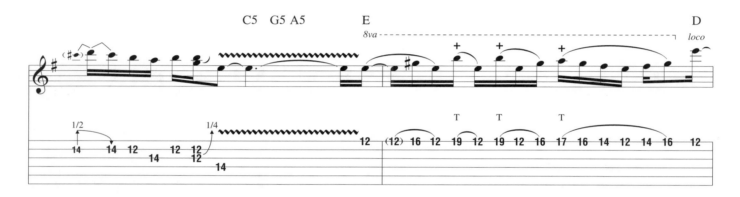

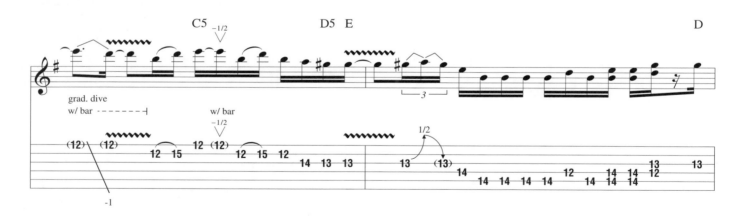

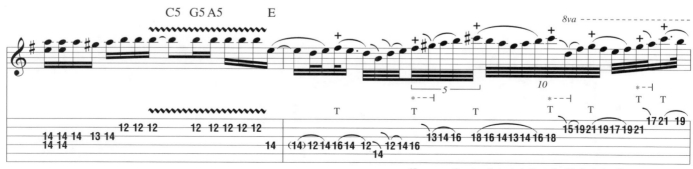

*In one motion, tap the note indicated with the index finger
of the pick hand, then pluck the adjacent string with the same
finger while pulling off.

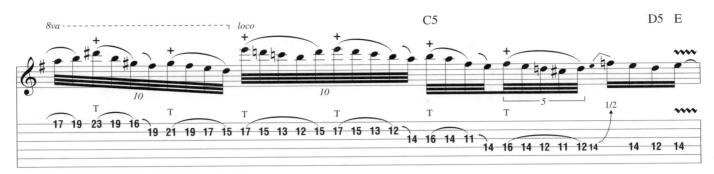

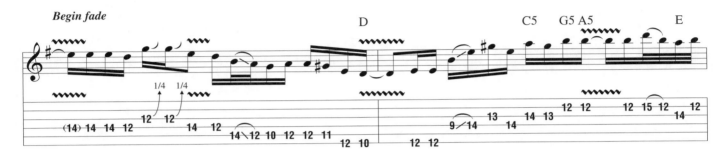

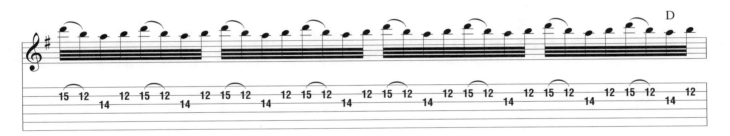

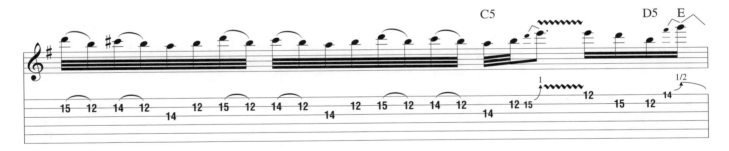

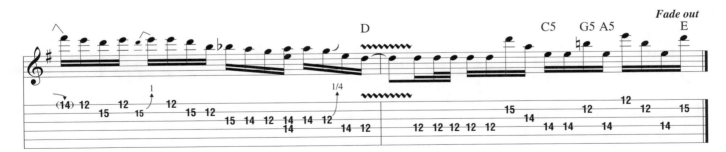

Additional Lyrics

2. Mm, come to my place; we can talk it over, oh,
Ev'rything going down in your head.
She says, "Take it easy, I need some time.
Time to work it out, to make you mine."

3. Yeah, such a bad girl, loves to work me overtime.
Feels good, hah, dancing close to the borderline.
She's a magic mountain, she's a leather glove.
Oh, she's my soul. It must be love.

Shake Me

Words and Music by Tom Keifer

Coda 1

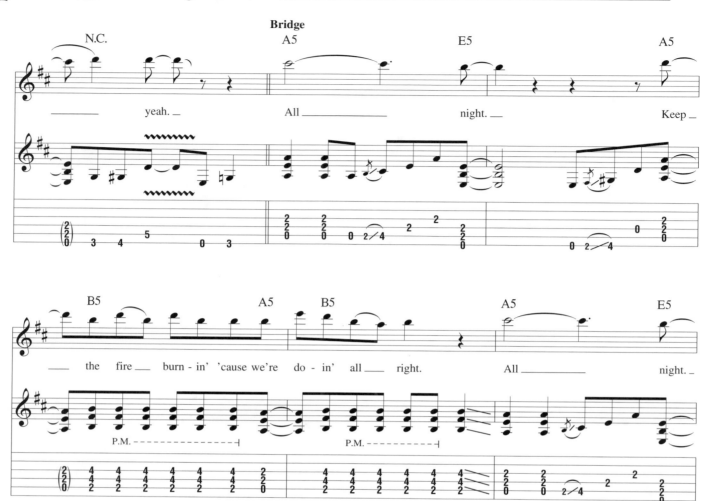

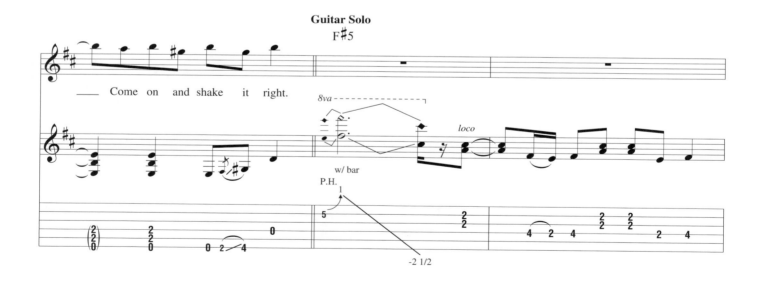

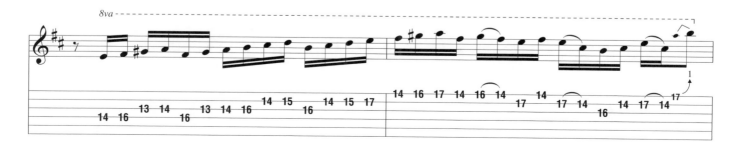

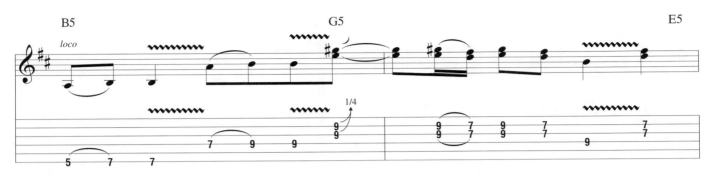

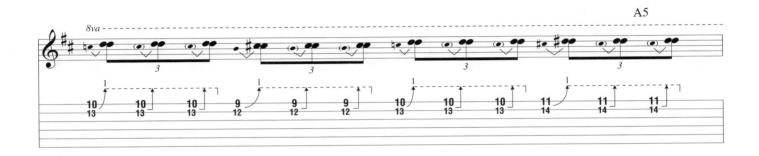

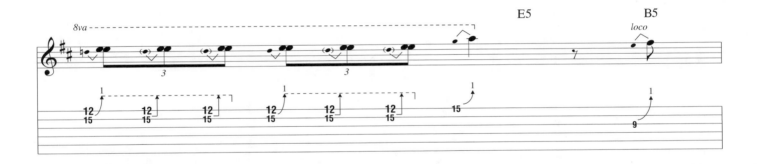

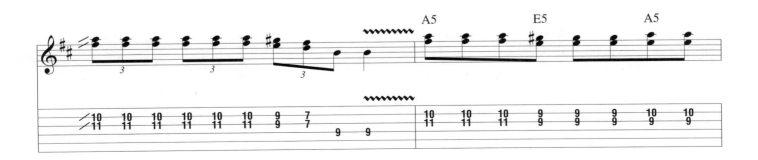

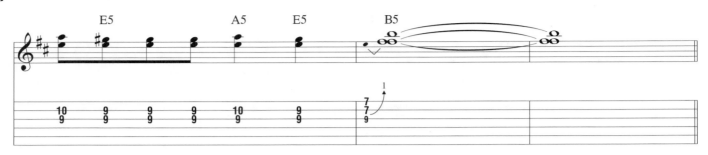

Interlude

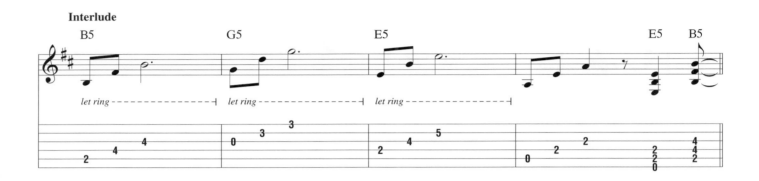

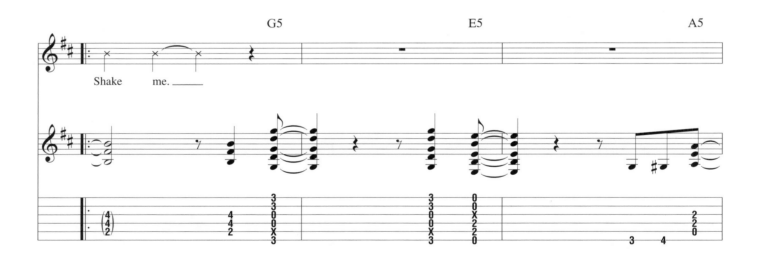

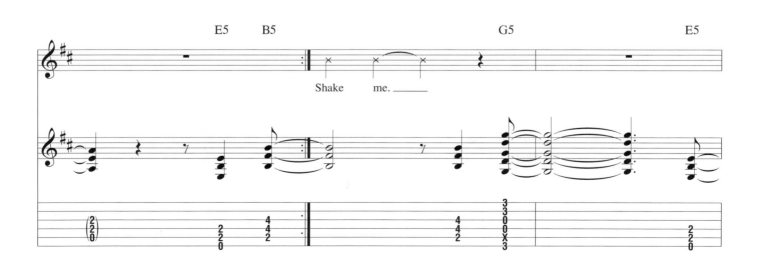

D.S.S. al Coda 2

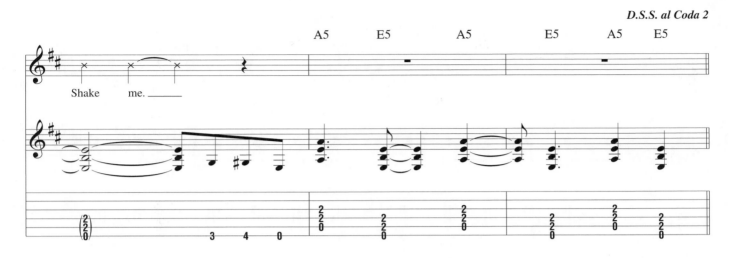

⊕ **Coda 2**

Outro-Guitar Solo

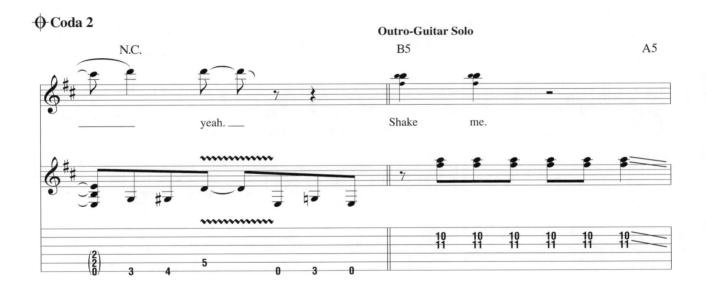

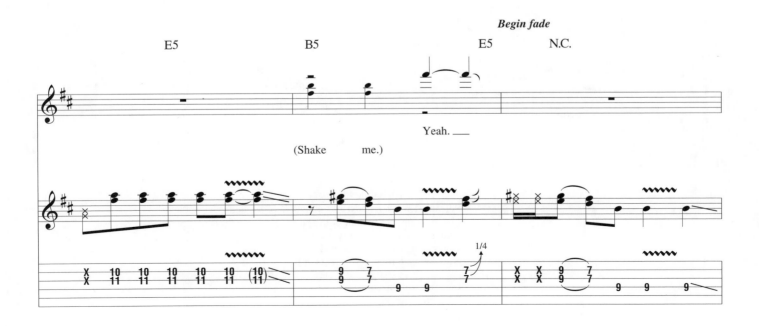

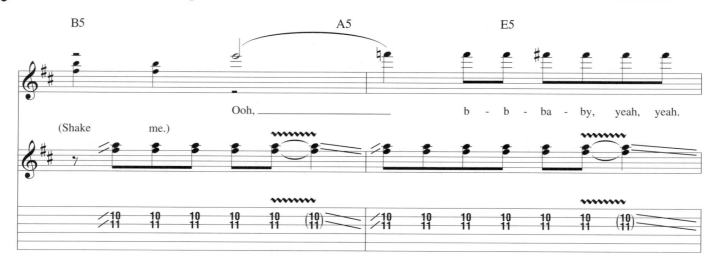

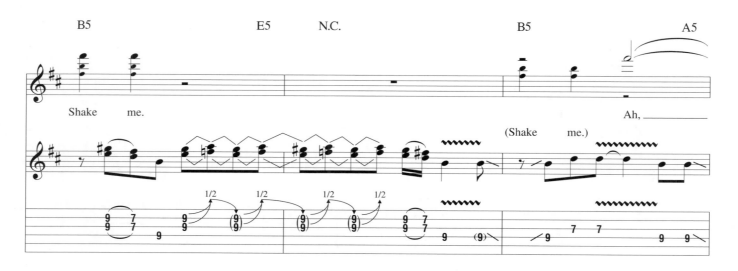

Additional Lyrics

2. Screamed and scratched and rolled out of the bed,
I never really got her out of my head.
And now and then she makes those social calls,
Gives me a squeeze, gets me kickin' the walls.
Now let me tell ya, it still feels tight,
And we were shakin' after every bite.
I feel her comin' in the middle of the night,
Screamin' higher.

Smokin' in the Boys Room

Words and Music by Michael Koda and Michael Lutz

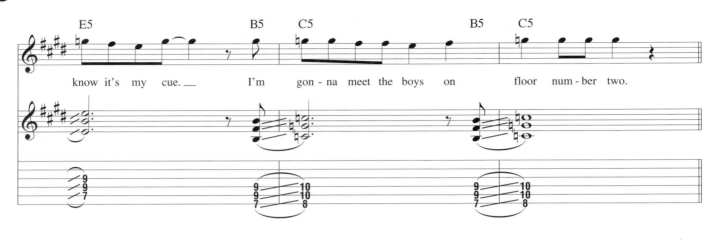

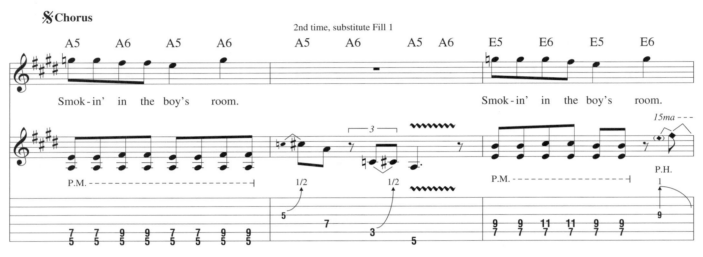

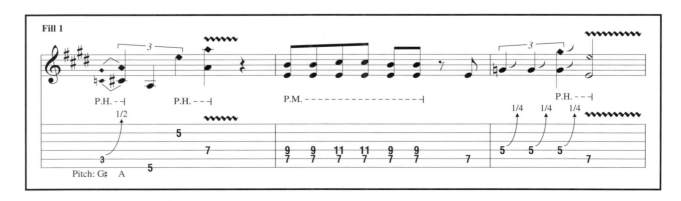

3. Well,

Verse

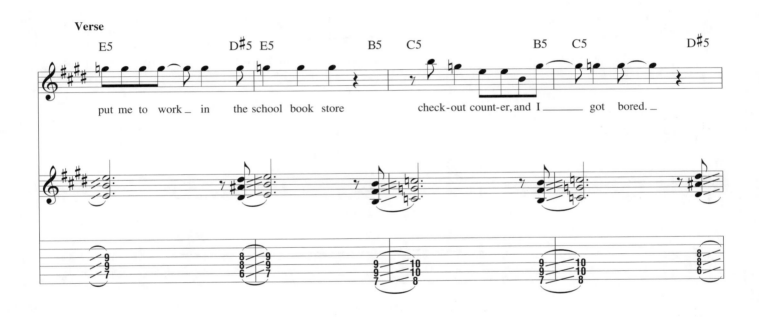

put me to work ___ in   the school book store   check-out count-er, and I _____ got   bored. ___

D.S. al Coda

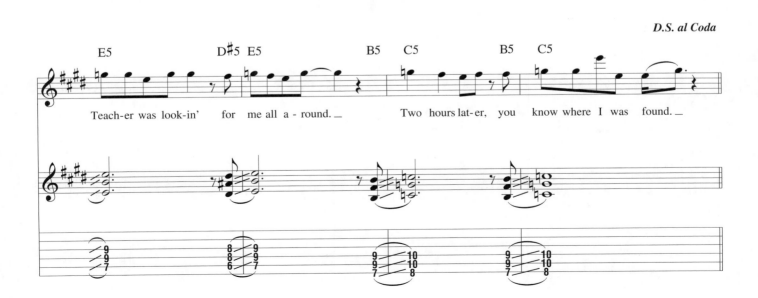

Teach-er was look-in'   for   me all a - round. ___   Two hours lat-er, you   know where I was   found. ___

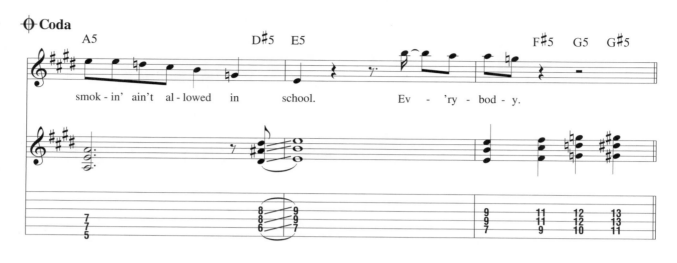

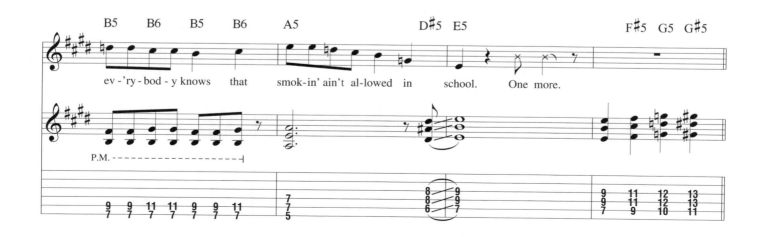

Additional Lyrics

2. Checkin' out the hall, makin' sure the coast is clear.
   Lookin' in the stalls, nah, there ain't nobody here.
   My buddies Sixx, Mick and Tom,
   To get caught would surely be the death of us all.

Sweet Child o' Mine

Words and Music by W. Axl Rose, Slash, Izzy Stradlin', Duff McKagan and Steven Adler

Tune down 1/2 step:
(low to high) E♭-A♭-D♭-G♭-B♭-E♭

Intro
Moderate Rock ♩ = 122

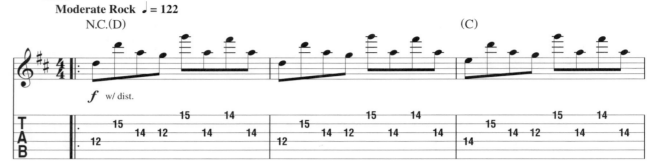

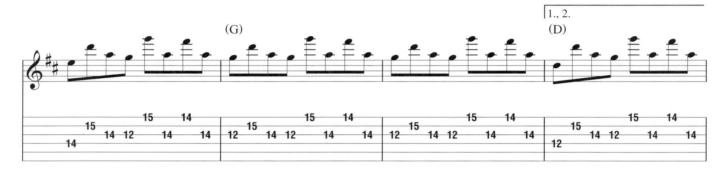

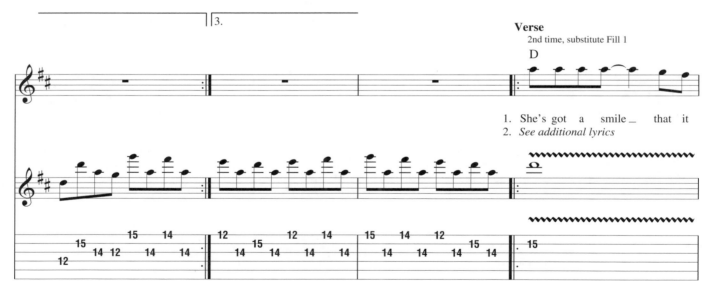

1. She's got a smile ＿ that it
2. *See additional lyrics*

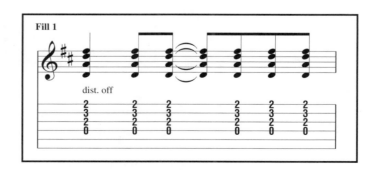

Guitar Solo

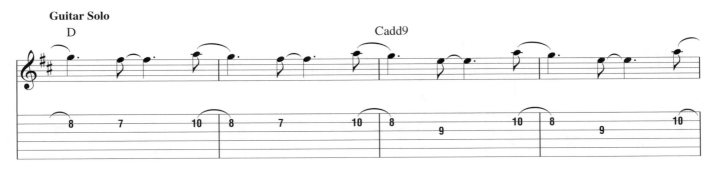

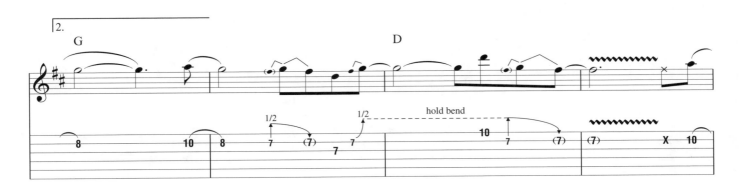

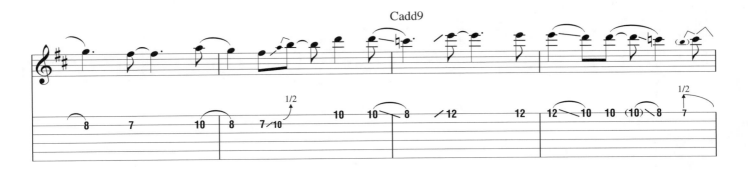

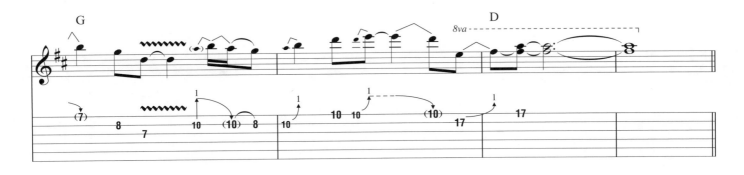

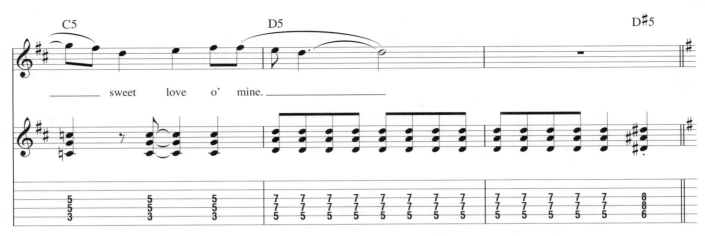

sweet   love   o' mine.

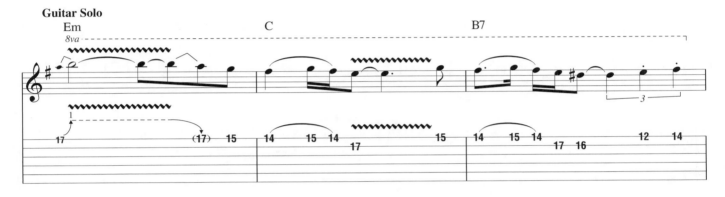

Guitar Solo

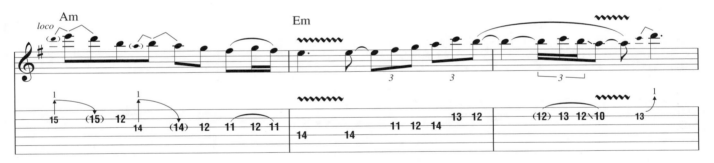

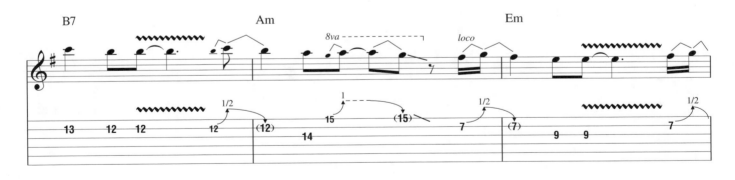

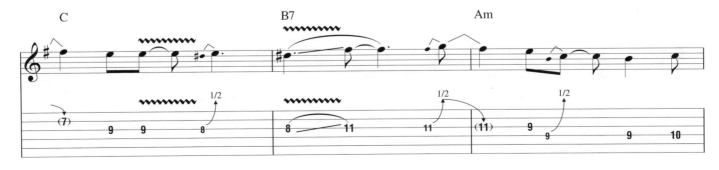

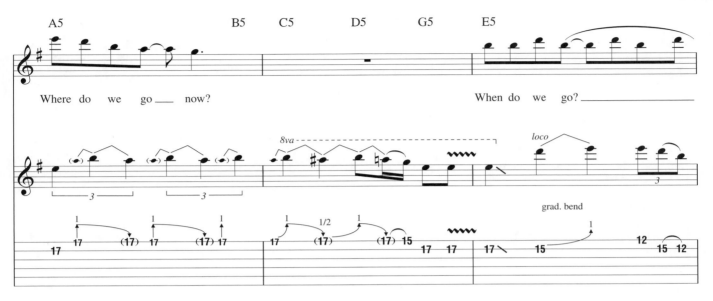

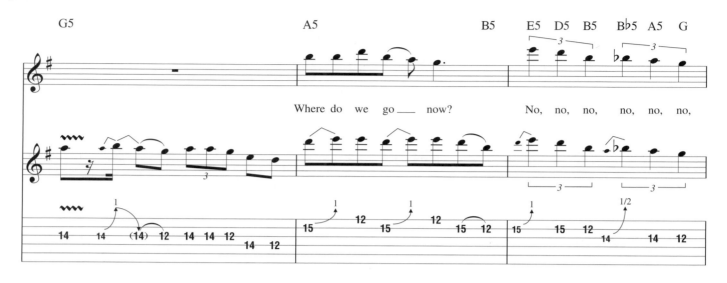

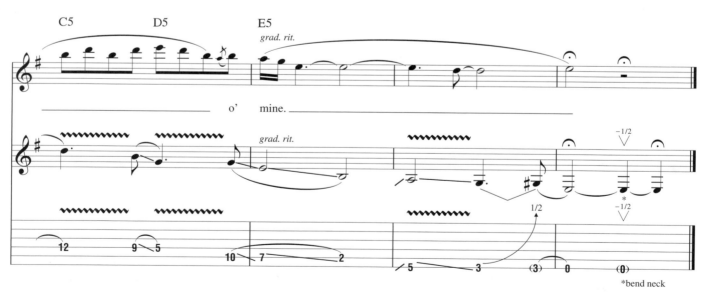

*bend neck

Additional Lyrics

2. She's got eyes of the bluest skies,
   As if they thought of rain.
   I'd hate to look into those eyes and see an ounce of pain.
   Her hair reminds me of a warm safe place
   Where as a child I'd hide,
   And pray for the thunder and the rain to quietly pass me by.

Talk Dirty to Me

Words and Music by Bobby Dall, Brett Michaels, Bruce Johannesson and Rikki Rockett

Tune down 1/2 step:
(low to high) E♭-A♭-D♭-G♭-B♭-E♭

Intro

Moderately fast ♩ = 124

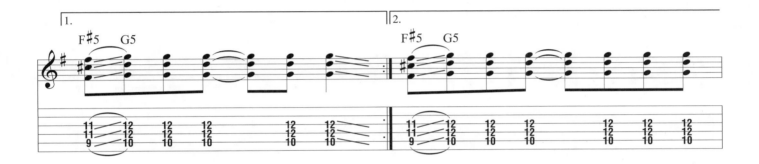

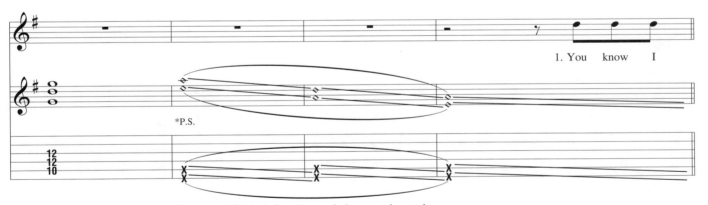

*Rub edge of pick down the strings, producing a scratchy sound.

Verse

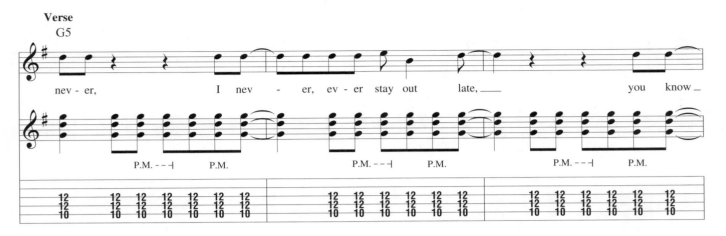

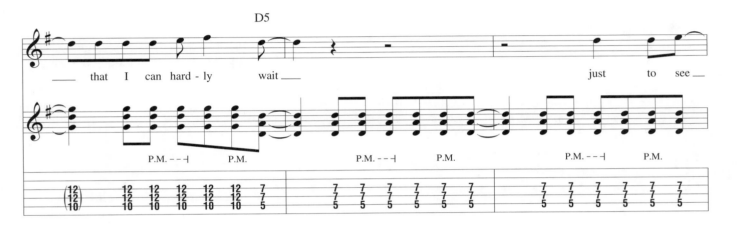

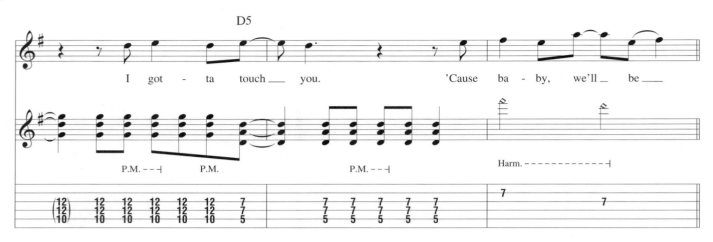

D5

I got - ta touch ___ you. 'Cause ba - by, we'll ___ be ___

P.M. - - -┤   P.M.   P.M. - - -┤   Harm. - - - - - - - - - - - - ┤

%: **Chorus**

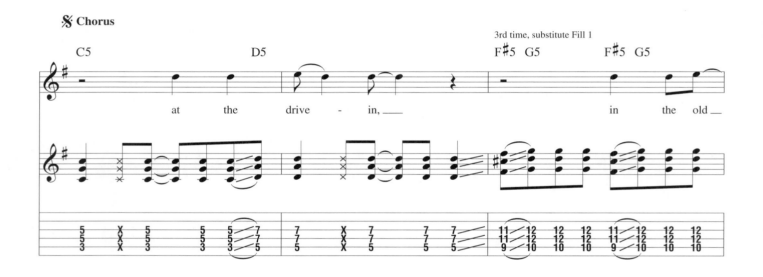

3rd time, substitute Fill 1

C5   D5   F#5 G5   F#5 G5

at   the   drive - in, ___   in   the   old ___

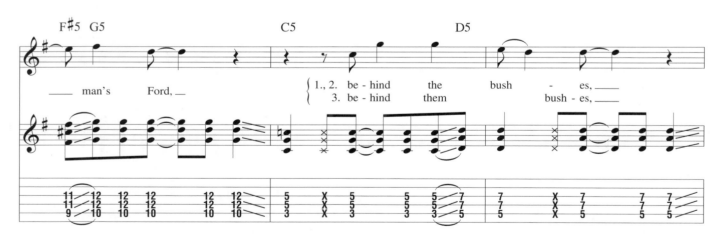

F#5 G5   C5   D5

___ man's   Ford, ___   { 1., 2. be - hind   the   bush - es, ___
                          3. be - hind   them   bush - es, ___

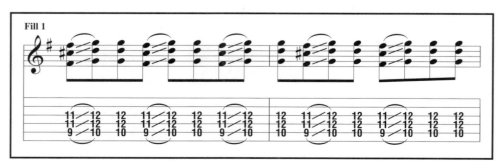

Fill 1

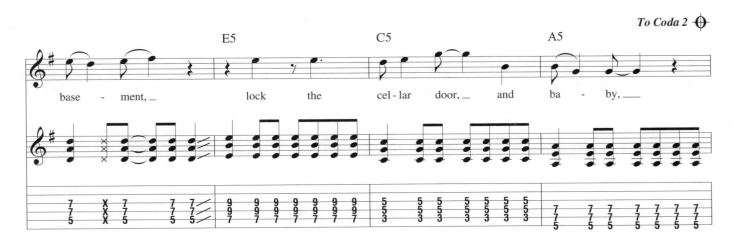

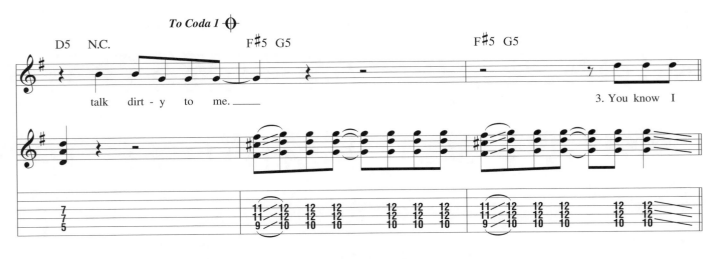

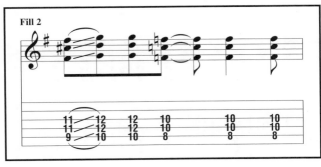

Verse

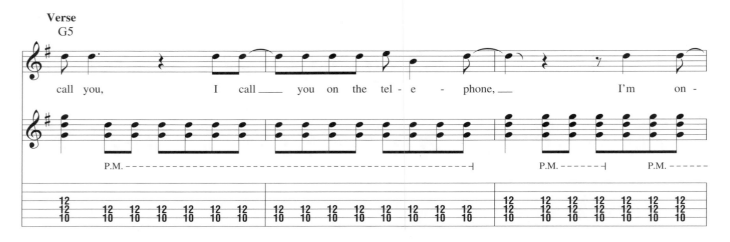

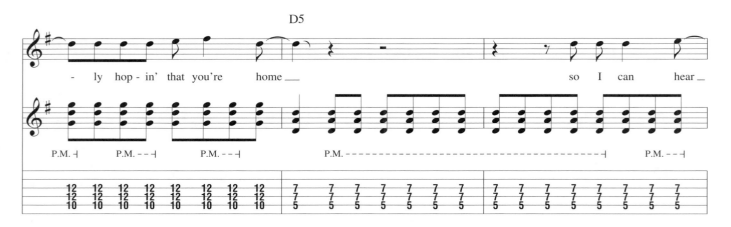

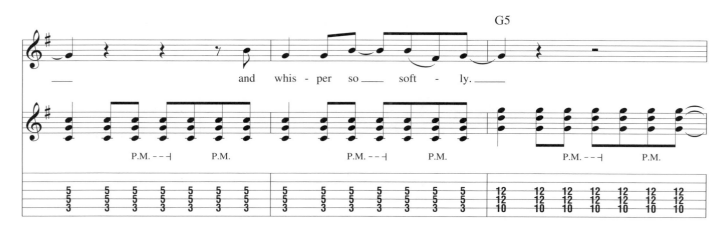

D.S. al Coda 1

Coda 1

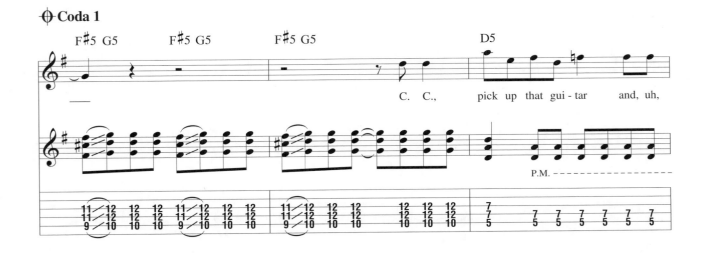

Guitar Solo

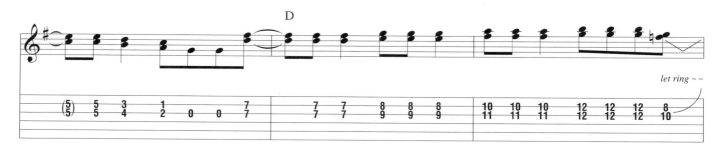

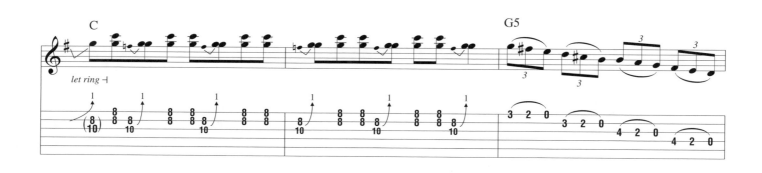

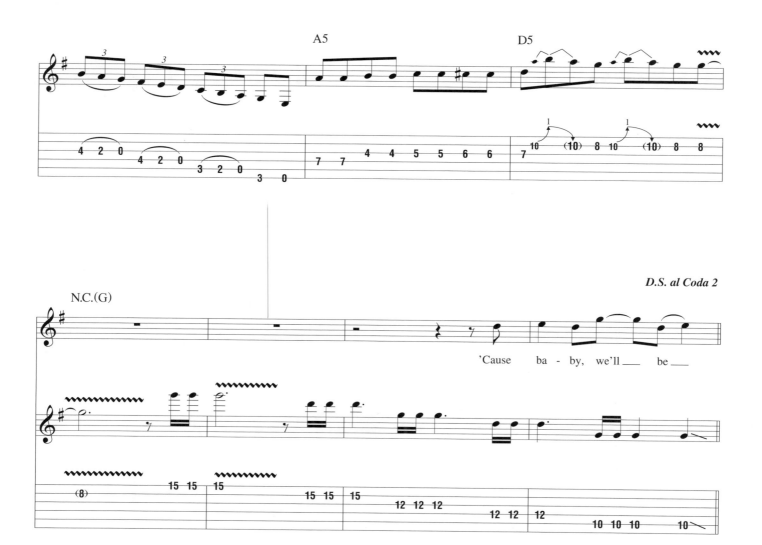

Coda 2

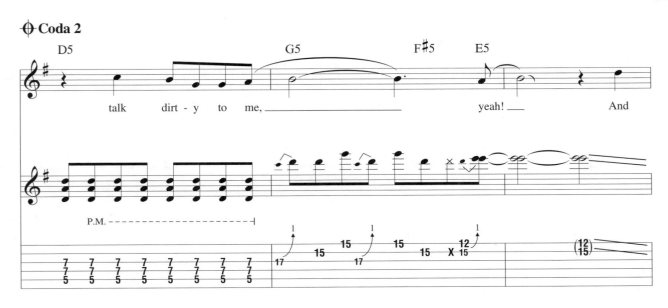

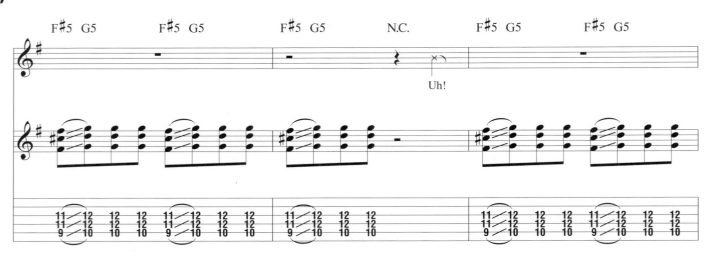

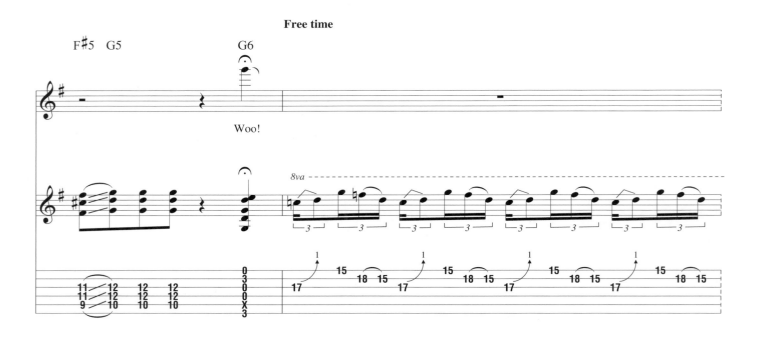

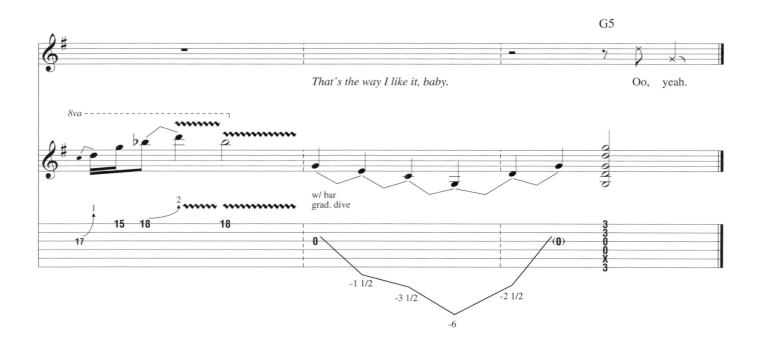

The Trooper
Words and Music by Steven Harris

Intro

Moderately fast Rock ♩ = 160

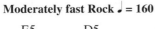

2nd time, substitute Fill 1

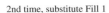

Fill 1

The smell of ac-rid smoke and hors-es' breath ____

as I plunge on in-to cer-tain death. ____ Oh. ____

𝄋 Chorus

2nd time, substitute Fill 2

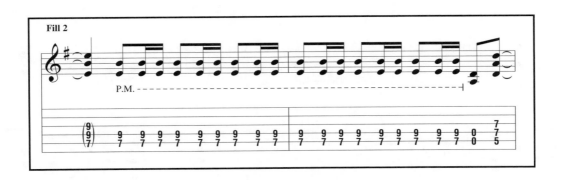

Fill 2

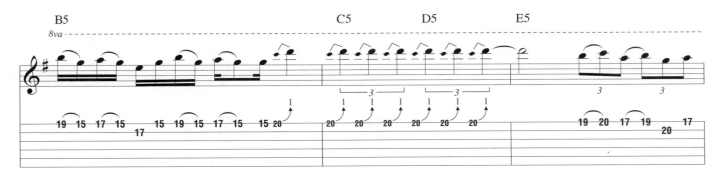

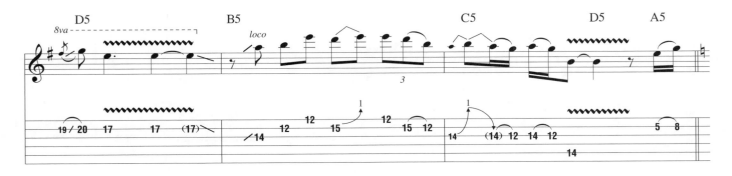

Guitar Solo

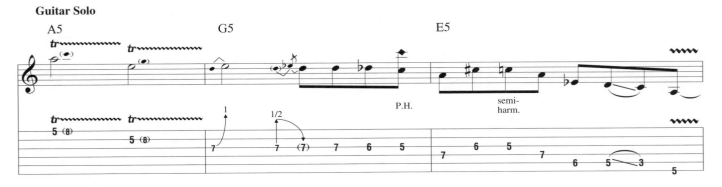

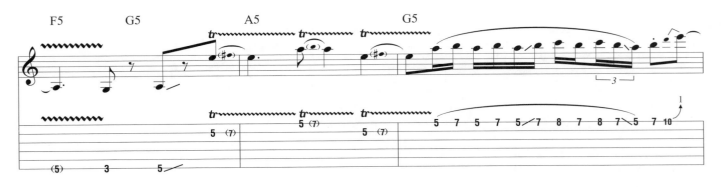

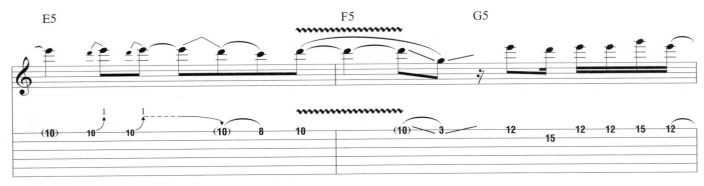

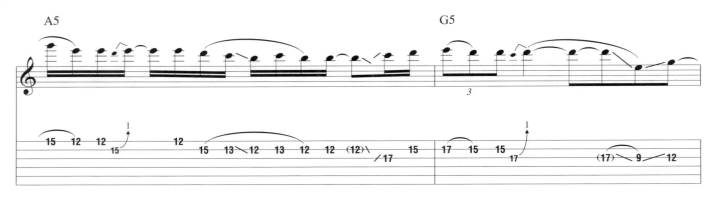

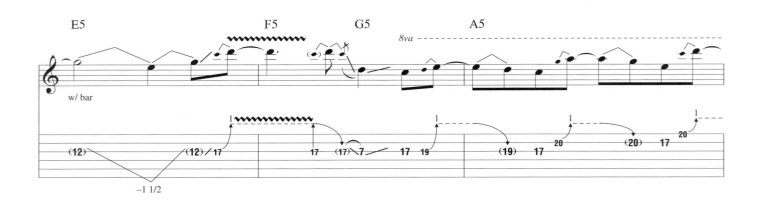

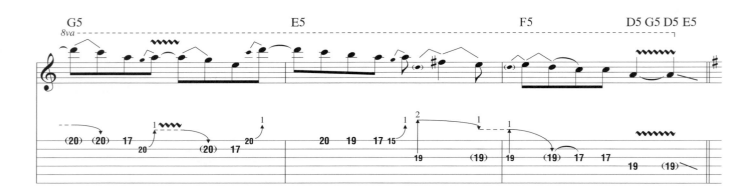

Interlude

2nd time, substitute Fill 1

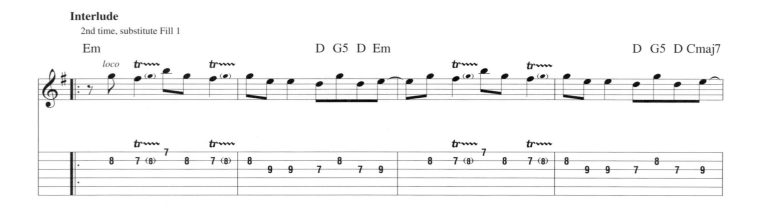

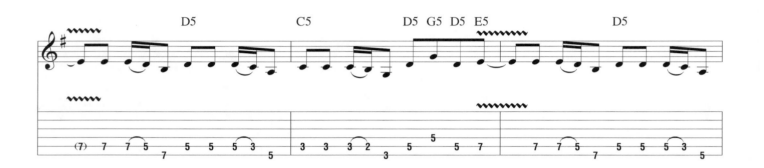

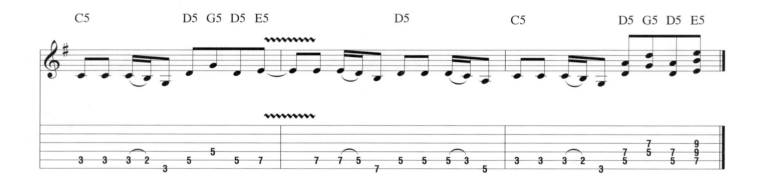

Additional Lyrics

3. We get so close, near enough to fight,
   When a Russian gets me in his sights.
   He pulls the trigger and I feel the blow,
   A burst of rounds takes my horse below.
   And as I lay there gazing at the sky,
   My body's numb and my throut is dry.
   And as I lay forgotten and alone,
   Without a tear I draw my parting groan.

Turn Up the Radio

Words and Music by Steve Isham, Steve Lynch, Steven Plunkett, Randy Rand and Keni Richards

Tune down 1/2 step:
(low to high) E♭-A♭-D♭-G♭-B♭-E♭

Intro
Moderate Rock ♩ = 113

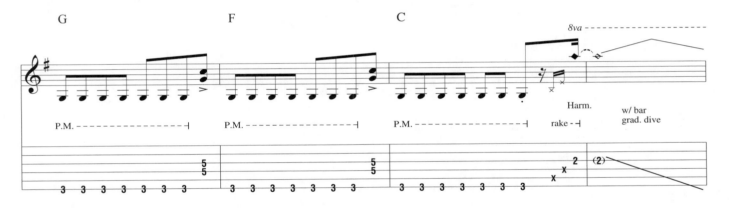

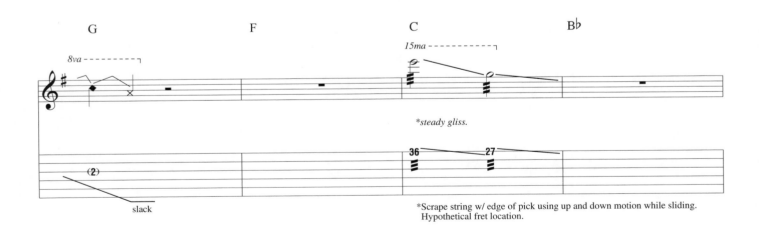

*steady gliss.

slack

*Scrape string w/ edge of pick using up and down motion while sliding.
Hypothetical fret location.

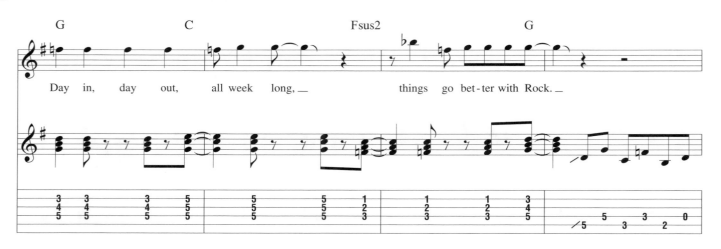

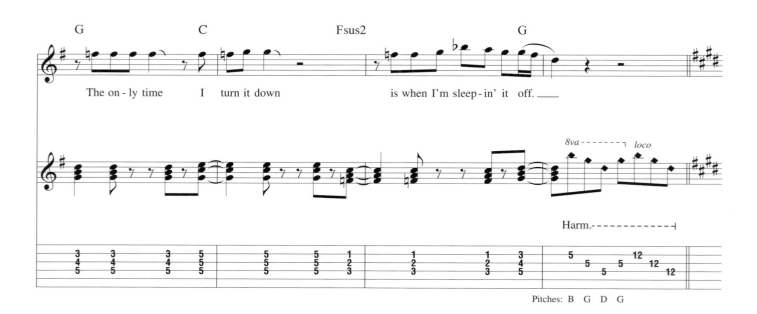

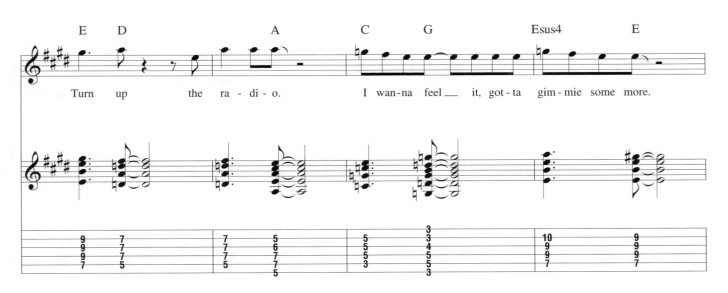

Turn up the ra-di-o. I wan-na feel __ it, got-ta gim-mie some more.

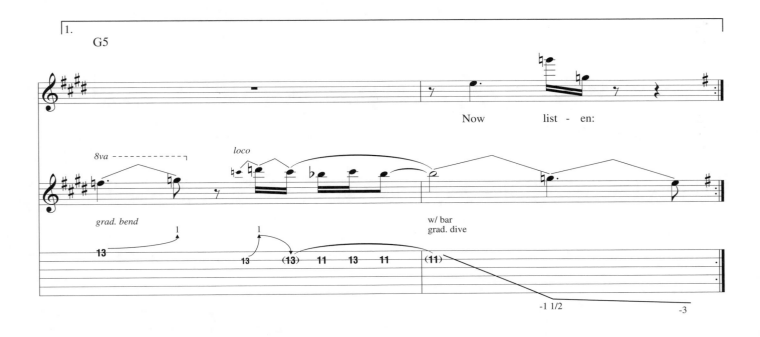

Now list - en:

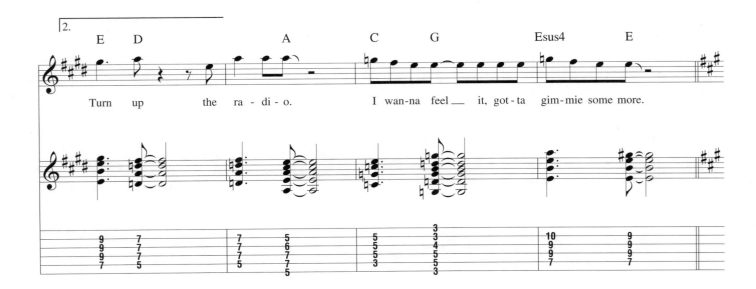

Turn up the ra-di-o. I wan-na feel __ it, got-ta gim-mie some more.

Guitar Solo

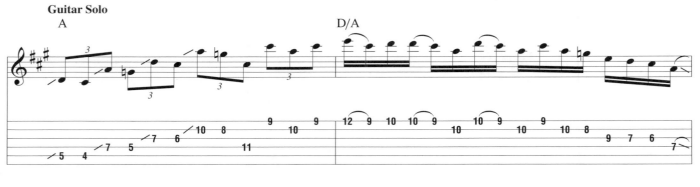

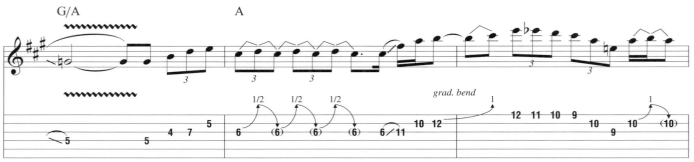

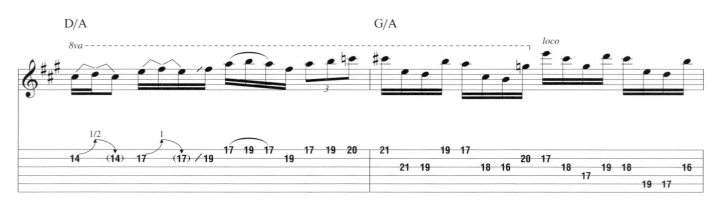

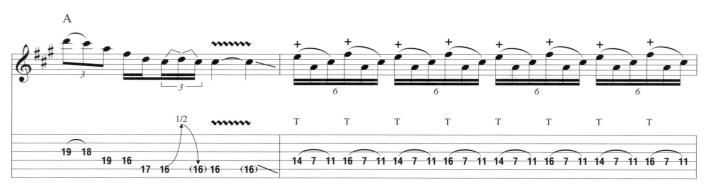

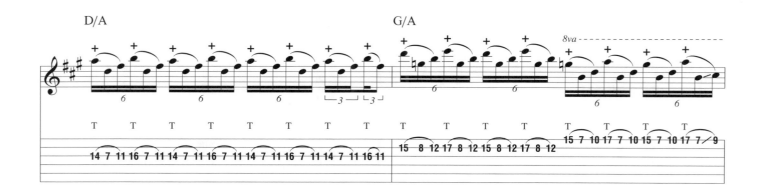

A

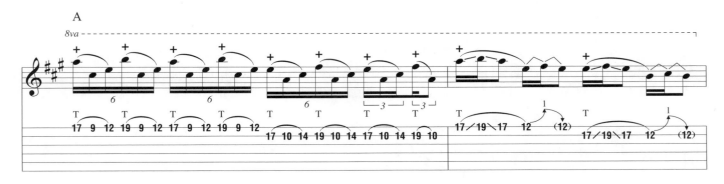

D/A   G/A   A

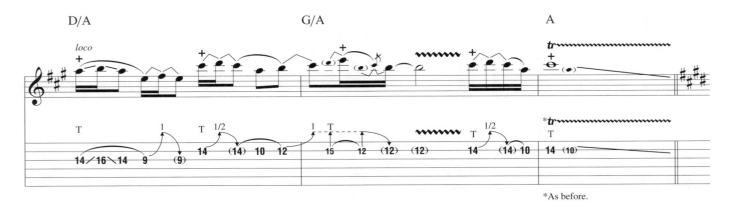

*As before.

Chorus

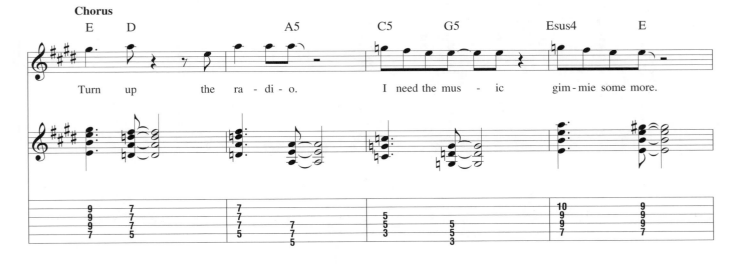

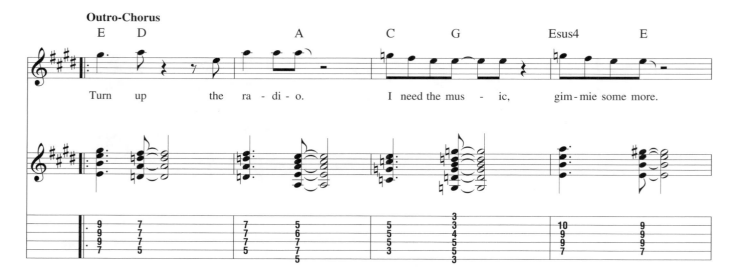

Outro-Chorus

Turn up the ra - di - o. I need the mus - ic, gim - mie some more.

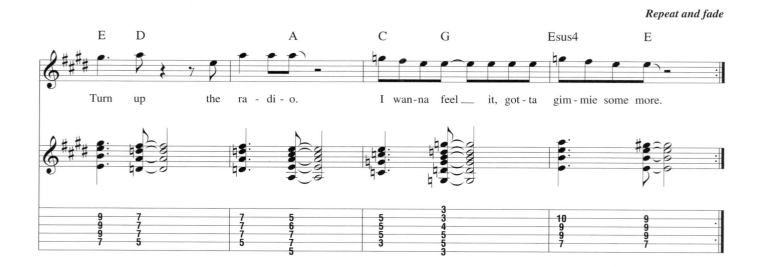

Repeat and fade

Turn up the ra - di - o. I wan-na feel __ it, got - ta gim - mie some more.

Additional Lyrics

2. I wanna shake, I wanna dance.
   So count it off, a, 1, 2, 3.
   I feel the beat, I'm in a trance;
   No better place to be.
   Daytime, nighttime, anytime.
   Things go better with Rock.
   I'm goin' 24 hours a day;
   I can't seem to stop.

Unchained

Words and Music by David Lee Roth, Edward Van Halen, Alex Van Halen and Michael Anthony

Drop D tuning, down 1/2 step:
(low to high) Db-Ab-Db-Gb-Bb-Eb

Intro
Moderate Rock ♩ = 138

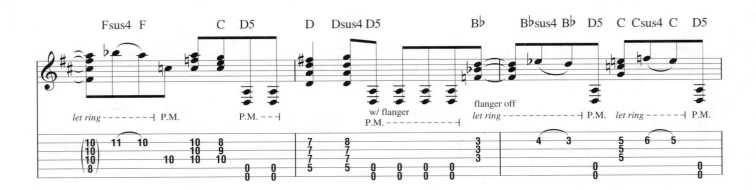

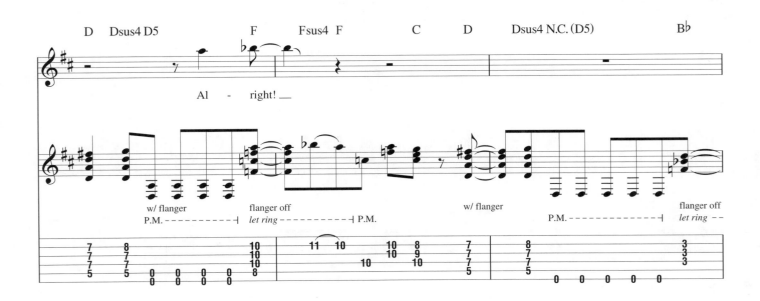

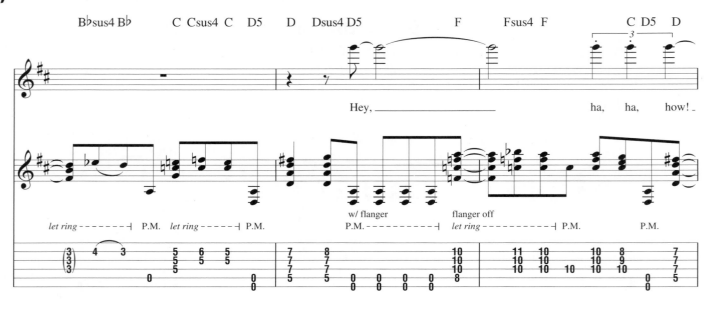

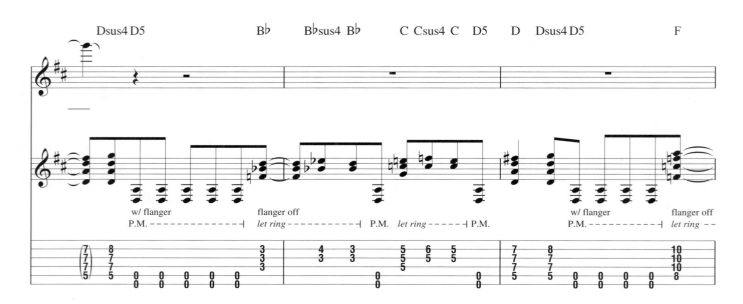

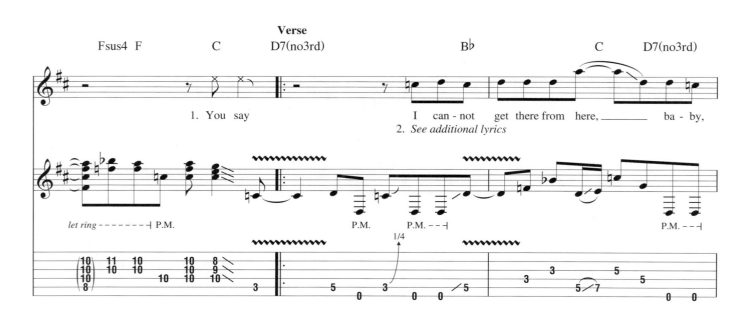

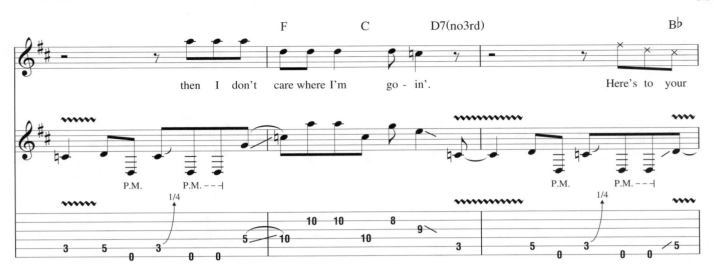

then I don't care where I'm go - in'. Here's to your

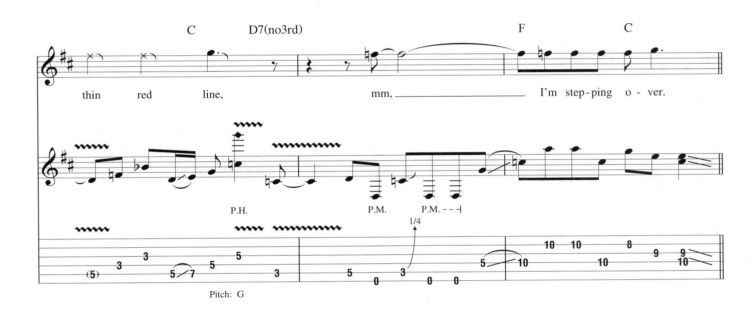

thin red line, mm, I'm step-ping o - ver.

Pitch: G

Pre-Chorus

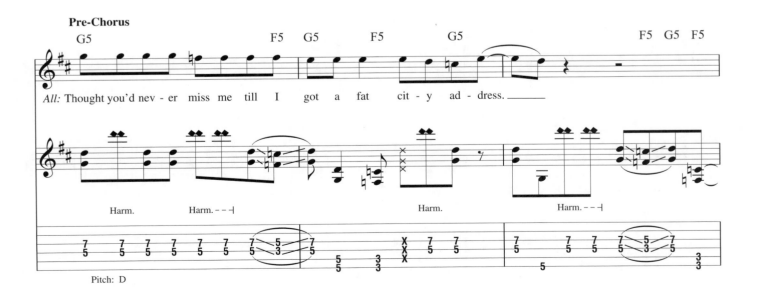

All: Thought you'd nev - er miss me till I got a fat cit - y ad - dress.

Pitch: D

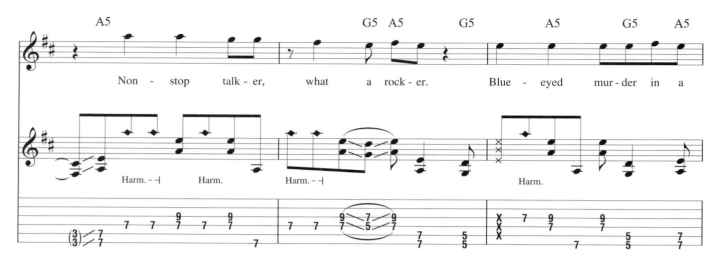

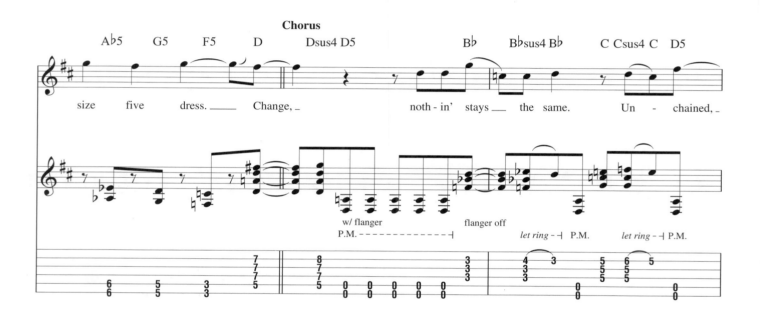

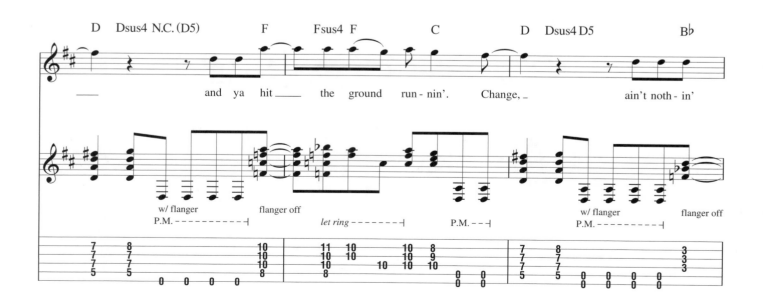

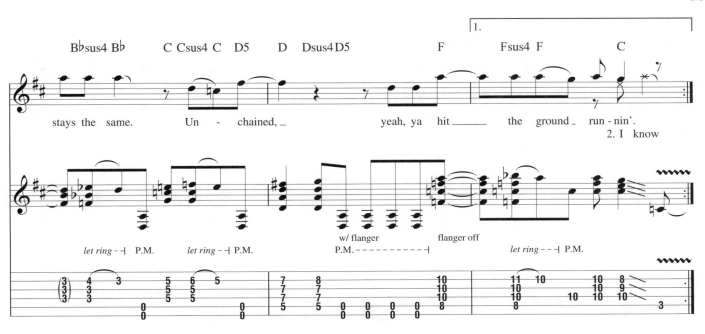

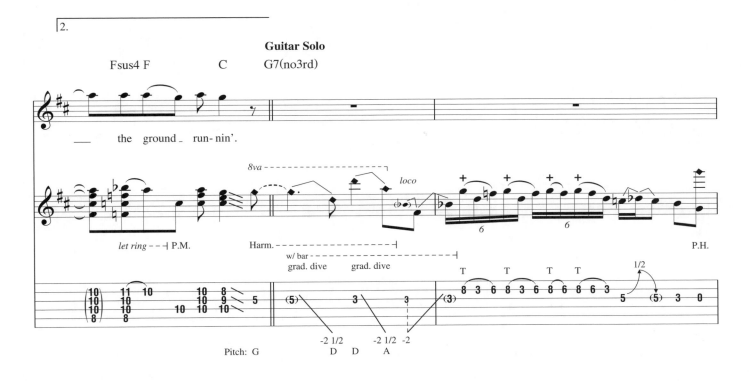

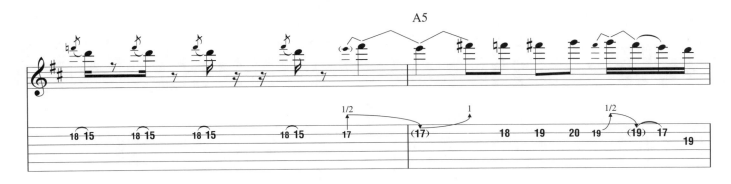

Bridge

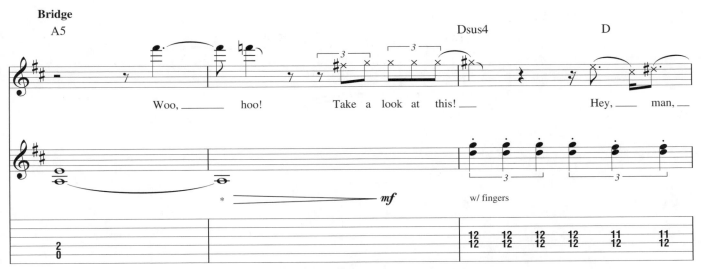

*Lower vol. know about halfway to produce a slightly distorted tone.

Woo, _____ hoo! Take a look at this! ___ Hey, ___ man, ___

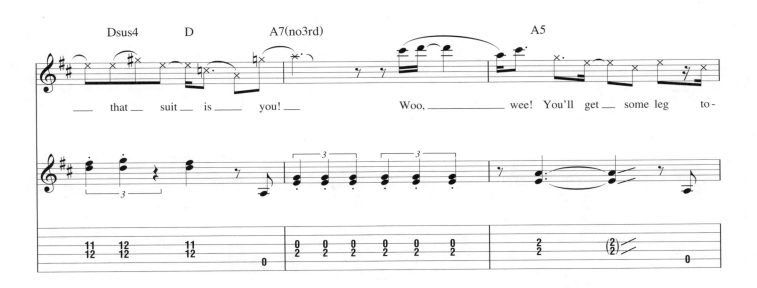

___ that ___ suit ___ is ___ you! ___ Woo, _____ wee! You'll get ___ some leg to-

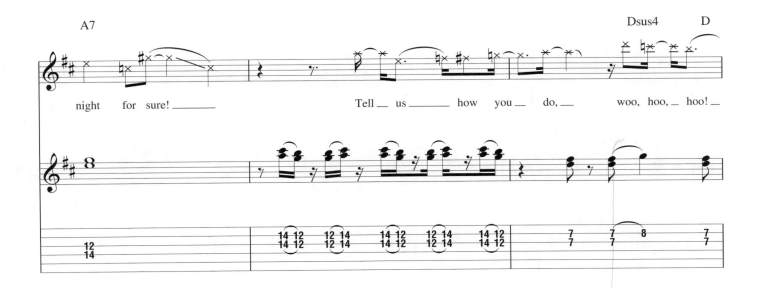

night for sure! _____ Tell ___ us _____ how you ___ do, ___ woo, hoo, ___ hoo! ___

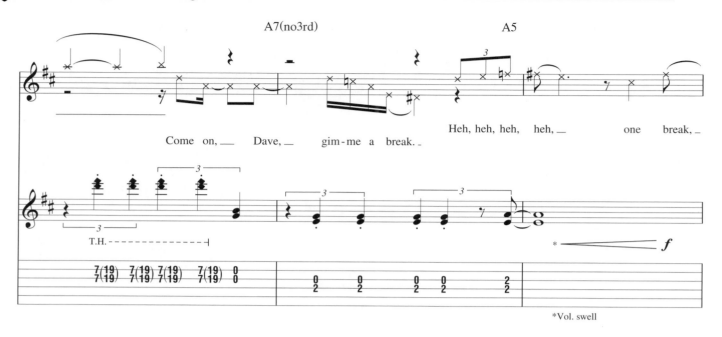

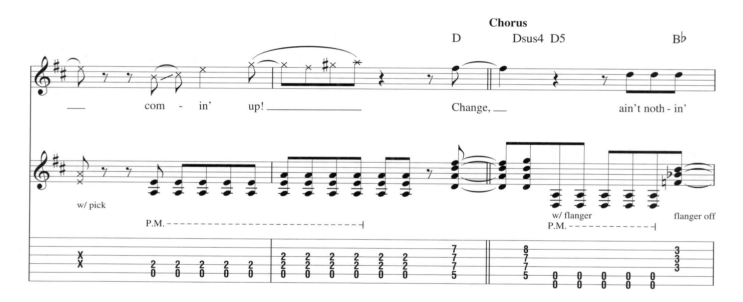

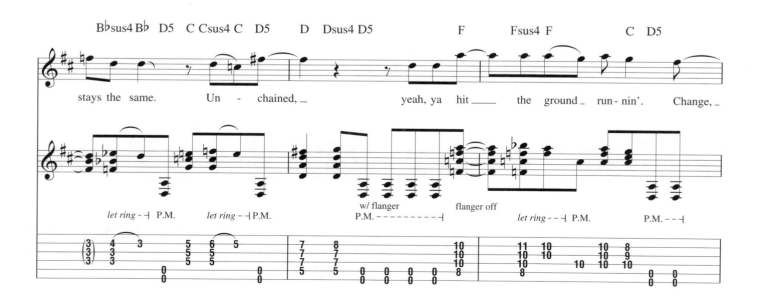

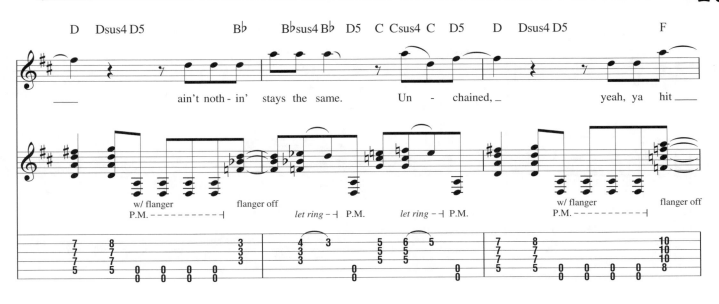

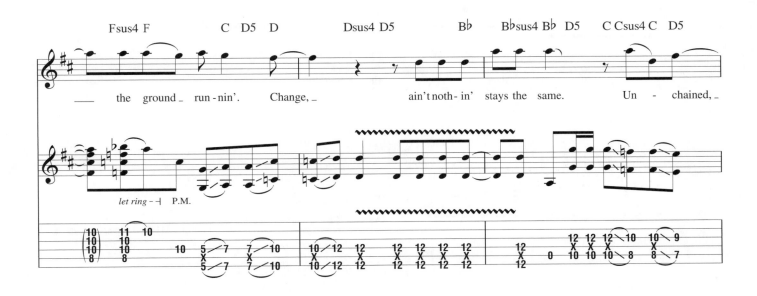

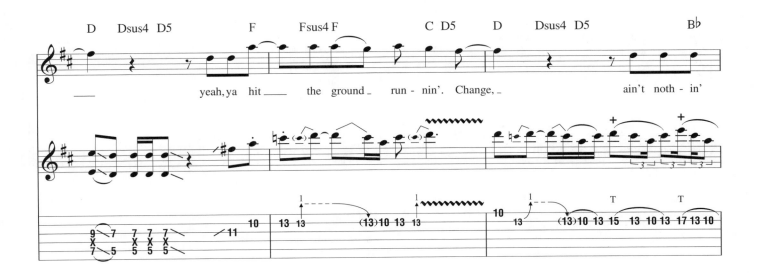

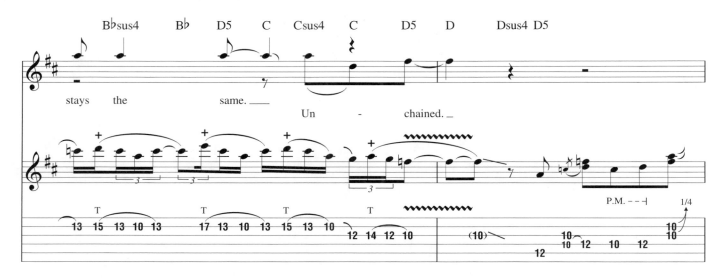

stays   the   same. ____   Un - chained. _

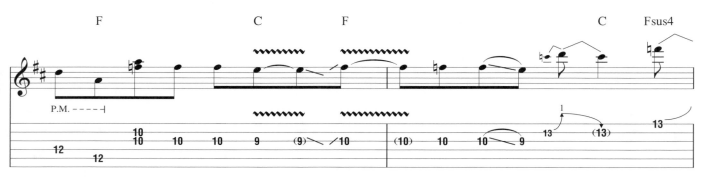

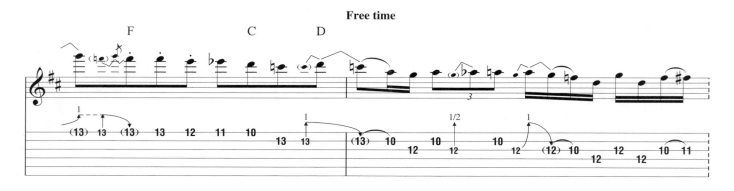

Free time

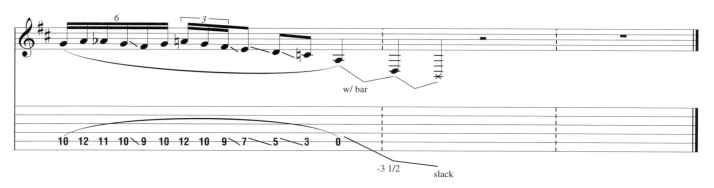

Additional Lyrics

2. I know I don't ask for permission,
This is my chance to fly.
Maybe enough ain't enough for you,
But it's my turn to fly.

Up All Night

Words and Music by Mark Slaughter and Dana Strum

Tune down 1 step:
(low to high) D-G-C-F-A-D

Intro

Moderately slow ♩ = 98

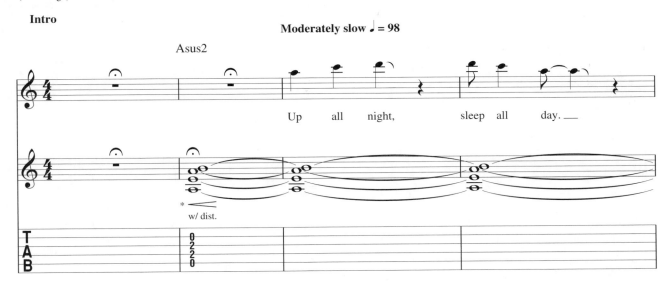

Asus2

Up all night, sleep all day. ___

*w/ dist.

*Vol. swell (Gradually increase vol. over the next 4 meas.)

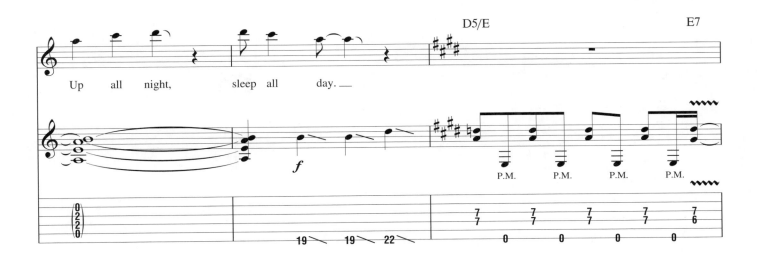

Up all night, sleep all day. ___

D5/E   E7

P.M.   P.M.   P.M.   P.M.

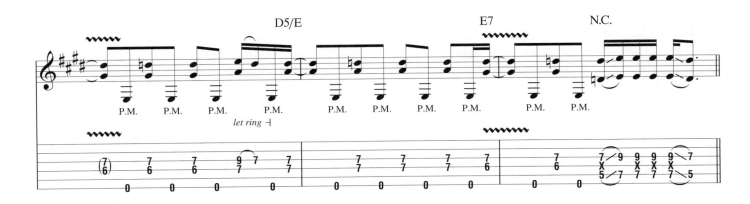

D5/E   E7   N.C.

P.M.   P.M.   P.M.   P.M.   P.M.   P.M.   P.M.   P.M.   P.M.   P.M.

let ring

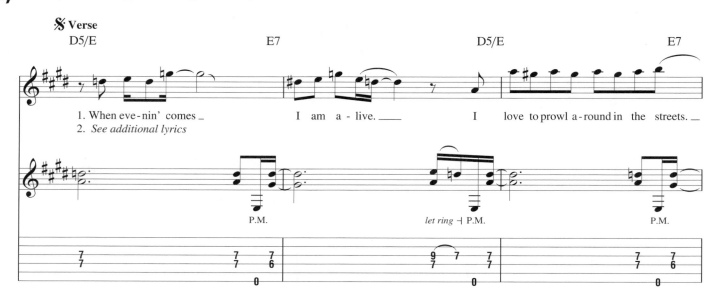

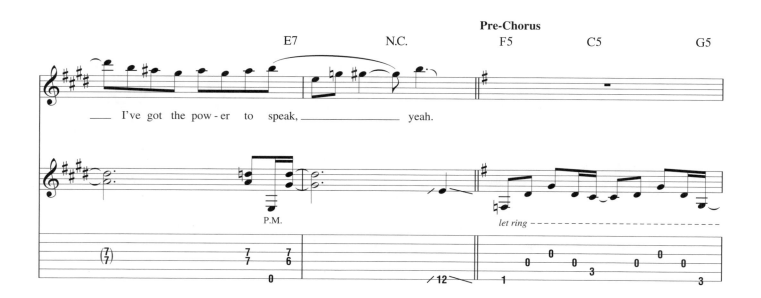

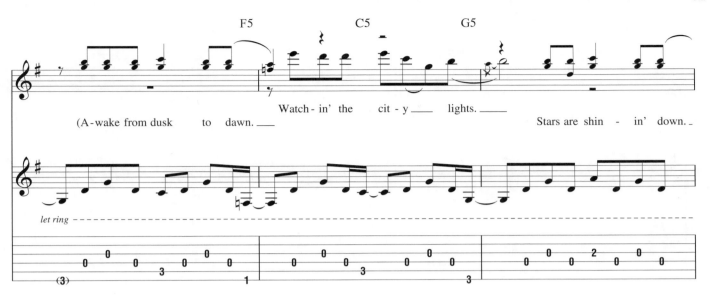

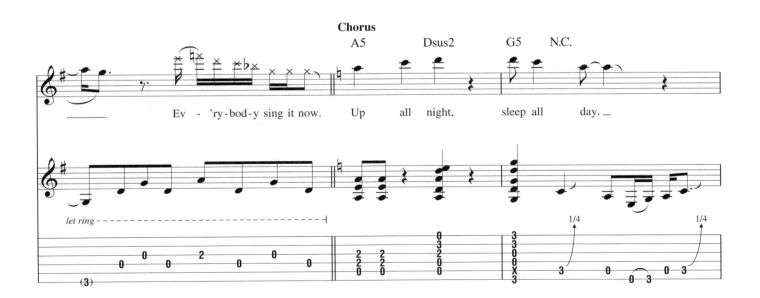

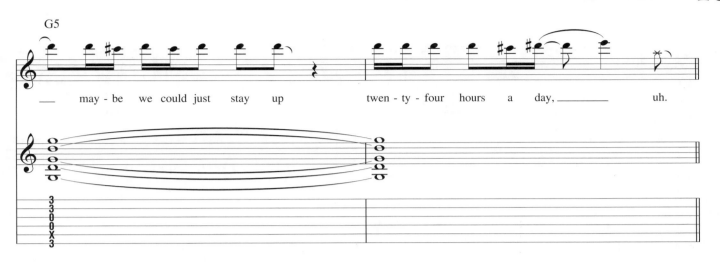

may - be we could just stay up twen - ty - four hours a day, _____ uh.

Interlude
N.C.

Huh!

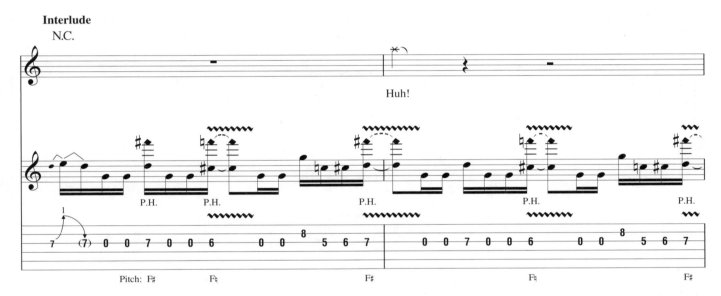

Guitar Solo

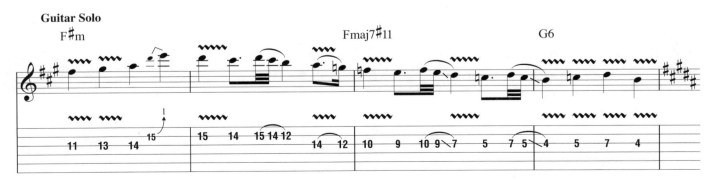

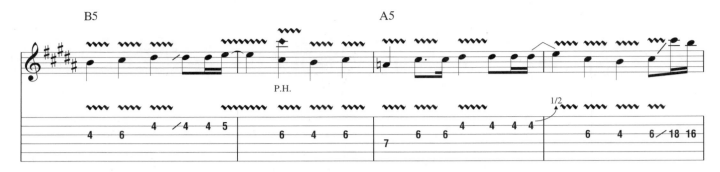

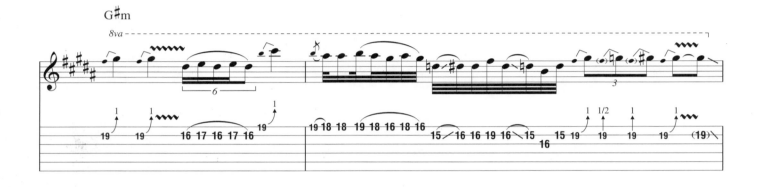

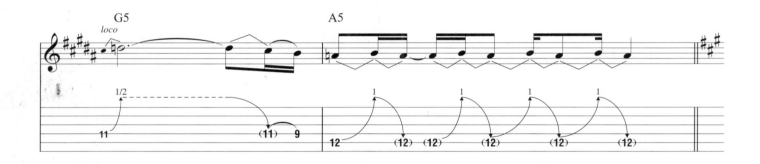

Pre-Chorus

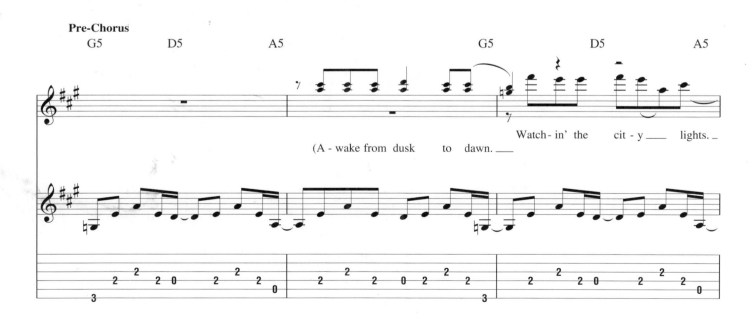

Additional Lyrics

2. Drivin' down the boulevard, all alone.
The neon signs are callin' your name.
Find me in the corner havin' the time of my life.
You'd think you'd want to do the same.

Wait

Words and Music by Mike Tramp and Vito Bratta

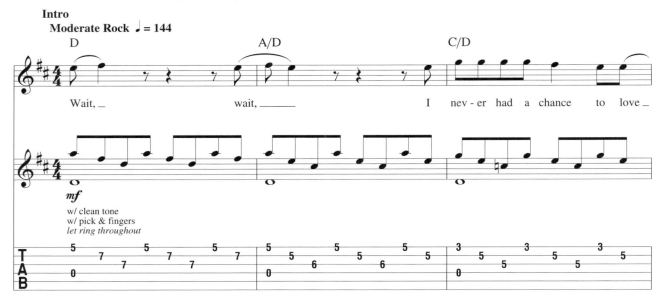

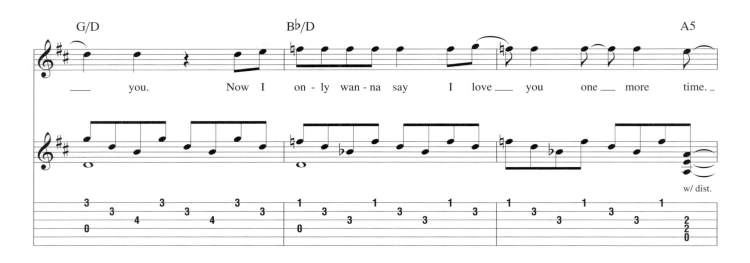

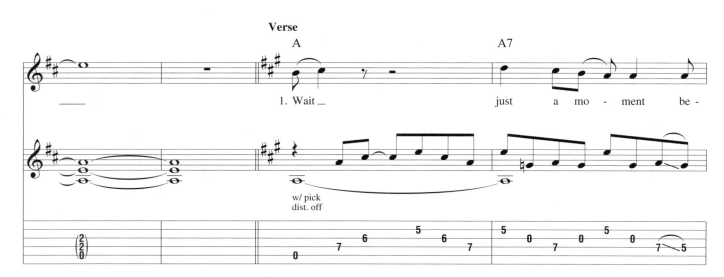

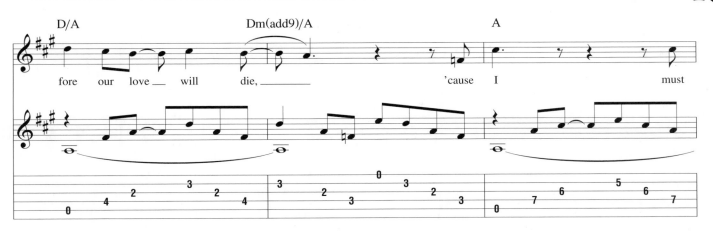

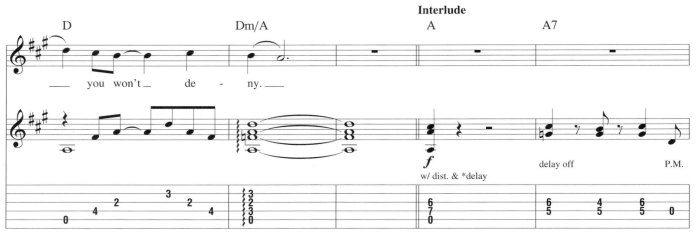

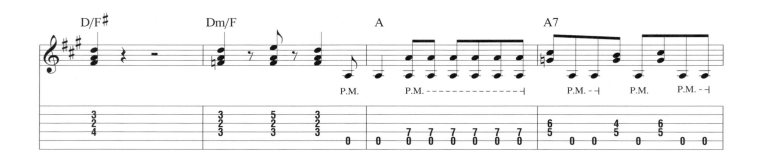

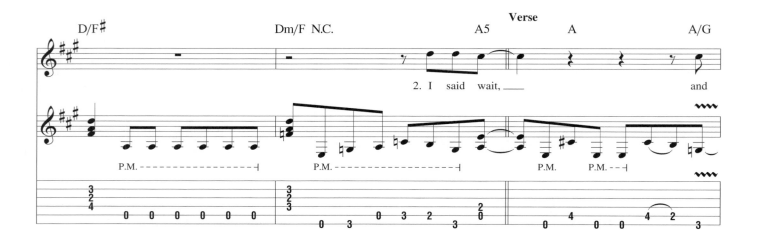

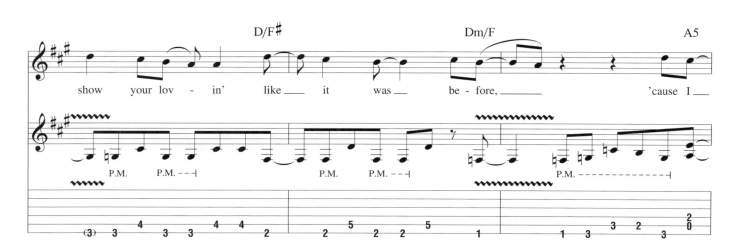

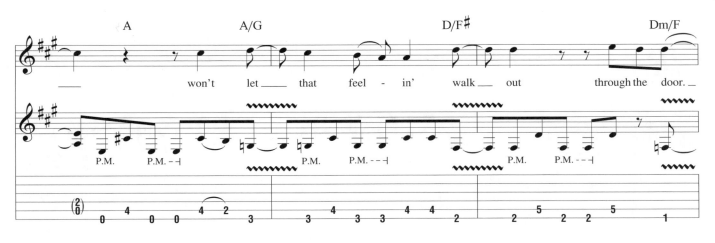

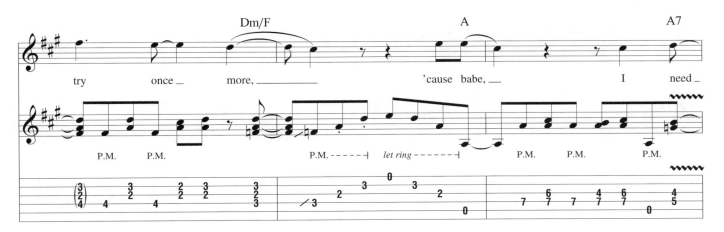

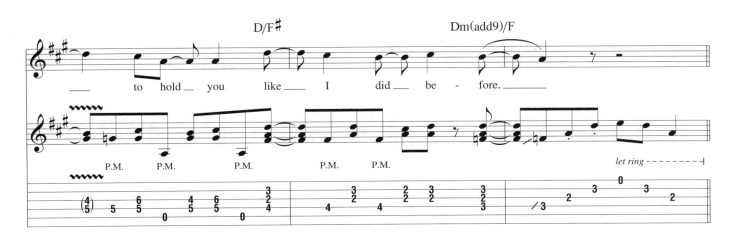

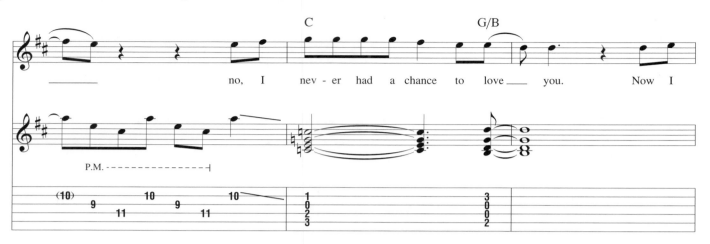

no, I nev-er had a chance to love ____ you.   Now I

on-ly wan-na say I love ____ you   one more   time. ____

Guitar Solo

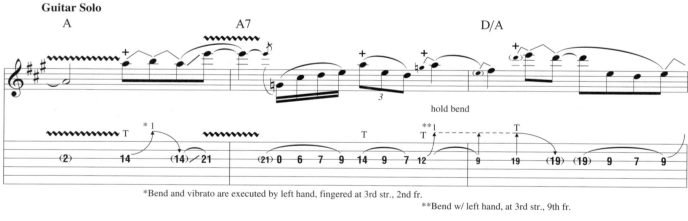

*Bend and vibrato are executed by left hand, fingered at 3rd str., 2nd fr.

**Bend w/ left hand, at 3rd str., 9th fr.

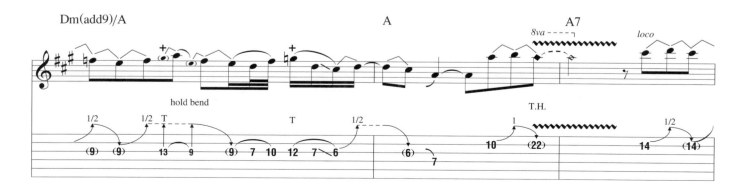

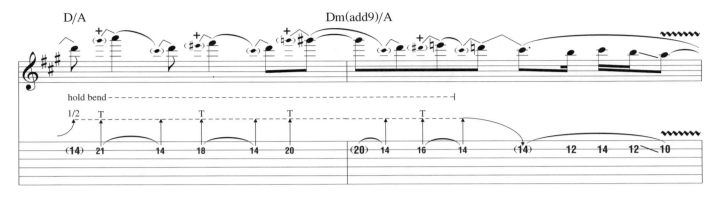

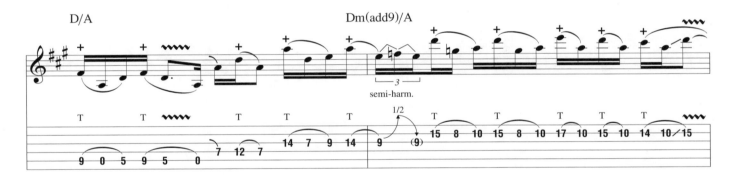

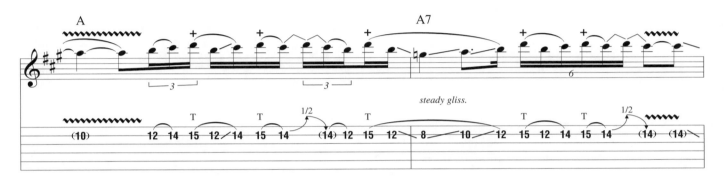

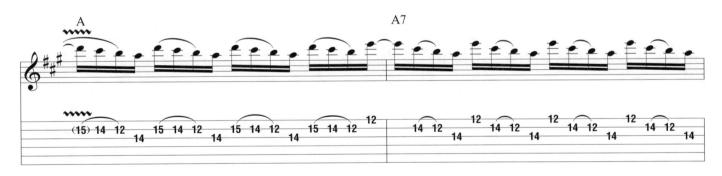

D.S. al Coda

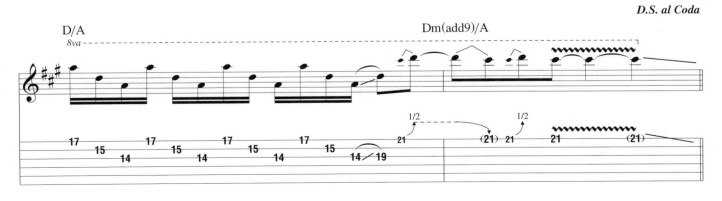

Coda

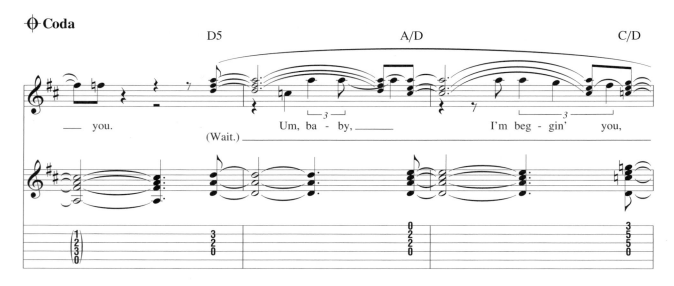

you.
(Wait.)
Um, ba - by, _____   I'm beg - gin' you,

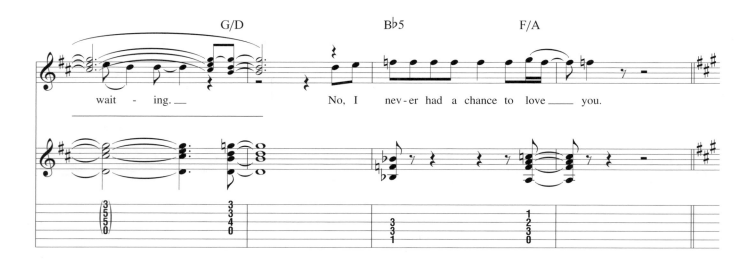

wait - ing. _____
No, I   nev - er had a chance to love _____ you.

Outro

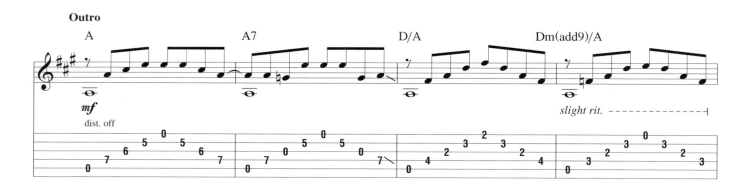

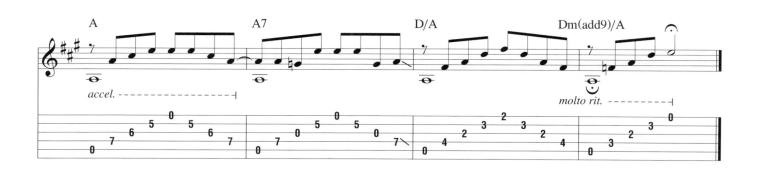

We're Not Gonna Take It

Words and Music by Daniel Dee Snider

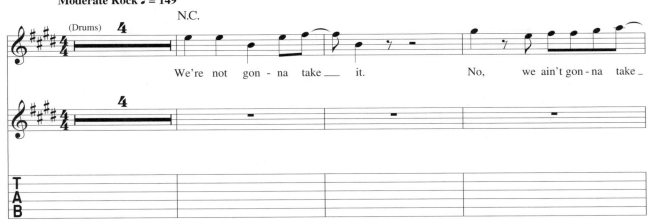

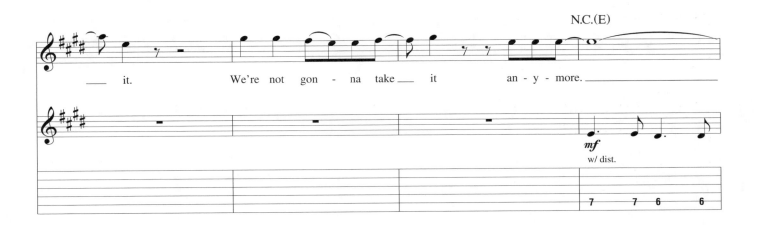

Guitar Solo

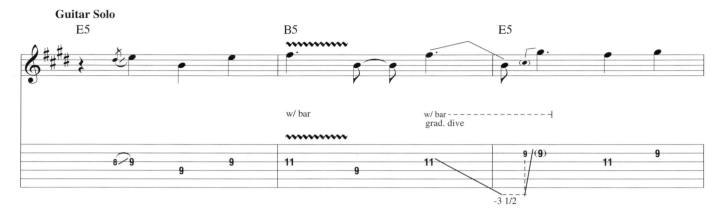

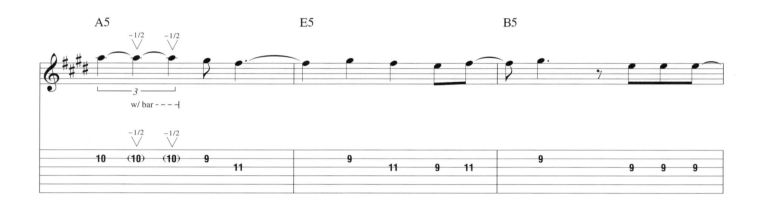

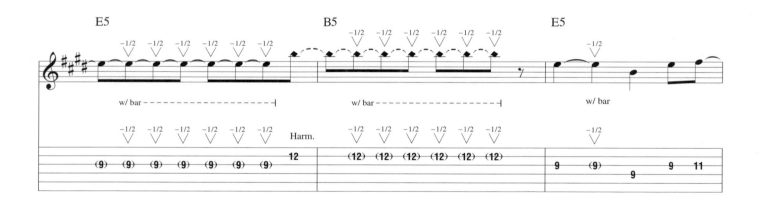

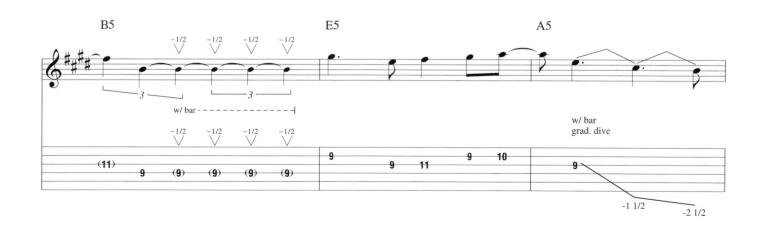

D.S.S. al Coda 2

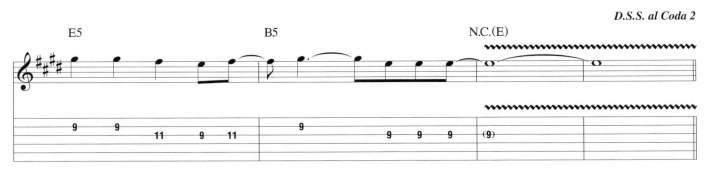

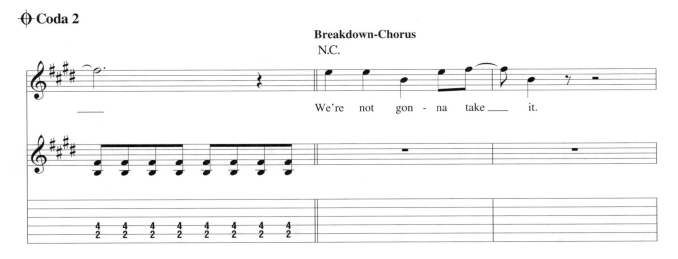

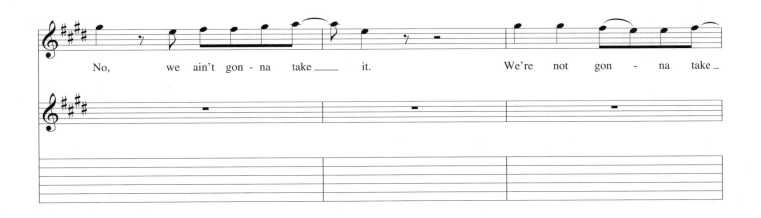

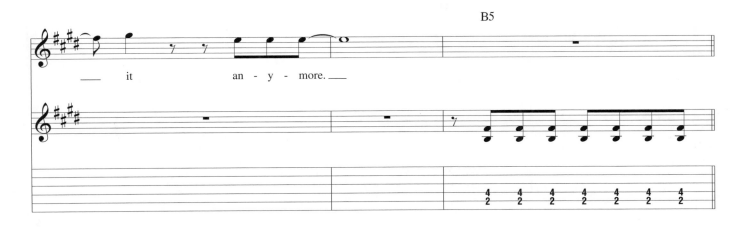

Additional Lyrics

2. Oh, you're so condescending.
   Your gall is never-ending.
   We don't want nothin'; not a thing from you.
   Your life is trite and jaded,
   Boring and confiscated.
   If that's your best, your best won't do.

Yankee Rose

Words by David Lee Roth
Music by Steve Vai

Intro
Free time

Moderately fast Rock ♩ = 126

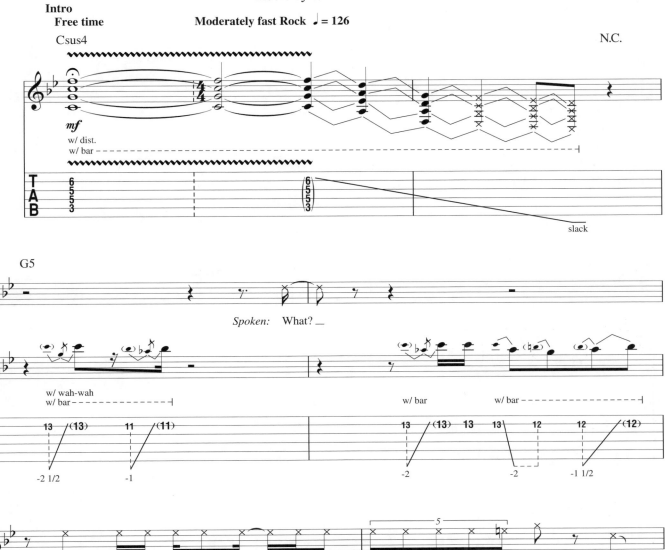

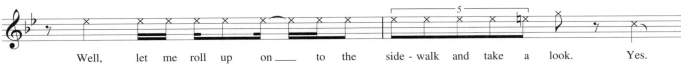

Well, let me roll up on ___ to the side-walk and take a look. Yes.

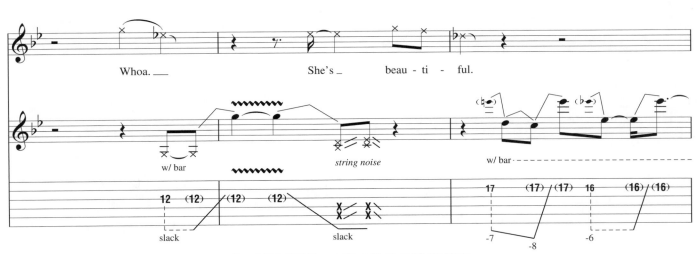

Whoa. ___ She's ___ beau-ti-ful.

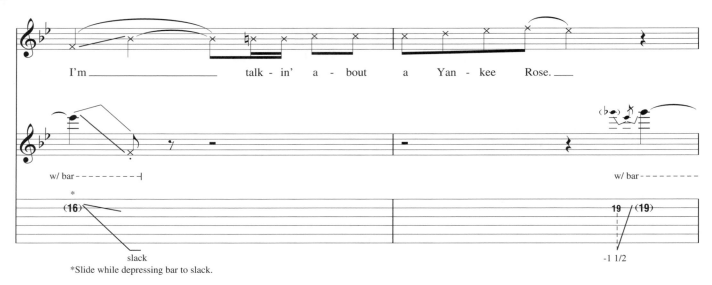

I'm_____ talk - in' a - bout a Yan - kee Rose. ___

w/ bar - - - - - - - -⌐   w/ bar - - - - - - -

* *Slide while depressing bar to slack.*

slack   -1 1/2

Laughed: Ah, ha, ha, ha, ha, ha, ha, ha, ha, ha, ha.   *Spoken:* And she __

w/ bar - - - - - - - - - - - - - -⌐

-1 1/2   -1/2

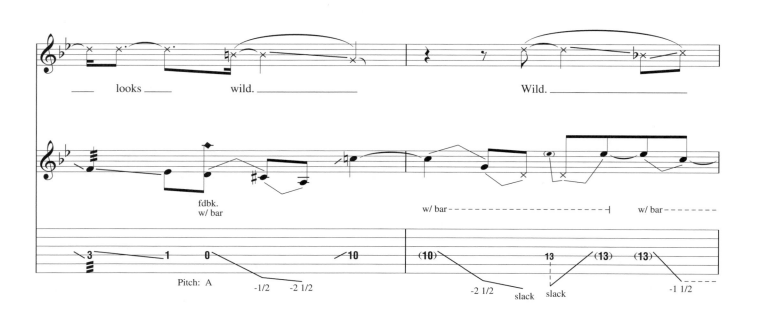

__ looks ____ wild. _____   Wild. _____

fdbk.   w/ bar - - - - - - - - - - - - - -⌐   w/ bar - - - - - - -
w/ bar

Pitch: A   -1/2   -2 1/2   -2 1/2   slack   slack   -1 1/2

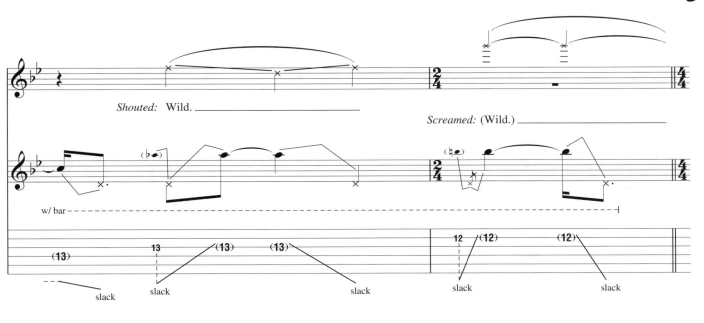

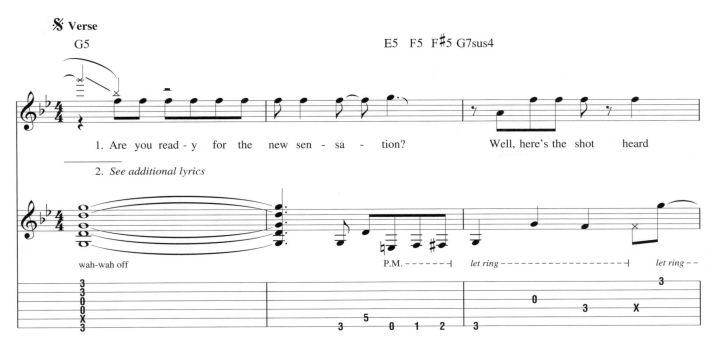

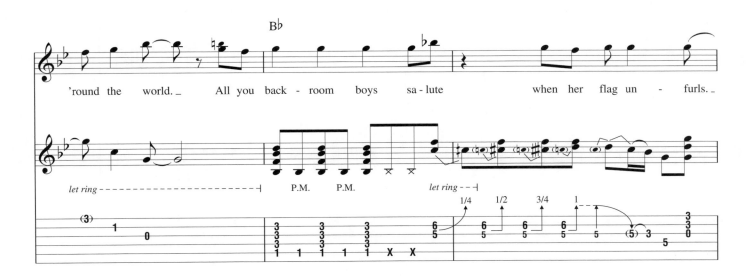

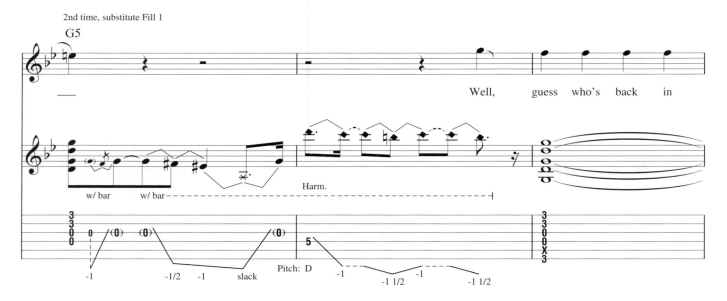

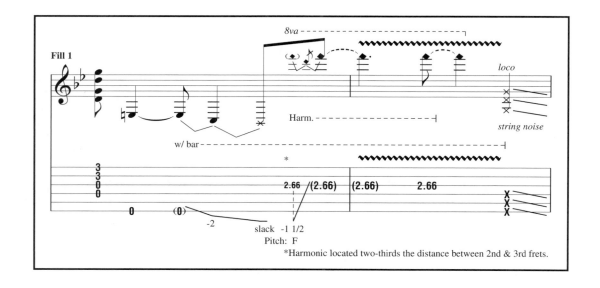

need right now is the o - rig - i - nal good time girl. ____

P.M.

let ring

Harm.

Pitch: D

Pre-Chorus

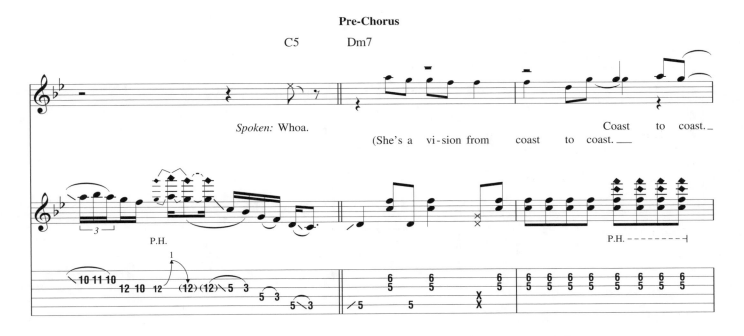

Spoken: Whoa.

(She's a vi-sion from coast to coast. ____

Coast to coast. ____

P.H.

P.H.

Fill 2

let ring

w/ bar

w/ bar

w/ bar

slack

*Vibrato bar scoops to slack (next 2 meas.).

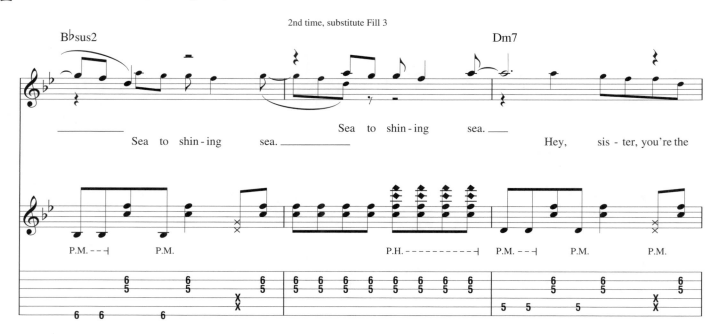

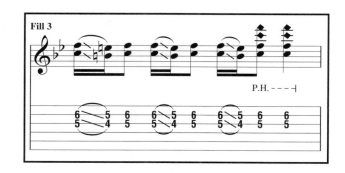

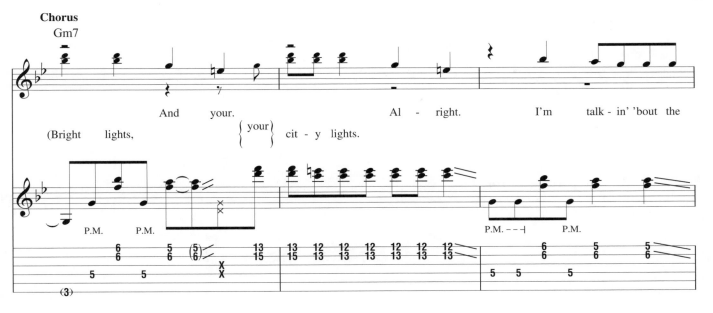

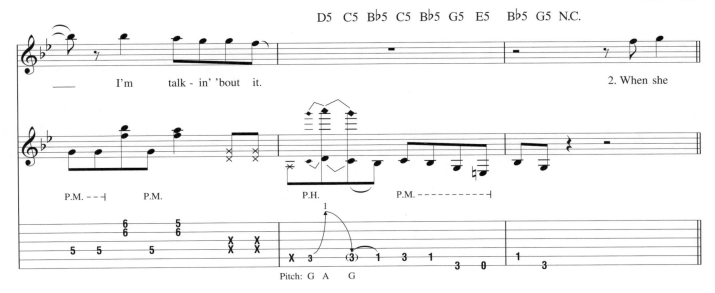

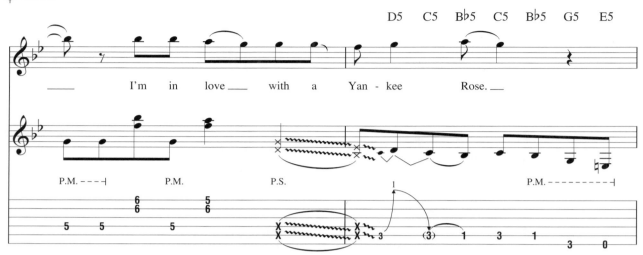

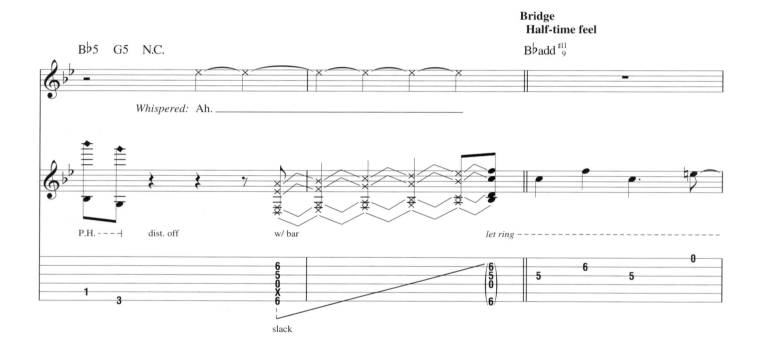

Breakdown
Gtr. tacet
N.C. (G5)

Ah, _____ raise them up,

now. Let's see who sa - lutes, ba - by. Yeah. ___ Yeah. _ Yeah.

Yeah. Yeah. Lit - tle bit, lit - tle bit, lit - tle bit high - er.

Outro
Csus4   C   B♭

Here's the na - tion-al an - them. Yeah, say. Come on!

w/ bar - ⅃

slack

A5   G5   F5   G5

I wan - na get a lit - tle bit of

w/ bar

P.H.

slack   Pitch: D

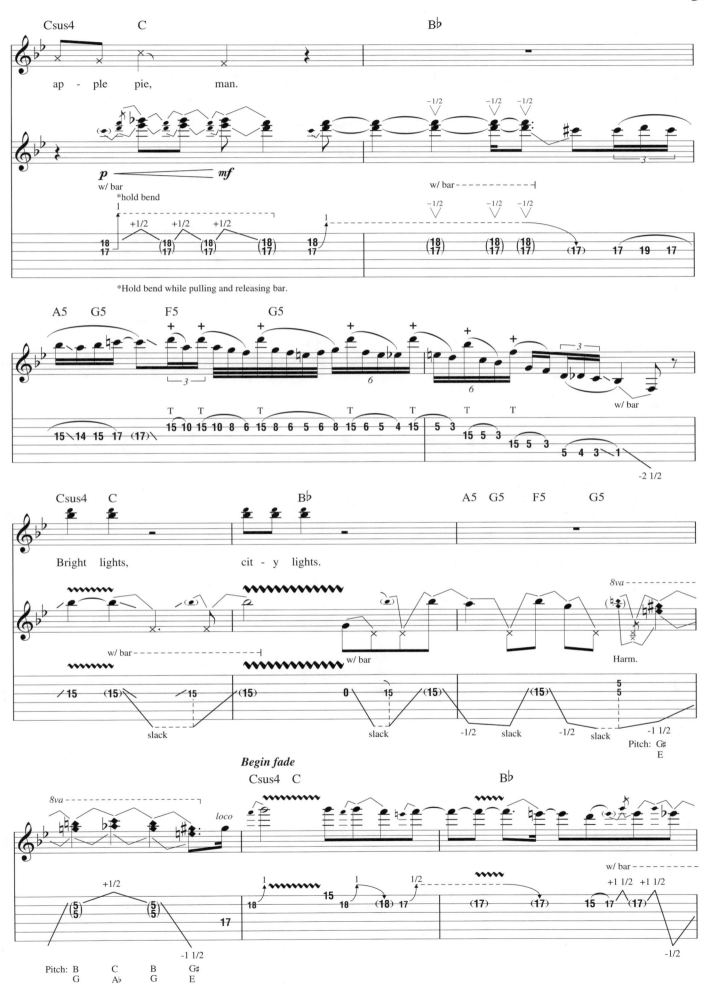

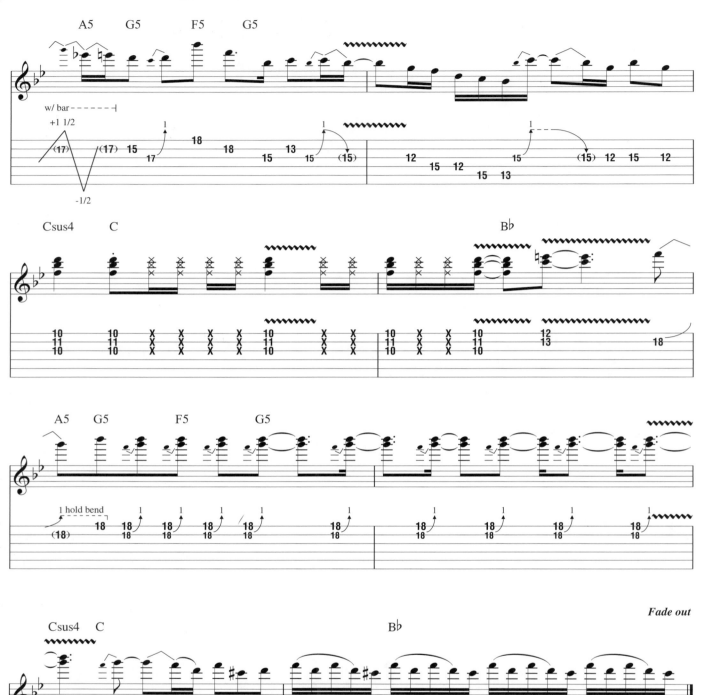

Additional Lyrics

2. When she walks, watch the sparks will fly.
Firecrackin' on the Fourth of July.
No sad songs tonight, something's in the air.
You can feel it, can't ya? Whoa.
A real state of independence.
So pretty when her rockets glare.
Still provin' any night that her flag's still there.

You Shook Me All Night Long

Words and Music by Angus Young, Malcolm Young, and Brian Johnson

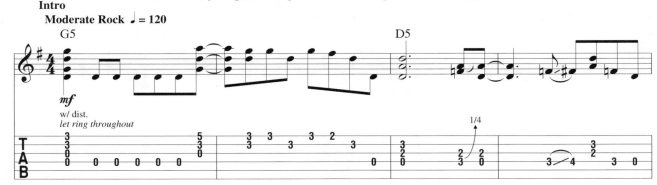

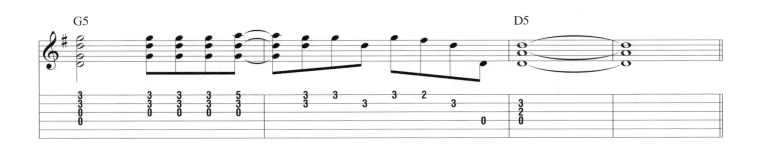

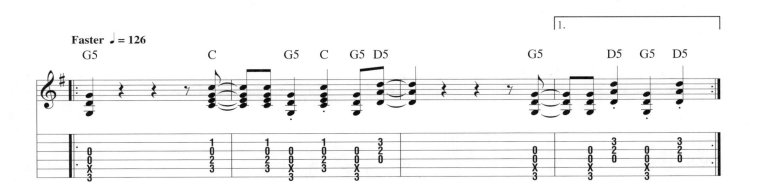

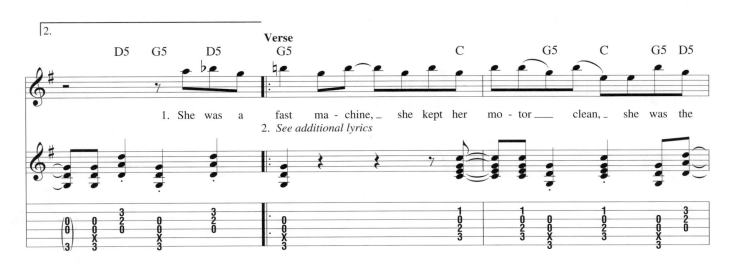

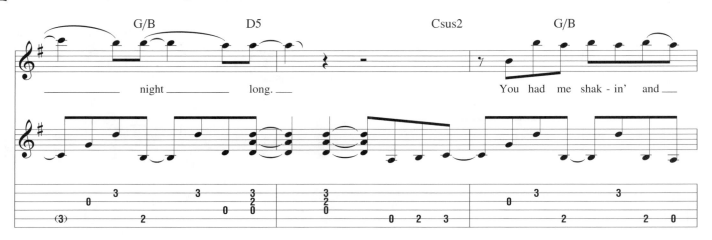

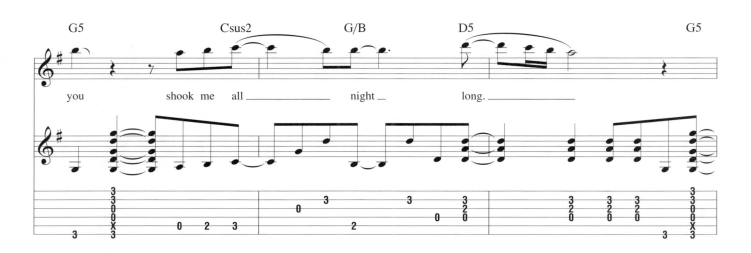

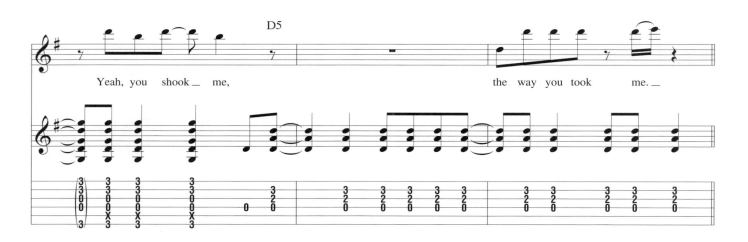

Guitar Solo

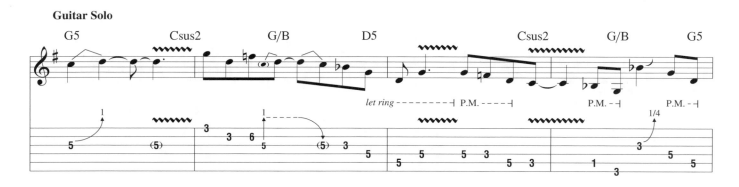

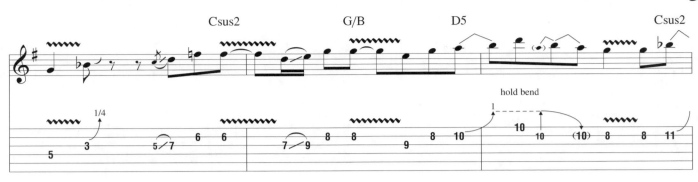

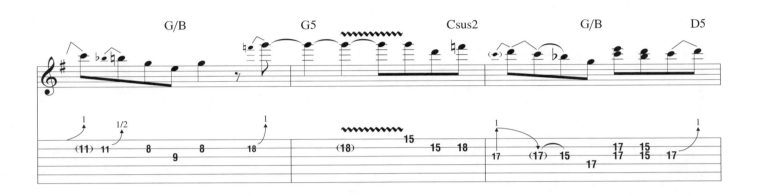

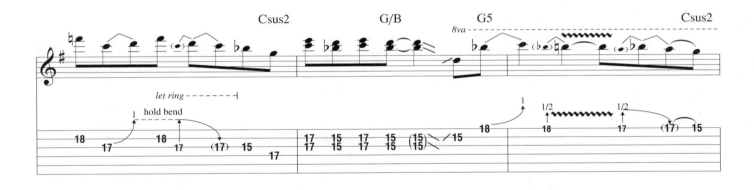

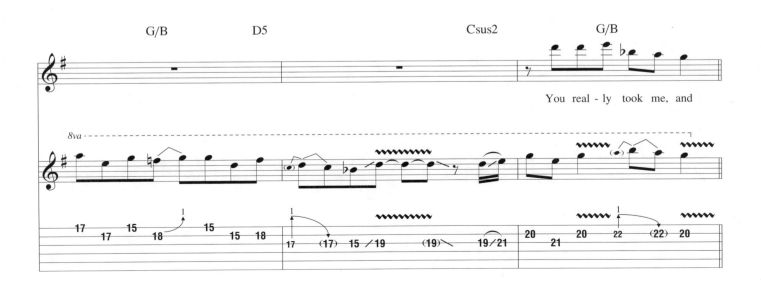

You real - ly took me, and

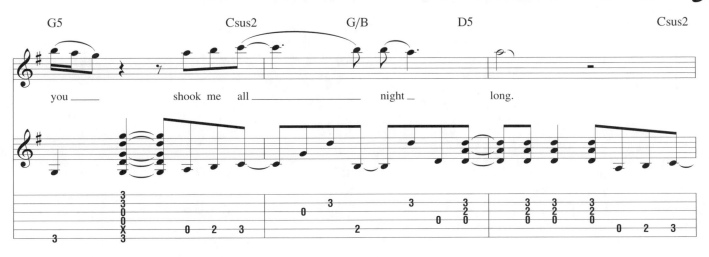

you _____ shook me all _____ night _____ long.

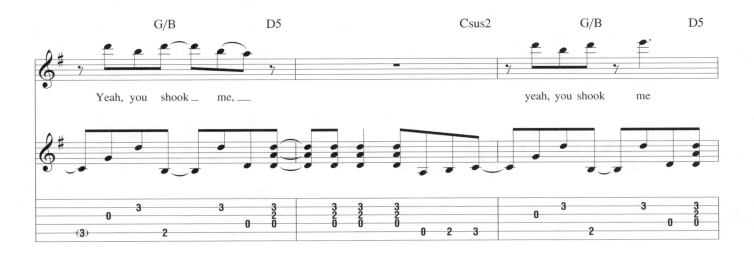

Yeah, you shook _____ me, _____   yeah, you shook   me

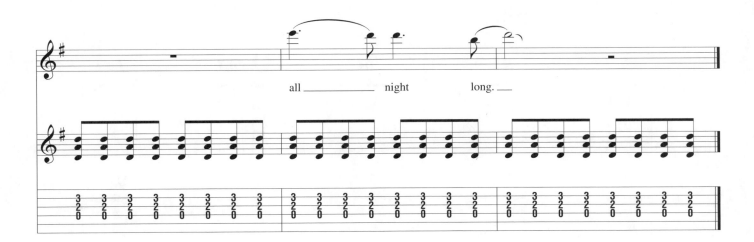

all _____ night   long. _____

Additional Lyrics

2. Workin' double-time on the seduction line.
    She was one of a kind; she's just a mine, all mine.
    Wanted no applause; just another cause.
    Made a meal out of me, and come back for more.
    Had to cool me down to take another round.
    Now I'm back in the ring to take another swing.
    'Cause the walls was shakin', the earth was quakin',
    My mind was achin', and we were makin' it. And you...

Chord and Scale Charts

C
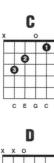
C E G C E

Cm
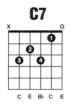
C G C E♭ G

C7
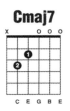
C E B♭ C E

Cmaj7
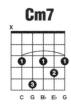
C E G B E

Cm7

C G B♭ E♭ G

D
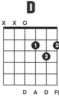
D A D F♯

Dm
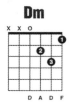
D A D F

D7
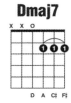
D A C F♯

Dmaj7
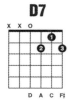
D A C♯ F♯

Dm7
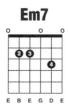
D A C F

E

E B E G♯ B E

Em

E B E G B E

E7
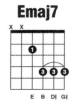
E B D G♯ B E

Emaj7
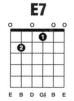
E B D♯ G♯

Em7

E B E G D E

F

F C F A C F

Fm
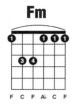
F C F A♭ C F

F7
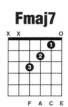
F C E♭ A C F

Fmaj7
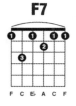
F A C E

Fm7
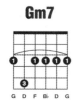
F C E♭ A♭ C F

G
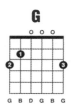
G B D G B G

Gm
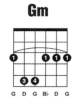
G D G B♭ D G

G7
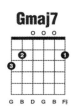
G B D G B F

Gmaj7
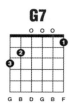
G B D G B F♯

Gm7
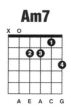
G D F B♭ D G

A
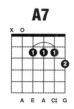
A E A C♯ E

Am
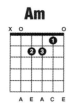
A E A C E

A7
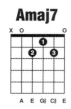
A E A C♯ G

Amaj7
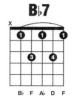
A E G♯ C♯ E

Am7

A E A C G

B♭
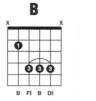
B♭ F B♭ D

B♭m

B♭ F B♭ D♭ F

B♭7

B♭ F A♭ D F

B♭maj7
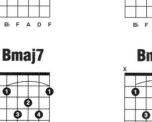
B♭ F A D F

B♭m7

B♭ F A♭ D♭ F

B
B F♯ B D♯

Bm
B F♯ B D F♯

B7
B D♯ A B F♯

Bmaj7
B F♯ A♯ D♯ F♯

Bm7
B F♯ A D F♯

Power Chords

Power chords, or "5" chords, are made of two notes (the "1" and "5" intervals), sometimes stacked and repeated in different orders and octaves. "Closed" power chord positions can be played on any fret. On these diagrams the root note is circled, and notes in parentheses (●) are extra "stacked" octaves that can turn a two-note power chord into a thicker-sounding one with three or more notes. Open-position chords are rooted on the open strings.

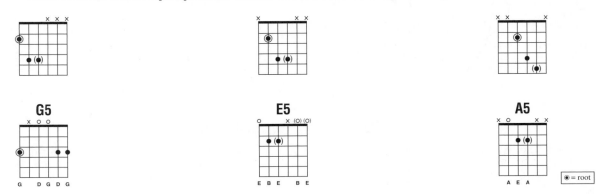

G5

G   D G D G

E5

E B E   B E

A5

A E A

● = root

The Minor Pentatonic Scale

The skeleton of rock riffs and solos, the *minor pentatonic scale* is made of five notes ("penta"=5), played and repeated in any order. Just like moveable power chords, you can play this scale all over the neck, depending on where the root note is. There are five "boxes" or positions of the scale — box 1 is the one you'll use the most. (A common key is A, where box 1 is rooted on fret 5.) Notice how box 2 begins where box 1 ends, and so on, so you can shift up the neck to play all five positions.

 You might hear some talk of the *major pentatonic scale* in these pages. Think of it as the same scale, with a different root — for example, if you play box 1 as a major pentatonic scale, the top note is your root.

 Want to learn to shred? Run up and down these box positions, over and over, until you can do it cleanly at blazing speed (or your neighbors start complaining).

Box 1

Box 2

Box 3

Box 4

Box 5

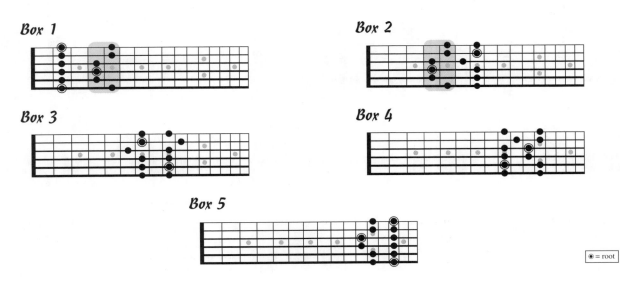

● = root

Guitar Notation Legend

Guitar Music can be notated three different ways: on a *musical staff*, in *tablature*, and in *rhythm slashes*.

RHYTHM SLASHES are written above the staff. Strum chords in the rhythm indicated. Use the chord diagrams found at the top of the first page of the transcription for the appropriate chord voicings. Round noteheads indicate single notes.

THE MUSICAL STAFF shows pitches and rhythms and is divided by bar lines into measures. Pitches are named after the first seven letters of the alphabet.

TABLATURE graphically represents the guitar fingerboard. Each horizontal line represents a a string, and each number represents a fret.

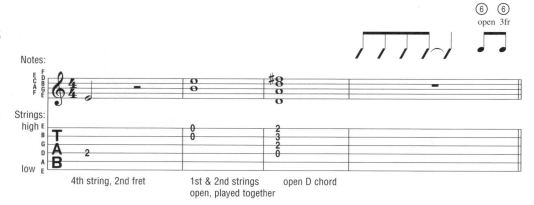

4th string, 2nd fret

1st & 2nd strings open, played together

open D chord

Definitions for Special Guitar Notation

HALF-STEP BEND: Strike the note and bend up 1/2 step.

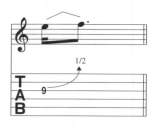

WHOLE-STEP BEND: Strike the note and bend up one step.

GRACE NOTE BEND: Strike the note and immediately bend up as indicated.

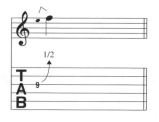

SLIGHT (MICROTONE) BEND: Strike the note and bend up 1/4 step.

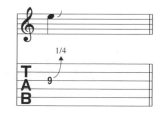

BEND AND RELEASE: Strike the note and bend up as indicated, then release back to the original note. Only the first note is struck.

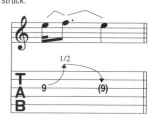

PRE-BEND: Bend the note as indicated, then strike it.

PRE-BEND AND RELEASE: Bend the note as indicated. Strike it and release the bend back to the original note.

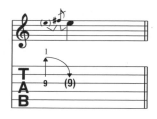

UNISON BEND: Strike the two notes simultaneously and bend the lower note up to the pitch of the higher.

VIBRATO: The string is vibrated by rapidly bending and releasing the note with the fretting hand.

WIDE VIBRATO: The pitch is varied to a greater degree by vibrating with the fretting hand.

HAMMER-ON: Strike the first (lower) note with one finger, then sound the higher note (on the same string) with another finger by fretting it without picking.

PULL-OFF: Place both fingers on the notes to be sounded. Strike the first note and without picking, pull the finger off to sound the second (lower) note.

LEGATO SLIDE: Strike the first note and then slide the same fret-hand finger up or down to the second note. The second note is not struck.

SHIFT SLIDE: Same as legato slide, except the second note is struck.

TRILL: Very rapidly alternate between the notes indicated by continuously hammering on and pulling off.

TAPPING: Hammer ("tap") the fret indicated with the pick-hand index or middle finger and pull off to the note fretted by the fret hand.

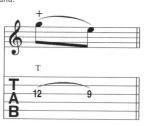

NATURAL HARMONIC: Strike the note while the fret-hand lightly touches the string directly over the fret indicated.

Harm.

TAB
12

PINCH HARMONIC: The note is fretted normally and a harmonic is produced by adding the edge of the thumb or the tip of the index finger of the pick hand to the normal pick attack.

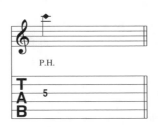

P.H.

TAB
5

HARP HARMONIC: The note is fretted normally and a harmonic is produced by gently resting the pick hand's index finger directly above the indicated fret (in parentheses) while the pick hand's thumb or pick assists by plucking the appropriate string.

8va

H.H.

TAB
7(19)

PICK SCRAPE: The edge of the pick is rubbed down (or up) the string, producing a scratchy sound.

P.S.

TAB
x

MUFFLED STRINGS: A percussive sound is produced by laying the fret hand across the string(s) without depressing, and striking them with the pick hand.

TAB
x x
x x

PALM MUTING: The note is partially muted by the pick hand lightly touching the string(s) just before the bridge.

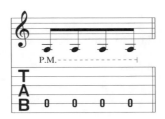

P.M. - - - - - - - - - - - - - - - - - - -

TAB
0   0   0   0

RAKE: Drag the pick across the strings indicated with a single motion.

rake - - - -

TAB
x   5
x

TREMOLO PICKING: The note is picked as rapidly and continuously as possible.

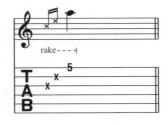

TAB
5   7

ARPEGGIATE: Play the notes of the chord indicated by quickly rolling them from bottom to top.

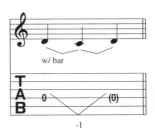

TAB
5
5
5
5

VIBRATO BAR DIVE AND RETURN: The pitch of the note or chord is dropped a specified number of steps (in rhythm) then returned to the original pitch.

w/ bar

TAB
0   (0)

-1

VIBRATO BAR SCOOP: Depress the bar just before striking the note, then quickly release the bar.

w/ bar - - - - - - - - - - -

TAB
4   5   7

VIBRATO BAR DIP: Strike the note and then immediately drop a specified number of steps, then release back to the original pitch.

-1/2   -1/2   -1/2
∨   ∨   ∨

w/ bar - - - - - - - - - - - - - - -

-1/2   -1/2   -1/2
∨   ∨   ∨

TAB
7   7   7

Additional Musical Definitions

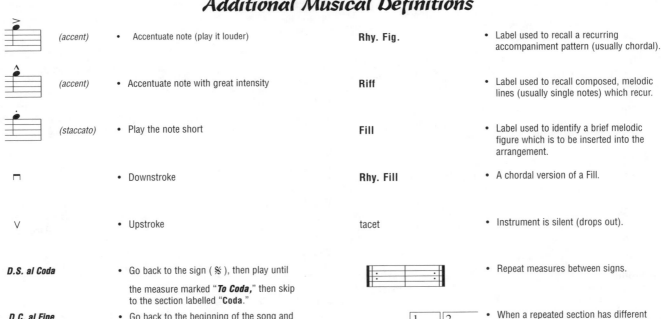

> (accent)	•	Accentuate note (play it louder)
^ (accent)	•	Accentuate note with great intensity
(staccato)	•	Play the note short
⊓	•	Downstroke
∨	•	Upstroke
D.S. al Coda	•	Go back to the sign (𝄋), then play until the measure marked "**To Coda,**" then skip to the section labelled "**Coda.**"
D.C. al Fine	•	Go back to the beginning of the song and play until the measure marked "***Fine***" (end).

Rhy. Fig.	• Label used to recall a recurring accompaniment pattern (usually chordal).
Riff	• Label used to recall composed, melodic lines (usually single notes) which recur.
Fill	• Label used to identify a brief melodic figure which is to be inserted into the arrangement.
Rhy. Fill	• A chordal version of a Fill.
tacet	• Instrument is silent (drops out).
	• Repeat measures between signs.
	• When a repeated section has different endings, play the first ending only the first time and the second ending only the second time.

NOTE: Tablature numbers in parentheses mean:
1. The note is being sustained over a system (note in standard notation is tied), or
2. The note is sustained, but a new articulation (such as a hammer-on, pull-off, slide or vibrato begins), or
3. The note is a barely audible "ghost" note (note in standard notation is also in parentheses).

HAL•LEONARD GUITAR PLAY·ALONG®

This series will help you play your favorite songs quickly and easily. Just **INCLUDES TAB** follow the tab and listen to the CD to hear how the guitar should sound, and then play along using the separate backing tracks. Mac or PC users can also slow down the tempo without changing pitch by using the CD in their computer. The melody and lyrics are included in the book so that you can sing or simply follow along.

VOL. 1 – ROCK 00699570 / $14.95
Day Tripper • Message in a Bottle • Refugee • Shattered • Sunshine of Your Love • Takin' Care of Business • Tush • Walk This Way.

VOL. 2 – ACOUSTIC 00699569 / $16.95
Angie • Behind Blue Eyes • Best of My Love • Blackbird • Dust in the Wind • Layla • Night Moves • Yesterday.

VOL. 3 – HARD ROCK 00699573 / $16.95
Crazy Train • Iron Man • Living After Midnight • Rock You like a Hurricane • Round and Round • Smoke on the Water • Sweet Child o' Mine • You Really Got Me.

VOL. 4 – POP/ROCK 00699571 / $14.95
Breakdown • Crazy Little Thing Called Love • Hit Me with Your Best Shot • I Want You to Want Me • Lights • R.O.C.K. in the U.S.A. • Summer of '69 • What I Like About You.

VOL. 5 – MODERN ROCK 00699574 / $14.95
Aerials • Alive • Bother • Chop Suey! • Control • Last Resort • Take a Look Around (Theme from *M:I-2*) • Wish You Were Here.

VOL. 6 – '90s ROCK 00699572 / $14.95
Are You Gonna Go My Way • Come out and Play • I'll Stick Around • Know Your Enemy • Man in the Box • Outshined • Smells like Teen Spirit • Under the Bridge.

VOL. 7 – BLUES 00699575 / $16.95
All Your Love (I Miss Loving) • Born Under a Bad Sign • Hide Away • I'm Tore Down • I'm Your Hoochie Coochie Man • Pride and Joy • Sweet Home Chicago • The Thrill Is Gone.

VOL. 8 – ROCK 00699585 / $14.95
All Right Now • Black Magic Woman • Get Back • Hey Joe • Layla • Love Me Two Times • Won't Get Fooled Again • You Really Got Me.

VOL. 9 – PUNK ROCK 00699576 / $14.95
All the Small Things • Fat Lip • Flavor of the Weak • I Feel So • Lifestyles of the Rich and Famous • Say It Ain't So • Self Esteem • (So) Tired of Waiting for You.

VOL. 10 – ACOUSTIC 00699586 / $16.95
Here Comes the Sun • Landslide • The Magic Bus • Norwegian Wood (This Bird Has Flown) • Pink Houses • Space Oddity • Tangled Up in Blue • Tears in Heaven.

VOL. 11 – EARLY ROCK 00699579 / $14.95
Fun, Fun, Fun • Hound Dog • Louie, Louie • No Particular Place to Go • Oh, Pretty Woman • Rock Around the Clock • Under the Boardwalk • Wild Thing.

VOL. 12 – POP/ROCK 00699587 / $14.95
867-5309/Jenny • Every Breath You Take • Money for Nothing • Rebel, Rebel • Run to You • Ticket to Ride • Wonderful Tonight • You Give Love a Bad Name.

VOL. 13 – FOLK ROCK 00699581 / $14.95
Annie's Song • Leaving on a Jet Plane • Suite: Judy Blue Eyes • This Land Is Your Land • Time in a Bottle • Turn! Turn! Turn! • You've Got a Friend • You've Got to Hide Your Love Away.

VOL. 14 – BLUES ROCK 00699582 / $16.95
Blue on Black • Crossfire • Cross Road Blues (Crossroads) • The House Is Rockin' • La Grange • Move It on Over • Roadhouse Blues • Statesboro Blues.

VOL. 15 – R&B 00699583 / $14.95
Ain't Too Proud to Beg • Brick House • Get Ready • I Can't Help Myself • I Got You (I Feel Good) • I Heard It Through the Grapevine • My Girl • Shining Star.

VOL. 16 – JAZZ 00699584 / $15.95
All Blues • Bluesette • Footprints • How Insensitive • Misty • Satin Doll • Stella by Starlight • Tenor Madness.

VOL. 17 – COUNTRY 00699588 / $15.95
Amie • Boot Scootin' Boogie • Chattahoochee • Folsom Prison Blues • Friends in Low Places • Forever and Ever, Amen • T-R-O-U-B-L-E • Workin' Man Blues.

VOL. 18 – ACOUSTIC ROCK 00699577 / $15.95
About a Girl • Breaking the Girl • Drive • Iris • More than Words • Patience • Silent Lucidity • 3 AM.

VOL. 19 – SOUL 00699578 / $14.95
Get Up (I Feel like Being) a Sex Machine • Green Onions • In the Midnight Hour • Knock on Wood • Mustang Sally • Respect • (Sittin' On) The Dock of the Bay • Soul Man.

VOL. 20 – ROCKABILLY 00699580 / $14.95
Be-Bop-A-Lula • Blue Suede Shoes • Hello Mary Lou • Little Sister • Mystery Train • Rock This Town • Stray Cat Strut • That'll Be the Day.

VOL. 21 – YULETIDE 00699602 / $14.95
Angels We Have Heard on High • Away in a Manger • Deck the Hall • The First Noel • Go, Tell It on the Mountain • Jingle Bells • Joy to the World • O Little Town of Bethlehem.

VOL. 22 – CHRISTMAS 00699600 / $14.95
The Christmas Song • Frosty the Snow Man • Happy Xmas • Here Comes Santa Claus • Jingle-Bell Rock • Merry Christmas, Darling • Rudolph the Red-Nosed Reindeer • Silver Bells.

VOL. 23 – SURF 00699635 / $14.95
Let's Go Trippin' • Out of Limits • Penetration • Pipeline • Surf City • Surfin' U.S.A. • Walk Don't Run • The Wedge.

VOL. 24 – ERIC CLAPTON 00699649 / $16.95
Badge • Bell Bottom Blues • Change the World • Cocaine • Key to the Highway • Lay Down Sally • White Room • Wonderful Tonight.

VOL. 25 – LENNON & McCARTNEY 00699642 / $14.95
Back in the U.S.S.R. • Drive My Car • Get Back • A Hard Day's Night • I Feel Fine • Paperback Writer • Revolution • Ticket to Ride.

VOL. 26 – ELVIS PRESLEY 00699643 / $14.95
All Shook Up • Blue Suede Shoes • Don't Be Cruel • Heartbreak Hotel • Hound Dog • Jailhouse Rock • Little Sister • Mystery Train.

VOL. 27 – DAVID LEE ROTH 00699645 / $16.95
Ain't Talkin' 'bout Love • Dance the Night Away • Hot for Teacher • Just like Paradise • A Lil' Ain't Enough • Runnin' with the Devil • Unchained • Yankee Rose.

VOL. 28 – GREG KOCH 00699646 / $14.95
Chief's Blues • Death of a Bassman • Dylan the Villain • The Grip • Holy Grail • Spank It • Tonus Diabolicus • Zoiks.

VOL. 29 – BOB SEGER 00699647 / $14.95
Against the Wind • Betty Lou's Gettin' out Tonight • Hollywood Nights • Mainstreet • Night Moves • Old Time Rock & Roll • Rock and Roll Never Forgets • Still the Same.

VOL. 30 – KISS 00699644 / $14.95
Cold Gin • Detroit Rock City • Deuce • Firehouse • Heaven's on Fire • Love Gun • Rock and Roll All Nite • Shock Me.

VOL. 31 – CHRISTMAS HITS 00699652 / $14.95
Blue Christmas • Do You Hear What I Hear • Happy Holiday • I Saw Mommy Kissing Santa Claus • I'll Be Home for Christmas • Let It Snow! Let It Snow! Let It Snow! • Little Saint Nick • Snowfall.

VOL. 32 – THE OFFSPRING 00699653 / $14.95
Bad Habit • Come out and Play • Gone Away • Gotta Get Away • Hit That • The Kids Aren't Alright • Pretty Fly (For a White Guy) • Self Esteem.

VOL. 33 – ACOUSTIC CLASSICS 00699656 / $16.95
Across the Universe • Babe, I'm Gonna Leave You • Crazy on You • Heart of Gold • Hotel California • I'd Love to Change the World • Thick as a Brick • Wanted Dead or Alive.

VOL. 34 – CLASSIC ROCK 00699658 / $16.95
Aqualung • Born to Be Wild • The Boys Are Back in Town • Brown Eyed Girl • Reeling in the Years • Rock'n Me • Rocky Mountain Way • Sweet Emotion.

VOL. 35 – HAIR METAL 00699660 / $16.95
Decadence Dance • Don't Treat Me Bad • Down Boys • Seventeen • Shake Me • Up All Night • Wait • Talk Dirty to Me.

VOL. 36 – SOUTHERN ROCK 00699661 / $16.95
Can't You See • Flirtin' with Disaster • Hold on Loosely • Jessica • Mississippi Queen • Ramblin' Man • Sweet Home Alabama • What's Your Name.

VOL. 37 – ACOUSTIC METAL 00699662 / $16.95
Every Rose Has Its Thorn • Fly to the Angels • Hole Hearted • Love Is on the Way • Love of a Lifetime • Signs • To Be with You • When the Children Cry.

VOL. 38 – BLUES 00699663 / $16.95
Boom Boom • Cold Shot • Crosscut Saw • Everyday I Have the Blues • Frosty • Further on up the Road • Killing Floor • Texas Flood.

VOL. 39 – '80s METAL 00699664 / $16.95
Bark at the Moon • Big City Nights • Breaking the Chains • Cult of Personality • Lay It Down • Living on a Prayer • Panama • Smokin' in the Boys Room.

VOL. 40 – INCUBUS 00699668 / $16.95
Are You In? • Drive • Megalomaniac • Nice to Know You • Pardon Me • Stellar • Talk Shows on Mute • Wish You Were Here.

VOL. 41 – ERIC CLAPTON 00699669 / $16.95
After Midnight • Can't Find My Way Home • Forever Man • I Shot the Sheriff • I'm Tore Down • Pretending • Running on Faith • Tears in Heaven.

VOL. 42 – CHART HITS 00699670 / $16.95
Are You Gonna Be My Girl • Heaven • Here Without You • I Believe in a Thing Called Love • Just like You • Last Train Home • This Love • Until the Day I Die.

VOL. 43 – LYNYRD SKYNYRD 00699681 / $16.95
Don't Ask Me No Questions • Free Bird • Gimme Three Steps • I Know a Little • Saturday Night Special • Sweet Home Alabama • That Smell • You Got That Right.

VOL. 44 – JAZZ 00699689 / $14.95
I Remember You • I'll Remember April • Impressions • In a Mellow Tone • Moonlight in Vermont • On a Slow Boat to China • Things Ain't What They Used to Be • Yesterdays.

VOL. 45 – TV THEMES 00699718 / $14.95
Themes from shows such as: The Addams Family • Hawaii Five-O • King of the Hill • Charlie Brown • Mission: Impossible • The Munsters • The Simpsons • Star Trek®.

VOL. 46 – MAINSTREAM ROCK 00699722 / $16.95
Just a Girl • Keep Away • Kryptonite • Lightning Crashes • 1979 • One Step Closer • Scar Tissue • Torn.

VOL. 47 – HENDRIX SMASH HITS 00699723 / $17.95
All Along the Watchtower • Can You See Me? • Crosstown Traffic • Fire • Foxey Lady • Hey Joe • Manic Depression • Purple Haze • Red House • Remember • Stone Free • The Wind Cries Mary.

VOL. 48 – AEROSMITH CLASSICS 00699724 / $14.95
Back in the Saddle • Draw the Line • Dream On • Last Child • Mama Kin • Same Old Song & Dance • Sweet Emotion • Walk This Way.

VOL. 49 – STEVIE RAY VAUGHAN 00699725 $16.95
Couldn't Stand the Weather • Empty Arms • Lenny • Little Wing • Look at Little Sister • Love Struck Baby • The Sky Is Crying • Tightrope.

VOL. 50 – NÜ METAL 00699726 / $14.95
Duality • Here to Stay • In the End • Judith • Nookie • So Cold • Toxicity • Whatever.

VOL. 51 – ALTERNATIVE '90s 00699727 / $12.95
Alive • Cherub Rock • Come As You Are • Give It Away • Jane Says • No Excuses • No Rain • Santeria.

VOL. 56 – FOO FIGHTERS 00699749 / $14.95
All My Life • Best of You • DOA • I'll Stick Around • Learn to Fly • Monkey Wrench • My Hero • This Is a Call.

VOL. 57 – SYSTEM OF A DOWN 00699751 / $14.95
Aerials • B.Y.O.B. • Chop Suey! • Innervision • Question! • Spiders • Sugar • Toxicity.

VOL. 58 – BLINK-182 00699772 / $14.95
Adam's Song • All the Small Things • Dammit • Feeling This • Man Overboard • The Rock Show • Stay Together for the Kids • What's My Age Again?

VOL. 59 – GODSMACK 00699773 / $14.95
Awake • Bad Religion • Greed • I Stand Alone • Keep Away • Running Blind • Straight out of Line • Whatever.

VOL. 60 – 3 DOORS DOWN 00699774 / $14.95
Away from the Sun • Duck and Run • Here Without You • Kryptonite • Let Me Go • Live for Today • Loser • When I'm Gone.

VOL. 61 – SLIPKNOT 00699775 / $14.95
Before I Forget • Duality • The Heretic Anthem • Left Behind • My Plague • Spit It Out • Vermilion • Wait and Bleed.

VOL. 62 – CHRISTMAS CAROLS 00699798 / $12.95
God Rest Ye Merry, Gentlemen • Hark! The Herald Angels Sing • It Came upon the Midnight Clear • O Come, All Ye Faithful (Adeste Fideles) • O Holy Night • Silent Night • We Three Kings of Orient Are • What Child Is This?

VOL. 63 – CREEDENCE CLEARWATER REVIVAL 00699802 / $14.95
Bad Moon Rising • Born on the Bayou • Down on the Corner • Fortunate Son • Green River • Lodi • Proud Mary • Up Around the Bend.

VOL. 66 – THE ROLLING STONES 00699807 / $16.95
Beast of Burden • Happy • It's Only Rock 'N' Roll (But I Like It) • Miss You • Shattered • She's So Cold • Start Me Up • Tumbling Dice.

VOL. 67 – BLACK SABBATH 00699808 / $14.95
Black Sabbath • Children of the Grave • Iron Man • N.I.B. • Paranoid • Sabbath, Bloody Sabbath • Sweet Leaf • War Pigs (Interpolating Luke's Wall).

VOL. 68 – PINK FLOYD – DARK SIDE OF THE MOON 00699809 / $14.95
Any Colour You Like • Brain Damage • Breathe • Eclipse • Money • Time • Us and Them.

VOL. 74 – PAUL BALOCHE 00699831 / $14.95
Above All • All the Earth Will Sing Your Praises • Because of Your Love • My Reward • Offering • Open the Eyes of My Heart • Praise Adonai • Rise up and Praise Him.

Prices, contents, and availability subject to change without notice.

FOR MORE INFORMATION, SEE YOUR LOCAL MUSIC DEALER,
OR WRITE TO:

HAL•LEONARD®
CORPORATION
7777 W. BLUEMOUND RD. P.O. BOX 13819 MILWAUKEE, WI 53213

Visit Hal Leonard online at www.halleonard.com

0507

GUITAR BIBLES

from HAL•LEONARD®

Hal Leonard proudly presents the Guitar Bible series. Each volume contains great songs in authentic, note-for-note transcriptions with lyrics and tablature.

ACOUSTIC GUITAR BIBLE
35 acoustic classics: Angie • Building a Mystery • Change the World • Dust in the Wind • Hold My Hand • Iris • Maggie May • Southern Cross • Tears in Heaven • Wild World • and more.
00690432..$19.95

ACOUSTIC ROCK GUITAR BIBLE
35 classics: And I Love Her • Behind Blue Eyes • Come to My Window • Free Fallin' • Give a Little Bit • More Than Words • Night Moves • Pink Houses • Slide • 3 AM • and more.
00690625..$19.95

BABY BOOMER'S GUITAR BIBLE
35 songs: Angie • Can't Buy Me Love • Happy Together • Hey Jude • Imagine • Laughing • Longer • My Girl • New Kid in Town • Rebel, Rebel • Wild Thing • and more.
00690412..$19.95

BLUES GUITAR BIBLE
35 blues tunes: Boom Boom • Hide Away • I Can't Quit You Baby • I'm Your Hoochie Coochie Man • Killing Floor • Pride and Joy • Sweet Little Angel • The Thrill Is Gone • and more.
00690437..$19.95

BLUES-ROCK GUITAR BIBLE
35 songs: Cross Road Blues (Crossroads) • Hide Away • The House Is Rockin' • Love Struck Baby • Move It On Over • Piece of My Heart • Statesboro Blues • You Shook Me • more.
00690450..$19.95

CLASSIC ROCK GUITAR BIBLE
33 essential rock songs: Beast of Burden • Cat Scratch Fever • Double Vision • Free Ride • Hard to Handle • Life in the Fast Lane • The Stroke • Won't Get Fooled Again • and more.
00690662..$19.95

COUNTRY GUITAR BIBLE
35 country classics: Ain't Goin' Down • Blue Eyes Crying in the Rain • Boot Scootin' Boogie • Friends in Low Places • I'm So Lonesome I Could Cry • T-R-O-U-B-L-E • and more.
00690465..$19.95

DISCO GUITAR BIBLE
30 stand-out songs from the disco days: Brick House • Disco Inferno • Funkytown • Get Down Tonight • I Love the Night Life • Le Freak • Stayin' Alive • Y.M.C.A. • and more.
00690627..$17.95

EARLY ROCK GUITAR BIBLE
35 fantastic classics: Blue Suede Shoes • Do Wah Diddy Diddy • Hang On Sloopy • I'm a Believer • Louie, Louie • Oh, Pretty Woman • Surfin' U.S.A. • Twist and Shout • and more.
00690680..$17.95

FOLK-ROCK GUITAR BIBLE
35 songs: At Seventeen • Blackbird • Fire and Rain • Happy Together • Leaving on a Jet Plane • Our House • Time in a Bottle • Turn! Turn! Turn! • You've Got a Friend • more.
00690464..$19.95

GRUNGE GUITAR BIBLE
30 songs: All Apologies • Counting Blue Cars • Glycerine • Jesus Christ Pose • Lithium • Man in the Box • Nearly Lost You • Smells like Teen Spirit • This Is a Call • Violet • and more.
00690649..$17.95

HARD ROCK GUITAR BIBLE
35 songs: Ballroom Blitz • Bang a Gong • Barracuda • Living After Midnight • Rock You like a Hurricane • School's Out • Welcome to the Jungle • You Give Love a Bad Name • more.
00690453..$19.95

INSTRUMENTAL GUITAR BIBLE
37 great instrumentals: Always with Me, Always with You • Green Onions • Hide Away • Jessica • Linus and Lucy • Perfidia • Satch Boogie • Tequila • Walk Don't Run • and more.
00690514..$19.95

JAZZ GUITAR BIBLE
31 songs: Body and Soul • In a Sentimental Mood • My Funny Valentine • Nuages • Satin Doll • So What • Star Dust • Take Five • Tangerine • Yardbird Suite • and more.
00690466..$19.95

MODERN ROCK GUITAR BIBLE
26 rock favorites: Aerials (System of a Down) • Alive (P.O.D.) • Cold Hard Bitch (Jet) • Kryptonite (3 Doors Down) • Like a Stone (Audioslave) • Whatever (Godsmack) • and more.
00690724..$19.95

NÜ METAL GUITAR BIBLE
25 edgy metal hits: Aenema • Black • Edgecrusher • Last Resort • People of the Sun • Schism • Southtown • Take a Look Around • Toxicity • Youth of the Nation • and more.
00690569..$19.95

POP/ROCK GUITAR BIBLE
35 pop hits: Change the World • Heartache Tonight • Money for Nothing • Mony, Mony • Pink Houses • Smooth • Summer of '69 • 3 AM • What I Like About You • and more.
00690517..$19.95

R&B GUITAR BIBLE
35 R&B classics: Brick House • Fire • I Got You (I Feel Good) • Love Rollercoaster • Shining Star • Sir Duke • Super Freak • and more.
00690452..$19.95

ROCK GUITAR BIBLE
33 songs: All Day and All of the Night • Born to Be Wild • Day Tripper • Hey Joe • Jailhouse Rock • Money • Paranoid • Sultans of Swing • Walk This Way • You Really Got Me • more!
00690313..$19.95

ROCKABILLY GUITAR BIBLE
31 songs from artists such as Elvis, Buddy Holly and the Brian Setzer Orchestra: Blue Suede Shoes • Hello Mary Lou • Peggy Sue • Rock This Town • Travelin' Man • and more.
00690570..$19.95

SOUL GUITAR BIBLE
33 songs: Groovin' • I've Been Loving You Too Long • Let's Get It On • My Girl • Respect • Theme from Shaft • Soul Man • and more.
00690506..$19.95

SOUTHERN ROCK GUITAR BIBLE
25 southern rock classics: Can't You See • Free Bird • Hold On Loosely • La Grange • Midnight Rider • Sweet Home Alabama • and more.
00690723..$19.95

Prices, contents, and availability subject to change without notice.

FOR MORE INFORMATION, SEE YOUR LOCAL MUSIC DEALER,
OR WRITE TO:

HAL•LEONARD®
CORPORATION
7777 W. BLUEMOUND RD. P.O. BOX 13819 MILWAUKEE, WI 53213

Visit Hal Leonard online at **www.halleonard.com**

0606

GUITAR *signature licks*

Signature Licks book/CD packs provide a step-by-step breakdown of "right from the record" riffs, licks, and solos so you can jam along with your favorite bands. They contain performance notes and an overview of each artist's or group's style, with note-for-note transcriptions in notes and tab. The CDs feature full-band demos at both normal and slow speeds.

BEST OF ACOUSTIC GUITAR
00695640 ....$19.95

AEROSMITH 1973-1979
00695106 ....$22.95

AEROSMITH 1979-1998
00695219 ....$22.95

BEST OF AGGRO-METAL
00695592 ....$19.95

BEST OF CHET ATKINS
00695752 ....$22.95

THE BEACH BOYS DEFINITIVE COLLECTION
00695683 ....$22.95

BEST OF THE BEATLES FOR ACOUSTIC GUITAR
00695453 ....$22.95

THE BEATLES BASS
00695283 ....$22.95

THE BEATLES FAVORITES
00695096 ....$24.95

THE BEATLES HITS
00695049 ....$24.95

BEST OF GEORGE BENSON
00695418 ....$22.95

BEST OF BLACK SABBATH
00695249 ....$22.95

BEST OF BLINK - 182
00695704 ....$22.95

BEST OF BLUES GUITAR
00695846 ....$19.95

BLUES GUITAR CLASSICS
00695177 ....$19.95

BLUES/ROCK GUITAR MASTERS
00695348 ....$19.95

BEST OF CHARLIE CHRISTIAN
00695584 ....$22.95

BEST OF ERIC CLAPTON
00695038 ....$24.95

ERIC CLAPTON – THE BLUESMAN
00695040 ....$22.95

ERIC CLAPTON – FROM THE ALBUM UNPLUGGED
00695250 ....$24.95

BEST OF CREAM
00695251 ....$22.95

DEEP PURPLE – GREATEST HITS
00695625 ....$22.95

THE BEST OF DEF LEPPARD
00696516 ....$22.95

THE DOORS
00695373 ....$22.95

FAMOUS ROCK GUITAR SOLOS
00695590 ....$19.95

BEST OF FOO FIGHTERS
00695481 ....$22.95

GREATEST GUITAR SOLOS OF ALL TIME
00695301 ....$19.95

BEST OF GRANT GREEN
00695747 ....$22.95

GUITAR INSTRUMENTAL HITS
00695309 ....$19.95

GUITAR RIFFS OF THE '60S
00695218 ....$19.95

BEST OF GUNS N' ROSES
00695183 ....$22.95

HARD ROCK SOLOS
00695591 ....$19.95

JIMI HENDRIX
00696560 ....$24.95

HOT COUNTRY GUITAR
00695580 ....$19.95

BEST OF JAZZ GUITAR
00695586 ....$24.95

ERIC JOHNSON
00699317 ....$22.95

ROBERT JOHNSON
00695264 ....$22.95

THE ESSENTIAL ALBERT KING
00695713 ....$22.95

B.B. KING – THE DEFINITIVE COLLECTION
00695635 ....$22.95

THE KINKS
00695553 ....$22.95

BEST OF KISS
00699413 ....$22.95

MARK KNOPFLER
00695178 ....$22.95

BEST OF YNGWIE MALMSTEEN
00695669 ....$22.95

BEST OF PAT MARTINO
00695632 ....$22.95

MEGADETH
00695041 ....$22.95

WES MONTGOMERY
00695387 ....$22.95

BEST OF NIRVANA
00695483 ....$24.95

THE OFFSPRING
00695852 ....$24.95

VERY BEST OF OZZY OSBOURNE
00695431 ....$22.95

BEST OF JOE PASS
00695730 ....$22.95

PINK FLOYD – EARLY CLASSICS
00695566 ....$22.95

THE POLICE
00695724 ....$22.95

THE GUITARS OF ELVIS
00696507 ....$22.95

BEST OF QUEEN
00695097 ....$22.95

BEST OF RAGE AGAINST THE MACHINE
00695480 ....$22.95

RED HOT CHILI PEPPERS
00695173 ....$22.95

RED HOT CHILI PEPPERS – GREATEST HITS
00695828 ....$24.95

BEST OF DJANGO REINHARDT
00695660 ....$22.95

BEST OF ROCK
00695884 ....$19.95

BEST OF ROCK 'N' ROLL GUITAR
00695559 ....$19.95

BEST OF ROCKABILLY GUITAR
00695785 ....$19.95

THE ROLLING STONES
00695079 ....$22.95

BEST OF JOE SATRIANI
00695216 ....$22.95

BEST OF SILVERCHAIR
00695488 ....$22.95

THE BEST OF SOUL GUITAR
00695703 ....$19.95

BEST OF SOUTHERN ROCK
00695703 ....$19.95

ROD STEWART
00695663 ....$22.95

BEST OF SYSTEM OF A DOWN
00695788 ....$22.95

STEVE VAI
00673247 ....$22.95

STEVE VAI – ALIEN LOVE SECRETS: THE NAKED VAMPS
00695223 ....$22.95

STEVE VAI – FIRE GARDEN: THE NAKED VAMPS
00695166 ....$22.95

STEVE VAI – THE ULTRA ZONE: NAKED VAMPS
00695684 ....$22.95

STEVIE RAY VAUGHAN
00699316 ....$24.95

THE GUITAR STYLE OF STEVIE RAY VAUGHAN
00695155 ....$24.95

BEST OF THE VENTURES
00695772 ....$19.95

THE WHO
00695561 ....$22.95

BEST OF ZZ TOP
00695738 ....$22.95

Complete descriptions and songlists online!

FOR MORE INFORMATION, SEE YOUR LOCAL MUSIC DEALER, OR WRITE TO:

HAL•LEONARD® CORPORATION
7777 W. BLUEMOUND RD. P.O. BOX 13819 MILWAUKEE, WI 53213

www.halleonard.com
Prices, contents and availability subject to change without notice.

0606

AUTHENTIC TRANSCRIPTIONS WITH NOTES AND TABLATURE

GUITAR RECORDED VERSIONS®

Guitar Recorded Versions® are note-for-note transcriptions of guitar music taken directly off recordings. This series, one of the most popular in print today, features some of the greatest guitar players and groups from blues and rock to country and jazz.

Guitar Recorded Versions are transcribed by the best transcribers in the business. Every book contains notes and tablature.

00690016 Will Ackerman Collection $19.95
00690501 Bryan Adams – Greatest Hits $19.95
00690002 Aerosmith – Big Ones $24.95
00692015 Aerosmith – Greatest Hits $22.95
00690603 Aerosmith – O Yeah! (Ultimate Hits) $24.95
00690147 Aerosmith – Rocks $19.95
00690139 Alice in Chains $19.95
00690178 Alice in Chains – Acoustic $19.95
00694865 Alice in Chains – Dirt $19.95
00660225 Alice in Chains – Facelift $19.95
00694925 Alice in Chains – Jar of Flies/Sap $19.95
00690387 Alice in Chains – Nothing Safe: Best of the Box $19.95
00690812 All American Rejects – Move Along $19.95
00694932 Allman Brothers Band – Definitive Collection for Guitar Volume 1 $24.95
00694933 Allman Brothers Band – Definitive Collection for Guitar Volume 2 $24.95
00694934 Allman Brothers Band – Definitive Collection for Guitar Volume 3 $24.95
00690755 Alter Bridge – One Day Remains $19.95
00690571 Trey Anastasio $19.95
00690158 Chet Atkins – Almost Alone $19.95
00694876 Chet Atkins – Contemporary Styles $19.95
00694878 Chet Atkins – Vintage Fingerstyle $19.95
00690865 Atreyu – A Deathgrip on Yesterday $19.95
00690609 Audioslave $19.95
00690804 Audioslave – Out of Exile $19.95
00690884 Audioslave – Revelations $19.95
00690820 Avenged Sevenfold – City of Evil $22.95
00694918 Randy Bachman Collection $22.95
00690366 Bad Company – Original Anthology – Book 1 $19.95
00690367 Bad Company – Original Anthology – Book 2 $19.95
00690503 Beach Boys – Very Best of $19.95
00694929 Beatles: 1962-1966 $24.95
00694930 Beatles: 1967-1970 $24.95
00690489 Beatles – 1 $24.95
00694880 Beatles – Abbey Road $19.95
00690110 Beatles – Book 1 (White Album) $19.95
00690111 Beatles – Book 2 (White Album) $19.95
00694832 Beatles – For Acoustic Guitar $22.95
00690137 Beatles – A Hard Day's Night $16.95
00690482 Beatles – Let It Be $17.95
00694891 Beatles – Revolver $19.95
00694914 Beatles – Rubber Soul $19.95
00694863 Beatles – Sgt. Pepper's Lonely Hearts Club Band $19.95
00690383 Beatles – Yellow Submarine $19.95
00690175 Beck – Odelay $17.95
00690632 Beck – Sea Change $19.95
00694884 Best of George Benson $19.95
00692385 Chuck Berry $19.95
00690835 Billy Talent $19.95
00690879 Billy Talent II $19.95
00690149 Black Sabbath $14.95
00690148 Black Sabbath – Master of Reality $14.95
00690142 Black Sabbath – Paranoid $14.95
00692200 Black Sabbath – We Sold Our Soul for Rock 'N' Roll $19.95
00690115 Blind Melon – Soup $19.95
00690674 blink-182 $19.95
00690389 blink-182 – Enema of the State $19.95
00690831 blink-182 – Greatest Hits $19.95
00690523 blink-182 – Take Off Your Pants and Jacket $19.95
00690028 Blue Oyster Cult – Cult Classics $19.95
00690008 Bon Jovi – Cross Road $19.95
00690491 Best of David Bowie $19.95
00690583 Box Car Racer $19.95
00690873 Breaking Benjamin – Phobia $19.95
00690764 Breaking Benjamin – We Are Not Alone $19.95
00690451 Jeff Buckley Collection $24.95
00690364 Cake – Songbook $19.95
00690564 The Calling – Camino Palmero $19.95
00690261 Carter Family Collection $19.95
00690293 Best of Steven Curtis Chapman $19.95
00690043 Best of Cheap Trick $19.95
00690171 Chicago – The Definitive Guitar Collection $22.95
00690567 Charlie Christian – The Definitive Collection $19.95
00690590 Eric Clapton – Anthology $29.95
00692391 Best of Eric Clapton – 2nd Edition $22.95
00690393 Eric Clapton – Selections from Blues $19.95
00690074 Eric Clapton – Cream of Clapton $24.95
00690265 Eric Clapton – E.C. Was Here $19.95
00690010 Eric Clapton – From the Cradle $19.95
00690716 Eric Clapton – Me and Mr. Johnson $19.95
00690263 Eric Clapton – Slowhand $19.95
00694873 Eric Clapton – Timepieces $19.95
00694869 Eric Clapton – Unplugged $22.95
00690415 Clapton Chronicles – Best of Eric Clapton $18.95
00694896 John Mayall/Eric Clapton – Bluesbreakers $19.95
00690162 Best of the Clash $19.95
00690828 Coheed & Cambria – Good Apollo I'm Burning Star, IV, Vol. 1: From Fear Through the Eyes of Madness $19.95
00690682 Coldplay – Live in 2003 $19.95
00690494 Coldplay – Parachutes $19.95
00690593 Coldplay – A Rush of Blood to the Head $19.95
00690806 Coldplay – X & Y $19.95
00694940 Counting Crows – August & Everything After $19.95
00690405 Counting Crows – This Desert Life $19.95
00694840 Cream – Disraeli Gears $19.95
00690838 Cream – Royal Albert Hall: London May 2-3-5-6 2005 $22.95
00690285 Cream – Those Were the Days $17.95
00690856 Creed – Greatest Hits $22.95
00690401 Creed – Human Clay $19.95
00690352 Creed – My Own Prison $19.95
00690551 Creed – Weathered $19.95
00690819 Best of Creedence Clearwater Revival $19.95
00690572 Steve Cropper – Soul Man $19.95
00690613 Best of Crosby, Stills & Nash $19.95
00690777 Crossfade $19.95
00699521 The Cure – Greatest Hits $24.95
00690637 Best of Dick Dale $19.95
00690184 dc Talk – Jesus Freak $19.95
00690822 Best of Alex De Grassi $19.95
00690289 Best of Deep Purple $17.95
00690784 Best of Def Leppard $19.95
00694831 Derek and the Dominos – Layla & Other Assorted Love Songs $19.95
00690384 Best of Ani DiFranco $19.95
00690322 Ani DiFranco – Little Plastic Castle $19.95
00690191 Dire Straits – Money for Nothing $24.95
00695382 Very Best of Dire Straits – Sultans of Swing $19.95
00690347 The Doors – Anthology $22.95
00690348 The Doors – Essential Guitar Collection $16.95
00690250 Best of Duane Eddy $16.95
00690533 Electric Light Orchestra Guitar Collection $19.95
00690555 Best of Melissa Etheridge $19.95
00690524 Melissa Etheridge – Skin $19.95
00690496 Best of Everclear $19.95
00690515 Extreme II – Pornograffitti $19.95
00690810 Fall Out Boy – From Under the Cork Tree $19.95
00690664 Best of Fleetwood Mac $19.95
00690870 Flyleaf $19.95
00690734 Franz Ferdinand $19.95
00694920 Best of Free $19.95
00690257 John Fogerty – Blue Moon Swamp $19.95
00690235 Foo Fighters – The Colour and the Shape $19.95
00690808 Foo Fighters – In Your Honor $19.95
00690595 Foo Fighters – One by One $19.95
00690394 Foo Fighters – There Is Nothing Left to Lose $19.95
00690805 Best of Robben Ford $19.95
00690222 G3 Live – Joe Satriani, Steve Vai, and Eric Johnson $22.95
00694807 Danny Gatton – 88 Elmira St $19.95
00690438 Genesis Guitar Anthology $19.95
00690753 Best of Godsmack $19.95
00120167 Godsmack $19.95
00690848 Godsmack – IV $19.95
00690338 Goo Goo Dolls – Dizzy Up the Girl $19.95
00690576 Goo Goo Dolls – Gutterflower $19.95
00690773 Good Charlotte – Chronicles of Life and Death $19.95
00690601 Good Charlotte – The Young and the Hopeless $19.95
00690117 John Gorka Collection $19.95
00690591 Patty Griffin – Guitar Collection $19.95
00690114 Buddy Guy Collection Vol. A-J $22.95
00690193 Buddy Guy Collection Vol. L-Y $22.95
00690697 Best of Jim Hall $19.95
00690840 Ben Harper – Both Sides of the Gun $19.95
00694798 George Harrison Anthology $19.95
00690778 Hawk Nelson – Letters to the President $19.95
00690068 Return of the Hellecasters $19.95
00692930 Jimi Hendrix – Are You Experienced? $24.95
00692931 Jimi Hendrix – Axis: Bold As Love $22.95
00690304 Jimi Hendrix – Band of Gypsys $22.95
00690321 Jimi Hendrix – BBC Sessions $22.95
00690608 Jimi Hendrix – Blue Wild Angel $24.95
00694944 Jimi Hendrix – Blues $24.95
00692932 Jimi Hendrix – Electric Ladyland $24.95
00660099 Jimi Hendrix – Radio One $24.95
00690602 Jimi Hendrix – Smash Hits $19.95
00690017 Jimi Hendrix – Woodstock $24.95
00690843 H.I.M. – Dark Light $19.95
00690869 Hinder – Extreme Behavior $19.95
00660029 Buddy Holly $19.95
00660169 John Lee Hooker – A Blues Legend $19.95
00694905 Howlin' Wolf $19.95
00690692 Very Best of Billy Idol $19.95
00690688 Incubus – A Crow Left of the Murder $19.95
00690457 Incubus – Make Yourself $19.95
00690544 Incubus – Morningview $19.95
00690136 Indigo Girls – 1200 Curfews $22.95
00690790 Iron Maiden Anthology $24.95
00690730 Alan Jackson – Guitar Collection $19.95
00694938 Elmore James – Master Electric Slide Guitar $19.95
00690652 Best of Jane's Addiction $19.95
00690721 Jet – Get Born $19.95
00690684 Jethro Tull – Aqualung $19.95
00690647 Best of Jewel $19.95
00694833 Billy Joel for Guitar $19.95
00690814 John5 – Songs for Sanity $19.95
00690751 John5 – Vertigo $19.95
00694912 Eric Johnson – Ah Via Musicom $19.95
00690660 Best of Eric Johnson $19.95
00690845 Eric Johnson – Bloom $19.95
00690169 Eric Johnson – Venus Isle $22.95
00690846 Jack Johnson and Friends – Sing-A-Longs and Lullabies for the Film Curious George $19.95
00690271 Robert Johnson – The New Transcriptions $24.95
00699131 Best of Janis Joplin $19.95
00690427 Best of Judas Priest $19.95
00690651 Juanes – Exitos de Juanes $19.95
00690277 Best of Kansas $19.95
00690742 The Killers – Hot Fuss $19.95
00690504 Very Best of Albert King $19.95
00690444 B.B. King & Eric Clapton – Riding with the King $19.95
00690134 Freddie King Collection $19.95
00690339 Best of the Kinks $19.95
00690157 Kiss – Alive! $19.95
00694903 Best of Kiss for Guitar $24.95
00690164 Mark Knopfler Guitar – Vol. 1 $19.95
00690163 Mark Knopfler/Chet Atkins – Neck and Neck $19.95
00690780 Korn – Greatest Hits, Volume 1 $22.95
00690836 Korn – See You on the Other Side $19.95
00690377 Kris Kristofferson Collection $17.95
00690861 Kutless – Hearts of the Innocent $19.95
00690834 Lamb of God – Ashes of the Wake $19.95
00690875 Lamb of God – Sacrament $19.95
00690823 Ray LaMontagne – Trouble $19.95
00690658 Johnny Lang – Long Time Coming $19.95
00690726 Avril Lavigne – Under My Skin $19.95
00690679 John Lennon – Guitar Collection $19.95
00690279 Ottmar Liebert + Luna Negra – Opium Highlights $19.95
00690785 Best of Limp Bizkit $19.95
00690781 Linkin Park – Hybrid Theory $22.95

FOR MORE INFORMATION, SEE YOUR LOCAL MUSIC DEALER, OR WRITE TO:

HAL•LEONARD® CORPORATION
7777 W. BLUEMOUND RD. P.O. BOX 13819 MILWAUKEE, WI 53213

Complete songlists and more at www.halleonard.com
Prices, contents, and availability subject to change without notice.

0607

THE DECADE SERIES

These Guitar Recorded Versions collections feature the top tunes that shaped a decade, transcribed note-for-note with tab.

The 1950s
35 pivotal songs from the early rock years: All Shook Up • Donna • Heartbreak Hotel • Hound Dog • I'm Movin' On • Lonesome Town • Matchbox • Moonlight in Vermont • My Babe • Poor Little Fool • Race With the Devil • Rebel 'Rouser • Rock Around the Clock • Rockin' Robin • Sleepwalk • Slippin' and Slidin' • Sweet Little Angel • Tequila • Wake Up Little Susie • Yankee Doodle Dixie • and more.

00690543..$15.95

The 1960s
30 songs that defined the '60s: Badge • Blackbird • Fun, Fun, Fun • Gloria • Good Lovin' • Happy Together • Hey Joe • Hush • I Can See for Miles • I Feel Fine • I Get Around • Louie, Louie • My Girl • Oh, Pretty Woman • On the Road Again • Somebody to Love • Soul Man • Suite: Judy Blue Eyes • Susie-Q • Wild Thing • and more.

00690542..$15.95

The 1970s
30 top songs from the '70s: Best of My Love • Breakdown • Dust in the Wind • Evil Woman • Landslide • Lay Down Sally • Let It Be • Maggie May • No Woman No Cry • Oye Como Va • Show Me the Way • Smoke on the Water • So Into You • Space Oddity • Stayin' Alive • Teach Your Children • Time in a Bottle • Walk This Way • Wheel in the Sky • You've Got a Friend • and more.

00690541..$16.95

The 1980s
30 songs that best represent the decade: 867-5309/Jenny • Every Breath You Take • Eye of the Tiger • Fight for Your Right (To Party) • Heart and Soul • Hit Me With Your Best Shot • I Love Rock 'N Roll • La Bamba • Money for Nothing • Mony, Mony • Refugee • Rock Me • Rock You Like a Hurricane • Start Me Up • Summer of '69 • Sweet Child O' Mine • Wait • What I Like About You • and more.

00690540..$16.95

The 1990s
30 essential '90s classics: All I Wanna Do • Barely Breathing • Building a Mystery • Come Out and Play • Cryin' • Fields of Gold • Friends in Low Places • Hold My Hand • I Can't Dance • Iris • Jump, Jive an' Wail • More Than Words • Santa Monica • Semi-Charmed Life • Silent Lucidity • Smells Like Teen Spirit • Smooth • Tears in Heaven • Two Princes • Under the Bridge • Wonderwall • and more.

00690539..$16.95

The 2000s
30 songs, including: Alive • All the Small Things • Are You Gonna Be My Girl • Californication • Click Click Boom • Complicated • Drive • Hanging by a Moment • Heaven • If You're Gone • Kryptonite • Lifestyles of the Rich and Famous • Maps • The Space Between • Take a Look Around (Theme from *M:I-2*) • Wherever You Will Go • Yellow • and more.

00690761..$15.95

More of the 1950s
30 top songs of the '50s, including: Blue Suede Shoes • Bye Bye Love • Don't Be Cruel (To a Heart That's True) • Hard Headed Woman • Jailhouse Rock • La Bamba • Peggy Sue • Rawhide • Say Man • See You Later, Alligator • That'll Be the Day • Yakety Yak • and more.

00690756..$14.95

More of the 1960s
30 great songs of the '60s: All Along the Watchtower • Born to Be Wild • Brown Eyed Girl • California Dreamin' • Do You Believe in Magic • Hang On Sloopy • I'm a Believer • Paperback Writer • Secret Agent Man • So You Want to Be a Rock and Roll Star • Sunshine of Your Love • Surfin' U.S.A. • Ticket to Ride • Travelin' Man • White Rabbit • With a Little Help from My Friends • and more.

00690757..$14.95

More of the 1970s
30 more hits from the '70s: Aqualung • Carry on Wayward Son • Evil Ways • Feel like Makin' Love • Fly like an Eagle • Give a Little Bit • I Want You to Want Me • Lights • My Sharona • One Way or Another • Rock and Roll All Nite • Roxanne • Saturday Night's Alright (For Fighting) • Suffragette City • Sultans of Swing • Sweet Emotion • Sweet Home Alabama • Won't Get Fooled Again • Wonderful Tonight • and more.

00690758..$17.95

More of the 1980s
30 songs that defined the decade: Call Me • Crazy Crazy Nights • Heartbreaker • Here I Go Again • It's Still Rock and Roll to Me • Jack and Diane • Jessie's Girl • Once Bitten Twice Shy • Rock the Casbah • Runnin' Down a Dream • Sharp Dressed Man • Smokin' in the Boys Room • Stray Cat Strut • Wanted Dead or Alive • White Wedding • and more.

00690759..$16.95

More of the 1990s
30 songs: Alive • Change the World • Come as You Are • The Freshmen • Hard to Handle • Hole Hearted • Just a Girl • Lightning Crashes • Mr. Jones • No Excuses • No Rain • Only Wanna Be with You • Pretty Fly (For a White Guy) • Push • Shimmer • Stay • Stupid Girl • What I Got • Whatever • Whiskey in the Jar • Zombie • and more.

00690760..$14.95

More of the 2000s
30 recent hits: All Downhill From Here • By the Way • Clocks • Cold Hard Bitch • Drops of Jupiter (Tell Me) • Harder to Breathe • I Did It • I Hate Everything About You • Learn to Fly • Ocean Avenue • St. Anger • Wasting My Time • When I'm Gone • Wish You Were Here • With Arms Wide Open • Youth of the Nation • and more.

00690762..$16.95